*Collection Development
in Libraries
A Treatise*

**FOUNDATIONS IN LIBRARY AND
INFORMATION SCIENCE   VOLUME 10 (Part A)**

Editor: Robert D. Stueart, *Dean, School of Library Science,
Simmons College*

FOUNDATIONS IN LIBRARY AND INFORMATION SCIENCE

A Series of Monographs, Texts and Treatises

Series Editor: Robert D. Stueart, *Dean, School of Library Science, Simmons College, Boston*

Collection Development
in Libraries ,
A Treatise

Edited by: ROBERT D. STUEART
Dean, School of Library Science
Simmons College—Boston

GEORGE B. MILLER, JR.
Assistant Director for Collection
Development
University of New Mexico Libraries

 JAI PRESS INC.

Greenwich, Connecticut

Library of Congress Cataloging in Publication Data

Main entry under title:

Collection development in libraries.

   (Foundations in library and information science
v. 10)
   Includes bibliographical references and index.
   1. Collection development (Libraries) I. Stueart,
Robert D. II. Miller, George Bertram, 1926-
III. Series
Z687.C64   025.2   79-93165
ISBN 0-89232-106-7 (pt. A)
ISBN 0-89232-162-8 (pt. B)

Copyright © 1980 JAI PRESS INC.
165 West Putnam Avenue
Greenwich, Connecticut 06830

ISBN NUMBER: 0-89232-106-7

Library of Congress Catalog Card Number: 79-93165

Manufactured in the United States of America

CONTENTS   Part A

PART III: COLLECTION DEVELOPMENT PROCESS

CONTENTS   Part B

PART VI: NEW DIRECTIONS IN COLLECTION DEVELOPMENT

CONTRIBUTORS

Baughman, James C.
Associate Professor, School of Library Science, Simmons College

*Chisholm, Margaret E.
Vice-President for University Relations and Development, University of Washington

*Clark, Alice S.
Assistant Dean for Reader Services, University of New Mexico Library

Darling, Pamela W.
Preservation Officer, Columbia University Libraries

Deal, Carl W.
Executive Director, Latin American Studies Association, and Latin American Librarian, University of Illinois

Dowd, Sheila T.
Assistant University Librarian for Collection Development, University of California—Berkeley

Dudley, Norman H.
Assistant University Librarian for Collection Development, University of California—Los Angeles

*Feller, Siegfried
Chief Bibliographer and Associate Director of Libraries for Collections and Research, University of Massachusetts

*Fitzgibbons, Shirley A.
Assistant Professor, College of Library and Information Services, University of Maryland

Hamlin, Jean Boyer
Director of Libraries, Rutgers, The State University—Newark

*Hannaford, William E., Jr.
Acquisitions Librarian, Middlebury College

*Hernon, Peter
Assistant Professor, School of Library Science, Simmons College

Hoffman, Andrea
Assistant Director and Head of Resources and Research Division, Teacher's College Library, Columbia University

xi

Kaiser, John R.
Coordinator for Collection Development and Area Programs, Pennsylvania State University Libraries

Larsen, A. Dean
Assistant Director for Collection Development, Brigham Young University

*McGrath, William E.
Dean of Library Services, University of Lowell

Martin, Murray S.
Associate University Librarian, Pennsylvania State University Libraries

*Miller, George B., Jr.
Director of Library Communications, University of New Mexico

Mosher, Paul H.
Assistant Director for Collection Development, Stanford University Libraries

*Osburn, Charles B.
Assistant University Librarian for Collection Development, Northwestern University

Rambler, Linda
Reference Librarian (Social Science Bibliographer), Pennsylvania State University Libraries

Stueart, Robert D.
Dean, School of Library Science, Simmons College

*Subramanyam, Kris
Associate Professor, School of Library and Information Science, Drexel University

Ungarelli, Donald
Director, C.W. Post Library, Long Island University

Varnet, Harvey
Assistant Director for Public Services, Bristol Community College Learning Resources Center

Welsch, Erwin
Social Science Bibliographer, University of Minnesota Libraries

*Authors appearing in Part A.

Preface

The need for a treatise on collection development has been felt for quite some time. Although recently a great deal has appeared in the literature about collection development and the selection of materials, there has been no systematic attempt to meld the theoretical foundations with the practical application of the art. Indeed, discussion has most often centered on the unique problems that types of libraries have in the development process, rather than looking at problems and prospects which are applicable to all types of institutions. The intent of this collection, each chapter of which is written by an expert in a particular area, is to present theories, techniques and state-of-the-art analysis which have wide application to academic, research, public, school and special libraries. It is intended not only as an information vehicle but also as a stimulus for discussion and decision. It should be as useful for the beginner as for the seasoned professional.

The editors wish to thank Herbert M. Johnson and Gayle Jerman of JAI for their patience and encouragement in the long struggle to complete this work, and to each of the authors who have contributed their expertise to make this treatise what it is. Special thanks is also extended to Jay McPherson for the indexing and to Fran Berger for her assistance on the manuscript.

George B. Miller, Jr.   Robert D. Stueart
Albuquerque, N.M.   Boston, Mass.

Introduction

According to sociologist Daniel Bell, we are moving from an industrial society into a post-industrial one where knowledge and information frame the problems (1). In such a world libraries certainly should occupy a central position in the universe by providing, as an adaptation of the old cliché states, the right bit of information to the right person at the right time, in the right location and in the right format. Under such changing and challenging conditions, librarians are charged with identifying trends which will have an impact on the way that libraries and other information centers function. Several such trends are already placing tremendous pressures on libraries to develop their collections and access to those materials in a more systematic way than had been necessary or even

possible in the more leisurely past. These trends are forcing a reconsideration of approaches and emphases that until very recently have
been taken for granted. One is acutely aware of the reasons: the
rapid pace of change; the steadily expanding, exploding—polluting if
you will—volume of recorded knowledge in the form of production
of books, journals and other media; the march of technologies,
including visual communication; the need for a larger portion of the
staff and others to bring expertise to the collection development
process; the spiraling costs of materials and their processing, including selecting and acquiring them; the impact of demands for foreign
language materials, both for area-studies programs in academic institutions and to satisfy the needs of non-English-speaking or English-
as-a-second-language populations; the greatly reduced buying power
of the dollar superimposed on dwindling materials budgets and keen
competition from other departments in the city, university, company
or school district for those dollars; and the demand for development
and sharing of library resources, through networking and other
consortia. To seriously ignore any one of these factors would be
devastating for a library's collection, which would soon lose some of
its interest and much of its value to patrons. But to recognize these
issues as catalysts may very well be the first step in the present
development of and renewed interest in the future of library collections. Indeed, collection development has become a hot and fascinating topic of discussion and debate. Much of the debate has centered
around previously held attitudes toward library collection development. For example, historically, one basic criterion for collection
development has been a knowledge of the community and its needs.
This mission is evident in statements by authorities over the years
who have maintained that discovering the needs of the community is
the librarian's first priority in establishing relationship with the
public. "How to select the books to fill those needs best is the
second; and this implies a third, how to judge the value of individual
books" (2). This idea is further reinforced if one agrees with the line
of reasoning that "every item acquired for use in a library collection . . . relate(s) directly to the needs, interests and abilities of the
clientele served by the institution, within the limits set by the
institution's conception of its scope and objectives" (3).

However, there has always existed some question as to whether the identified needs of present patrons or the potential needs of present and future patrons should have more influence on the development of a collection. Some writers maintain that those conditions are mutually exclusive. For example, Poole, writing about public libraries over a hundred years ago, declared that to meet "the varied wants of readers there must be on the shelves of the library books which persons of culture never read" (4), although they may want to do so at some future time. A speech, long since forgotten by most, further reflects this attitude toward the function of the library: "A good book is a permanent possession. Why should we get excited if we do not get a reader today? The book is there, it will attract a reader in due course—tomorrow; if not tomorrow, the day after. It is not of the may-fly order, which is born and dead in twenty-four hours; it is a permanent possession which sooner or later will find its reader" (5). This line of argument would lead to further questioning of whether any library could reasonably afford to or even be expected to maintain a "balanced, comprehensive" collection which is developed not only for present-day patrons but also for future potential needs whatever and wherever they may be. This conflict in basic philosophy has existed since the beginning of serious discussion about collection development and is perhaps best summed up by Andrews who, writing in the last century, stated that

> In the selection of the first book to form a new library, there is always a Scylla and Charybdis awaiting the unwary librarian or trustee. On one side is the great temptation to have the library represent the best thought and culture of the world in all ages. In the desire to fill the library with the very best, one fact is lost sight of, i.e., that it is not the abstract value of the book, but its adaptability to the needs of the reader, that make it the right book in the right place (6).

Goldhor, among others, has criticized the term *well-rounded* as being vague and open to numerous interpretations. He qualified the term by stating that "presumably what most librarians mean when they seek to make their collections 'well-rounded' is that, first of all, there be some material on every branch of knowledge and creative composition and that, second, purchases be apportioned among all the possible fields according to a rough, subjectively estimated composite of the amount of literature published in each field, the distribution of previous circulation between the various classes of the Dewey system, and what the librarian's experience indicates to him, in a general way, the registered public is likely to request" (7).

Disagreement still persists as to the desirability of "comprehensiveness" over that of recognized "need." Monroe cites what she calls a truism in librarianship as being able to create a good collection of materials related to the specific community and to develop that collection to fulfill the goals of the institution for information, recreation and education. She further states that "we've abandoned the artificially 'balanced collection' in favor of the community oriented collection with its own internal balance" (8). This point is certainly arguable if applied to all types and sizes of libraries across the board. It may be true that large public libraries must meet diverse needs and that their "subject coverage approaches the universal, selected to meet the recreational and informational, and to some extent, the educational and research needs of its readers" (9). But one must also consider that many small public libraries have the singular goal of recreation or, at the most, include basic reference materials, while academic libraries often exclude recreational materials, as do most types of special libraries. On the other hand, the "balanced collection" is still a goal of many large research libraries, both academic and public.

This concept of "balanced collection" is difficult to define and almost impossible to administer given the current fiscal realities. It is doubtful whether such a collection could ever be successfully developed if, indeed, it is even desirable. In addition, one would be very naive not to recognize that the quality as well as the quantity of a collection is related directly to the monetary support that the library receives from its parent institution, be that the college or university administration, the local town or city authority, the school board, or the management of a company or other corporation.

From the outset of any discussion a careful distinction needs to be made between selection of materials and the development of collections. "Mystery, maze and muddle" are all words which could easily be used to describe these concepts and the secret rites which have developed around the topic. Many are fumbling around in the process because little effort has been expended in finding out much about the past and little is currently being thought about the future. Collection development in its simplistic form is the systematic development of collections. The process is a standard one and includes the selection and/or rejection of current and retrospective materials, the deselection—or evaluation—of the collection as it now exists, the replacement of worn or vanished but useful materials, and the continuing process of surveying the collection to determine new fields to be developed or levels of intensity of collecting which should be revised. This process projects the future of collection development and poses certain major questions which must be answered in the process, questions such as whether the concept of access to, rather than ownership of, resources implies a change in the emphasis of an individual library's collection.

Such a task implies the broadest of approaches and the broadest of questions. We inquire into the directions our present collection activity is moving us; we examine the way in which our system functions, based on some empirical evidence; we evaluate the desirability of the results of our activity and our policies; and we examine the goals that they imply and the value they embody. This treatise, then, undertakes to explore the major issues relating to the history, state-of-the-art and future of library collection development. Although some issues relate primarily to one type of library, it is felt that the topics can be generalized to most types of institutions. The editors have chosen this treatise form to take full advantage of the expertise of individuals working in the field. Each chapter, therefore, is written by an individual who has been involved both in research and in the practical applications of the theory to the topics they have been assigned. In developing this work an outline was first prepared and then each author was asked to write on the issue with which he or she has been most closely identified. It is thought that this collective approach to a very complex subject will make for a much more authoritative and generalizable volume than would be otherwise possible. Even though most major topics have been addressed in separate chapters, certain topics out of necessity are woven into the fabric of several chapters rather than being assigned separate chapters. For example, "user satisfaction" and "mechanized information retrieval" are not treated in separate chapters but rather touched on in several chapters.

It is obviously impossible to reconstruct in such a subject manifold and varied practices and policies which have developed in all types of libraries and indeed that is not the intent of this work. Instead, what has been attempted here is to give a selective composite picture of the theory and practice of collection development. In a work such as this some overlapping is inevitable. It is hoped that the repetition in this volume is more informative than distracting because in most cases it has been necessary to repeat certain ideas so that discussion of the topic at hand can be fully developed. Also it should be recognized that authors' styles vary in a work of this magnitude.

The subject of collection development, for purposes of this treatise, have been subdivided into five broad categories: the *management* aspects, the *process* of development, the *use* of materials as a determinant to development, the *format* of certain materials, and finally a look at the *future* of collection development. Even though each of the subcategories is further divided into specific topics so that each chapter can be considered individually, the process of collection development is an integrating and ongoing exercise and therefore each chapter is only one part of the total process.

The first six chapters of this treatise introduce the basic management principles upon which the rest is developed, and set the framework for the remainder of the volume. With a broad overview in "Organizational Models for Collection Development," Dudley examines the state-of-the-art of responsibility for collection development in each type of library from university to school, from large public to special. In a thorough consideration of the budgeting process, "The Allocation of Money Within the Materials Budget," Martin discusses the reasons for budget planning, the kinds of things that must be considered, and various ways of making the allocation of material budgets. "The Formulation of Collection Development Policy Statements" explores the ramifications of a selection policy statement. Dowd maintains that a clear understanding of collection development policy is necessary for all who attempt to interpret the library's collections to users, not merely for those persons charged with responsibility for selection decisions. The chapter on "A Survey of Attitudes Toward Collection Development in College Libraries" by Baughman et al. takes a historic look at responsibilities for collection development and then, by way of a questionnaire, defines current attitudes of librarians, faculty, and administrators of colleges. The findings confirm that the library and the activity of collection development are a central part of the formal communications model in institutions of higher education. Kaiser's comments, in "Resource Sharing in Collection Development," based on work currently being done, lay down a blueprint for cooperative collection development and capstone a developing body of literature with a state-of-the-art analysis of resource sharing. Finally in this section, Mosher, in "Managing Library Collections: The Process of Review and Planning," addresses the need for collection review, how one goes about the process and the impact that a planned program can have on library services.

To understand the process of collection development one must look at the very practical everyday problems and at trends which have influenced this process. The second section of six chapters addresses those points. In "The Selection Process," Hamlin discusses, from a very practical point, the framework within which selection takes place and the structure of the selection process in all types of libraries. The chapter on "Mass Buying Programs in the Development Process" by Stueart presents the advantages and disadvantages of various types of approval plans and the "profile" definition which is so important to such an agreement. In the two chapters on "Collecting Foreign Materials from Latin America" and "Collecting Foreign Materials from Western Europe" Deal and Welsch cover the unique problems of collecting materials in non-English languages in two areas of the world where book production and distribution are at a reasonably sophisticated level. Both present problems peculiar to foreign materials and some problems can be generalized to other areas of the globe. Other "areas" have not been included because of space considerations. The chapter by Darling on "Preservation and Conservation of Materials in the Collection Process" addresses the problem that all libraries are having in preserving materials, even for limited use, and the even larger problem of conserving materials for future use. The acquisition of retrospective materials is one of the primary functions of a growing library. With this axiom in mind, Larsen's chapter on "The Role of Retrospective Materials in Collection Development" develops a step-by-step approach to developing collections through the purchase of retrospective materials.

The third section, the beginning of Volume 2, is composed of three chapters which discuss some of the techniques which have been used as indicators in the process. In a very thorough and extensive state-of-the-art survey of "Citation Studies in the Social Sciences," Fitzgibbons presents a composite picture of the broad social science areas and sample studies within each social science. It is evident from her discussions that monographs play a much greater role in citation analysis in the social sciences than in science and technology. Subramanyam, with an overview of bibliometric studies in "Citation Studies in Science and Technology" discusses their possible use as basis for policy formulation for the development of collections. An important discussion of Bradford's law of scattering, with which many librarians have little familiarity, provides a framework for decision-making in the area of development of serial collections. Humanities has not been included as a separate section since some of those disciplines are covered in the social sciences and because so little has been done with those "other disciplines" in the humanities. Finally in this section, the use of circulation data for the identification of use patterns of materials can be a useful tool in collection management operations. McGrath, in "Circulation Studies and Collection Development," addresses this issue in a solid theoretical chapter which relates well to his previous research and to those of others writing in the area.

The growth in information management has led libraries to examine and include formats of materials in their collections other than the traditional book materials. In many cases these types of materials have very important implications for developing collections. Clark considers all the advantages and disadvantages of "Microforms as a Substitute for the Original in the Collection Development Process" and suggests that libraries should be prepared to "sell" microforms as a valuable source of information. Hernon, in the chapter on "Developing Government the Publication Collection," makes an across-levels-of-government examination of the role that documents play in developing collections. Drawing on a survey that he has recently completed, he is able to develop a profile of government documents users and the intensity of that use and provides useful information concerning reviewing sources. In a chapter covering the complex subject of media, "Developing Non-Print Collections," Chisholm has woven together a unified media concept and has characterized the several models which currently exist for media selection. In "Developing the Serials Collection," Feller emphasizes the serials collection's value to the total resources.

The final four chapters take a futuristic look at collection development and address the questions facing us tomorrow. "Collection Evaluation or Analysis: Matching Library Acquisitions to Library Needs" by Mosher takes a rather unique approach to analyzing the collection according to need and makes some very valuable observations about the evaluation process. Miller, in a very insightful chapter on "Creativing in Collection Development," talks about creative ways of developing collections—including nontraditional financial sources, public relations, volunteers and gifts. After a brief look at past and current education components for collection development officers, Osburn, in "Education for Collection Development Officers," considers a rationale for expanding education for collection development in the context of library education and the evolving society. The final chapter, "Toward a Theory of Collection Development" by Hannaford explores the possibility of a theory emerging from collection development both as it relates to the normative which addresses what should be the bases of decisions and to the descriptive elements which relate to the bases of selecting items.

These chapters bring into a unified whole the importance of collection development in every type of library and point the direction to trends which are emerging.

Robert D. Stueart

REFERENCES

1. Daniel Bell, "Welcome to the Post-Industrial Society." *Physics Today* (February 1976): 46-49.

2. Helen E. Haines, *Living With Books.* (New York: Columbia University Press, 1950), p. 24.

3. Elanor Phinney, "Book Selection Theory." *Public Library Division Reporter* 4 (October 1955): 24.

4. William F. Poole, "The Organization and Management of Public Libraries." In *Public Libraries in the United States*, edited by the U.S. Bureau of Education. (Washington, D.C.: Government Printing Office, 1875), p. 479.

5. J.P. Lamb, "Books and the Public Library." *Library Journal* 60 (December 1, 1935): 913.

6. Elizabeth P. Andrews, "Book Selection." *Library Journal* 22 (October 1897): 71.

7. Herbert Goldhor, "A Note on the Theory of Book Selection." *Library Quarterly* 12 (April 1942): 157-158.

8. Margaret E. Monroe, "What Makes a Good Book Collection?" *Maryland Libraries* 30 (Spring 1964): 6.

9. *Encyclopedia of Library and Information Sciences*, s.v. "Collection Building," by Joseph C. Shipman.

PART I

OVERVIEW

Collection Development in the United States

Robert D. Stueart

GENESIS

During the early days of library development, expanded collections were encouraged mostly through gifts to libraries from monasteries, wealthy citizens, professors and later students, with almost no thought being given to a core of materials desirable for that particular community of users nor any planned collection building or deselection of materials—almost everything was kept regardless of its use or value. During those early days and even into the latter part of the nineteenth century, library resources were likely to duplicate private collections. In academic libraries the little selection that took place was performed mostly by professors. Shores points out that the "major portion of colonial library holdings resulted from direct or indirect benefactions" with direct purchase being less than a tenth of the total holdings (1). Public libraries were modeled on those of universities and private scholars and were for scholars in the humanities. The selection function was carried on by the "cultured" members of the community or in some few cases by the librarian. Needless to say there were few, if any, written policies regarding selection and very little regard to collection development as it is conceived and as it functions today. The collections themselves were probably inadequate for the needs of that day but since access was limited it is doubtful whether that inadequacy was widely recognized. The laissez-faire approach used by most libraries in those early days led to collections which were uneven in quality and varied greatly in quantity. However, there was one library which must be cited as a model for development of U.S. libraries. The Göttingen University Library in Germany was probably the most outstanding example of a well-planned and supported collection. As Dr. Christian Gottlob Heyne, its renowned librarian, stated at that time, "proper selection rather than mere numbers of books is what makes real worth in a university library. Therefore, the uninterrupted, planned purchase of all important native and foreign publications produced by the development of knowledge is essential for a library with a scholarly plan" (2). This sentiment has echoed through the ages and was taken up again 150 years later by Downs, who stated that "mere size does not guarantee a great library or even a good one. The quality and richness of the book collection are even more significant . . . [Nothing can] compensate for deficiencies in book resources" (3).

Even before Heyne, count Gerlach Adolph Von Münchhausen, chief administrative officer of Göttingen during the late 1600s and early 1700s, embodied major principles which Leibniz had advanced during his tenure as librarian of the ducal library at Wolfenbüttel, among those being that the collection should be of "scholarly quality, usefulness, and up-to-dateness . . . and book selection on a planned, regular and international basis" (4). This can be considered the prototype of collection development statements, for, as Danton notes, nowhere else, at that time or earlier, are there to be found in combination, the stated, firm principles, and their actual implementation, of a consistent, centrally administered book selection policy, designed to secure for a library every work of scholarly value, whenever and wherever published; enormous library staff time expended toward this end; and ample, regular budget to make the desired result possible (5).

HISTORICAL OVERVIEW

That collection development has for some time been a major concern of American librarians is evident in the proceedings of many American Library Association conferences, even from the first one in Philadelphia in 1876 where there was a lively debate on selection (6). The 1894 Lake Placid Conference was devoted primarily to selection, though at a somewhat mundane level. A series of short papers by several librarians set forth the method which they employed in the selection of books, the guides they found most helpful, the criticisms they placed most confidence in, and the considerations which determined their expenditures. One speaker concluded that "there are three things necessary to a successful library—good books, good methods, and a good librarian. . . . The real problem . . . is the selection of books" (7) She further enumerated the principles which she saw as underlying selection: Who shall select, what shall be selected, and how shall it be selected The "who" has three requisites, "abundance of time, knowledge of books, and sympathy with popular taste." Another proponent of "selection" decried professorial laxity and the tendency to select books in a limited field with the sad results that the inequities of the professors of today are visited upon future college generations" (8). No mention was made of the responsibility of the librarian to assure that inequities did not occur. With the "what" it was felt that "the idea of completeness . . . should be banished. It is perhaps an instinct of a scholarly mind. It is also the refuse of the lazy and ignorant buyer. I believe that ten years from now we shall be ashamed of the libraries of today, because they are collections, not selections" (9). The "what" was also addressed by Justin Winsor, writing a few years earlier, when he declared that "a collection of good books, with a soul to it in the shape of a good librarian, becomes a vitalized power among the impulses by which the world goes on to improvement" (10). The established European tradition of selectivity was being transformed into American ingenuity. As Edelman said about that tradition, "only the 'good' books and journals were allowed to become part of the collection. However, there has never been general agreement on what constitutes quality" (11). Thomas Jefferson had already laid down strict rules for the development of a "quality" collection at the University of Virginia Library when it was founded in the nineteenth century. His criteria included "only books of great reputation and too expensive for private purchase. Only authoritative expositions of science and translations of 'superior elegance' were permitted" (12). During that period of time, library resources were likely to duplicate rather than supplement user collections. The general library collection was essentially a projection on a large scale of the library of an educated man" (13). Public libraries, in seeking a new role for themselves, began to try "to provide the books people want—not those we think they ought to read" (14). This new direction began in the Boston Public Library, which by the late 1870s had begun to furnish "in such numbers of copies that many persons . . . could be reading the same book at the same time; in short . . . the pleasant literature of the day should be made accessible to the whole people at the only time when they care for it, i.e., when it is fresh and new" (15).

Most large academic libraries, on the other hand, were concentrating on providing materials which were potentially useful for research and favored gathering most materials. The character of those materials being collected—in the case of academic libraries the research materials and in the case of the public libraries the popular demand materials—continued to determine the library's service to the community it served through the collection policies of that day.

From the initial role as caretakers of materials selected for them by cultured men, academic libraries began to emerge as omnivorous collections of practically anything and everything in print. This growth, with the advent of modern scholarship, was still under faculty impetus and was often haphazard and unplanned (16). Little attention was paid to real needs, or if attention was paid it was to immediate research needs of individual faculty members. But new approaches to teaching—textbooks began to be replaced by reading lists and honors programs began to develop in small private colleges with emphasis on individual research—coupled with the development of classification schemes such as Dewey's, gave some direction to a systematic increase in the size and scope of the collections. John Green Cogswell was well before his time at Harvard when he proposed, in the 1820s, a vigorous plan for the development of the college library. Harvard had to wait until the 1870s, after the Ph.D. programs were introduced and after Justin Winsor became librarian, to begin "to realize its potentialities in systematic collecting and in usefulness to the university" (17). To anyone attempting a review of the history of collection development in American libraries as a group, it is apparent that their growth has been almost entirely individual, unplanned with reference to any other library or group of libraries. Edelman states, "each university library reflects very much the particular academic history of its institution and especially the influence of a relatively small number of scholars and librarians. On balance, it has always been the scholar who provided the impetus; the librarian has made it possible" (18). Similar statements can be made about early public libraries with only slight modifications.

Responsibility for selection of materials continued to be a major concern of librarians, although selection of materials for public libraries and to an extent school libraries, because of the demand for current popular titles, both fiction and nonfiction, began to be more the responsibility of the librarian who was probably more frustrated with being unable to develop the collection on any kind of long-range program rather than the frustration of academic librarians at not having the primary responsibility for development.

Many voices have been raised, over the past hundred years, concerning the responsibility of both faculty and librarians in selecting materials. From the extreme of denouncing "professorial laxity and the tendency to select books in a limited field with the sad results that the inequities of the professors of today are visited upon future college generations" (19) to the recognition that "as a matter of his own field, the instructor should initiate recommendations for books and periodicals needed by himself and his students" (20) it has become evident to most writers and researchers that it is "equally the duty of the librarian and his assistants to know books and their use, so that they may not only quickly supply, but even anticipate the needs of their patrons" (21). Studies on how books are acquired and how they are used began to appear in the 1920s and 1930s. In his survey of land grant college libraries, Brown (22) found that in almost 70 percent of them the librarian's only relation to book selection was to prevent the purchase of duplicates. The need for developing criteria for collections was clearly felt by the Advisory Group on College Libraries which, during 1929-1932, recommended to the Carnegie Corporation the awarding of grants to college libraries for their book collections. This concern led to the first standards relating to selection of materials which were codified by the Advisory Group in 1932 when they issued *College Library Standards* for "an adequate stock of reference, general, curricular and leisure reading materials" (23). Soon after, the *List of Books for College Libraries* was compiled to meet, in some measure, the need for objective criteria (24). In Danton's study it was found that librarians in the "more successful libraries" had "very much more direct responsibility for book selection and particularly responsibility for the systematic growth of the libraries book collections" (25) The *List of Books for College Libraries* (26) was a first attempt to list materials which had been selected by that code of objective criteria. Before that time there does not seem to have existed a criterion for evaluating the techniques used in collection development. However, the approach employed in the *List* or any such listing has certain inherent weaknesses: it is a rigid one, soon becomes outdated, is retroactive rather than forward-looking, and offers no principles for selection. The value of this check-list approach lies in the pooled judgment of books for specific users. It emphasizes "the desirability of the careful selection of books for appropriate courses rather than larger collections which bear no special relation to the curricula" (27).

The process of book selection for public libraries, likewise, developed, not as a recognized theory, but rather as a growing body of practice. Not until Haines stated her principles for selection under the retrenchment conditions of the 1930s was there a humanistic approach to the theory of selection. The principles she expounded

included: 1) maintain quality—books of authority in knowledge of
creative vitality and of excellence in literary expression should
consistently be given preference; 2) preserve appropriate values—
selection should respond, as far as possible, to leading trends of
public interest; and 3) determine essentials and reduce nonessentials
—in the present day of swift transition, the new is more important
than the old (28). These criteria have guided public libraries since
that time. Her *Living With Books* (29) is still the classic statement on
collection development. This statement of criteria was followed in
the early 1940s by new standards for public libraries (30).

In 1950 Enoch Pratt Free Library developed and adopted a
statement, reflecting many of Haines's thoughts, which provided the
key to the selection policy of that library. It was a model statement
which was used by many other public libraries. Four years later a
Book Selection Work Conference, part of ALA's activities, met in
Philadelphia to formulate some sort of statement for public libraries
to use as further guide. The revised *Standards of Public Libraries* (31)
would then include a statement that every library should have a
concrete statement of policy covering the selection and maintenance
of its collection of book and nonbook materials. It was about that
time, with the ALA Bill of Rights and the Freedom to Read statement, that public libraries began to concentrate on selection policy
statements. The same was true for academic libraries after the 1959
Standards for College Libraries (32). Librarians began agreeing
among themselves that nothing relieves the librarian—not reviewing
sources, nor recommended lists, nor faculty, nor pressure groups—
from the major responsibility of developing collections. In academic
libraries this lessening of faculty responsibility (33) was a major
happening and, indeed, many still dispute that it has happened.
Several things were happening to bring about this development. First,
a realization of the findings that the Waples and Lasswell study had
discovered in the mid 1930s. The study revealed that when the
primary selection responsibility rests with a group of subject
specialists librarians, as it did with the New York Public Library in
that survey, then, at least in the four social science fields they
observed, the library is more likely to have the research materials
deemed important by current scholars and of probable use to future

scholars than if the faculty had the primary responsibility (*34*). Criticism of an overreliance on faculty began to come from many sources, most echoing the sentiment that "the weakness of our collections, as well as the strength, has resulted from an over-dependence upon faculty members for purchase recommendations and faculty members have normally been interested and competent only in their areas" (*35*). The pattern of departmental allocation began to change and the responsibility moved more to the librarian. Formula for allocating resources began to emerge starting with an article by Clapp and Jordan (*36*). It was also during this period of time, the mid-1960s, that federal funds allowed libraries to expand their collections much faster than had ever been possible before. Interdisciplinary studies and an emphasis on area studies meant that the "scope and size of the selection process had grown well beyond the capabilities of part-time faculty selection" (*37*). The area specialist bibliography (*38*) and the subject specialist bibliographer began to assume major collection development responsibilities in academic libraries. These individuals became responsible for expanding collections and identifying weaknesses in existing collections.

With this increase in funding and specialists to define areas of interest and depth of coverage, approval plans and blanket order plans, with carefully developed profiles for individual libraries, began to replace the title-by-title selection which had previously occurred. The strongest argument for abandoning individual title selection was put forth by Thompson, who states "the dogma of book selection by individual title has yielded no significant results in university libraries. In fact, our growth seems to be the more haphazard on account of it. We cannot abolish selection by individual titles. . . . However, the major acquisition policy should be concerned with whole fields, and the key decisions should revolve around the intensity with which acquisition in these various fields should be pursued" (*39*). Also an acquisition program which employs a title-by-title selection system generates a number of sizable costs for the library (*40*).

This approach just described is opposite to that of many public and academic libraries, particularly small ones, which must choose every title with the greatest of care. If not, as Taube states, many feel that we would find ourselves assembling "the bad book, the cheap novel, the pompous genealogy, the insipid poem, the lying history, the dull report, the stupid diary, the ephemeral tract" (41) along with the valuable and useful materials. Public services librarians in public libraries have for a period of time prided themselves for reacting to changing community needs and have most often been responsible, to a large degree, for the collection development. The collection development process, however, is no easier in public libraries than in academic and in many cases may be more difficult:

> When you have a perfect people you can afford to have only perfect books, if there are such things. When you have a homogeneous public you can hope to have a stock of books exactly fitted to them all, and no book shall be unfitted to any one of them. But so long as there is a public of every diversity of mental capacity, previous education, habits of thought, taste, ideals, you must, if you are to give them satisfaction or do them any good, provide many books which will suit and benefit some and will do no good, perhaps in some cases may do harm, to others. It is inevitable. There is no escape from this fundamental difficulty (42).

The real confusion has been in terms of the role of the library— public or academic, school or special. Public libraries have generally assumed the educational, recreational, informational role, school libraries an educational role and special libraries an informational role. Like public libraries, most academic libraries have assumed a generalist role. "A college library must have, first of all, a collection of cultural and recreational materials that can expand students' horizons; second, a good basic collection that will meet most of their curricular needs, and third, a good reference collection that will serve as a key to the immediate library and to resources elsewhere . . . We should aim for a well-chosen basic collection that meets the first two needs . . . " (43)

By the 1970s primarily because of economic conditions, collection development plans were "being seriously disrupted and libraries have been forced either to sharply reduce their subscription lists or to decrease their book purchases disproportionately" (44). This fact brings libraries to a very precarious position where innovation and ingenuity are required, for as Leigh found almost thirty years ago in the *Public Library Inquiry*, as the size of the library budget decreases below a certain point the proportion of serious, significant authoritative materials in the library's collection as well as their amount, decreases. "Below this point the books and other materials purchased are selected more often on the basis of demand created by commercial promotion and mass popularity than on the basis of the judgment of experts as to their significance and reliability" (45).

A great deal more planning is now occurring in libraries with emphasis on codification of the development. This requires a hard look at the topics covered in the remainder of this treatise. Collection development officers and/or committees now place greater emphasis on quality than ever before and many would now argue with the statement in the latest standards which says that it "is not possible to have quality without quantity" (46). This attitude is also rejected by most who feel that too much faith has always been placed in "total coverage, inclusive listings, nondiscriminating completeness, whereas more rigorous standards of evaluation might well have resulted in reduced numbers of volumes without damaging content" (47). This quality is becoming even more difficult to judge objectively in terms of use and merit. Many would regard the only materials which have permanency as those "whose literary quality is of such merit that it outweighs the disadvantages of their outmoded ideas and background" (48). Bonn, among others, has identified more concrete methods of quality evaluation:

1) compiling statistics on holdings, use, expenditures;
2) checking lists, catalogs, bibliographies;
3) obtaining opinions from regular users;
4) examining the collection directly; and
5) applying standards, using various of the foregoing methods (49).

Other measurement studies (50, 51) have also begun to address the problem of measuring service capabilities of libraries and the importance that selection plays in that process.

In the last quarter of the twentieth century a good library cannot be built in a day, or a month, or even a year, but must be built through a carefully planned collection with one firm foot in the reality of today and the other raised for that giant step into the future. The principles, practices and trends in that process and the roles that librarians and patrons play are the subjects of the remainder of this work.

REFERENCES

1. Louis Shores, *Origins of the American College Library, 1638-1800*. (Nashville, Tenn.: George Peabody College, 1934), p. 101.
2. *Telehrte Anzeigen* (May 1800), pp. 849-852. Cited by J. Periam Danton in *Book Selection and Collections: A Comparison of German and American University Libraries*. (New York: Columbia University Press, 1963), p. 18.
3. Robert B. Downs, "The Implementation of Book Selection Policy in University and Research Libraries." In *Selection and Acquisition Procedures in Medium-Sized and Large Libraries*, Herbert Goldhor, ed. (Champaign, Ill.: Illini Union Bookstore, 1963), p. 2.
4. J. Periam Danton, *Book Selection and Collection: A Comparison of German and American University Libraries*. (New York: Columbia University Press, 1963), p. 15.
5. Ibid., p. 19.
6. Carl B. Roden, "Theories of Book Selection for Public Libraries." In *The Practice of Book Selection*, Louis R. Wilson, ed. (Chicago: University of Chicago Press, 1940), p. 6.
7. Mary S. Cutler, "Principles of Selection of Books." *Library Journal* 20 (October 1895): 340.
8. Alfred C. Potter, "Selection of Books for College Libraries." *Library Journal* 22 (October 1897): 39.
9. Cutler, op. cit., p. 341.
10. Justin Winsor, "The College Library and the Classes." *Library Journal* 3 (March 1878): 5.
11. Hendrik Edelman and G. Marvin Tatum, Jr., "The Development of Collections in American University Libraries." In *Libraries for Teaching, Libraries for Research*, Richard D. Johnson, ed. (Chicago: American Library Association, 1977), p. 37.
12. John S. Brubacher and Willis Rudy, *Higher Education in Transition*. (New York: Harper & Row, 1968.)
13. Arthur E. Bestor, "Transformation of American Scholarship, 1875-1917." *Library Quarterly* 23 (1953): 167.

14. F.M. Cruden, "Selection of Books." *Library Journal* 19 (December 1894): 41.
15. *Life, Letters and Journals of George Triknor.* (Boston: J.R. Osgood and Co., 1876), p. 302.
16. Bestor, op. cit.
17. Andrew D. Osborn, "The Development of Library Resources at Harvard: Problems and Potentialities." *Harvard Library Bulletin* 9 (1953): 198.
18. Edelman and Tatum, op. cit., p. 38.
19. Potter, op. cit.
20. Charles Edwin Friley, "College Library Control." *ALA Bulletin* 29 (February 1935): 70.
21. Ibid.
22. C.H. Brown, "The Library." In *Survey of Land Grant Colleges and Universities.* (Washington, D.C.: U.S. Department of Interior, Office of Education: Government Printing Office, 1930.)
23. Carnegie Corporation of New York, Advisory Group of College Libraries, *College Library Standards.* (New York: The Corporation, 1932), pp. 10-11.
24. J. Periam Danton, "The Selection of Books for College Libraries: An Examination of Certain Factors which Affect Excellence of Selection." *Library Quarterly* 5 (October 1935): 420.
25. Ibid., p. 446.
26. Charles B. Shaw, *List of Books for College Libraries.* (Chicago: American Library Association, 1930.)
27. Flora B. Luddington, "College Library Book Selection." *Library Journal* 60 (January 1, 1935): 11.
28. Helen E. Haines, "Book Selection in These Lean Years." *Book List* 31 (September 1934): 1.
29. Helen E. Haines, *Living With Books.* (New York: Columbia University Press, 1950.)
30. American Library Association, Committee on Post-War Planning, *Standards for Public Libraries.* (Chicago: American Library Association, 1943.)
31. American Library Association, Public Library Division, Coordinating Committee on Revision of Public Library Standards, *Public Library Service.* (Chicago: American Library Association, 1956), pp. 31-32.
32. American Library Association, Association of College and Research Libraries, Standards Committee, "Standards for College Libraries." *College and Research Libraries* 20 (July 1959): 74-80.
33. "The Selection of Academic Library Materials: A Literature Survey." *College and Research Libraries* 29 (September 1968): 364-372.
34. Douglas Waples and Harold D. Lasswell, *National Libraries and Foreign Scholarship.* (Chicago: University of Chicago Press, 1936), pp. 71-75.

35. Robert A. Miller, "A Look in the Mirror, Twenty-Five Years of University Librarianship." *Library Journal* 87 (October 1, 1963): 3381.
36. Verner W. Clapp and R.T. Jordan, "Quantitative Criteria for Adequacy of Academic Library Collections," *College and Research Libraries* 26 (September 1965): 371-380.
37. Edelman and Tatum, op. cit., p. 48.
38. Robert D. Stueart, *The Area Specialist Bibliographer: An Inquiry into His Role.* (Metuchen, N.J.: Scarecrow Press, 1972.)
39. Lawrence S. Thompson, "The Dogma of Book Selection in University Libraries." *College and Research Libraries* 21 (November 1960): 445.
40. Edelman and Tatum, op. cit., p. 38.
41. Mortimer Taube, "The Theory of Book Selection." *College and Research Libraries* 2 (June 1941): 224.
42. Mary Duncan Carter, et al., *Building Library Collections*, 4th ed. (Metuchen, N.J.: Scarecrow Press, 1974), pp. 12-13.
43. Evan Ira Farber, "Limiting College Library Growth: Bane or Boon?" In *Farewell to Alexandria*, Daniel Gore, ed. (Westport, Conn.: Greenwood Press, 1976), p. 39.
44. Bernard Fry and Herbert S. White, *Economics and Interaction of the Publisher-Library Relationship in the Production and Use of Scholarly and Research Journals.* Final Report. (Washington, D.C.: National Science Foundation, Office of Science Information Services, 1975), p. 1.
45. Robert D. Leigh, "The Public Library Inquiry and Sampling of Library Holdings of Books and Periodicals." *Library Quarterly* 21 (July 1959): 158.
46. American Library Association, Association of College and Research Libraries, "Standards for College Libraries," op. cit.
47. Blanche Prichard McCrum, "Book Selection in Relation to the Optimum Size of a College Library," *College and Research Libraries* 11 (April 1950): 139.
48. J.P. Lamb, "Books and the Public Library," *Library Journal* 60 (1933): 913.
49. George S. Bonn, "Evaluation of the Collection," *Library Trends* 22 (January 1974): 267.
50. F.W. Lancaster, *The Measurement and Evaluation of Library Services.* (Washington, D.C.: Information Resources Press, 1977).
51. Ernest R. DeProspo, Ellen Altman, and Kenneth E. Beasley, *Performance Measures for Public Libraries.* (Chicago: American Library Association, 1973.)

PART II

COLLECTION MANAGEMENT

Organizational Models for Collection Development

Norman H. Dudley

INTRODUCTION

Collection development, the selection of materials which make up a library's collection, has always been a major if not the primary responsibility of the librarian. In public libraries, school libraries, and special libraries, this responsibility has either been assumed by the head librarian or delegated to the library staff according to patterns which have changed very little in the past sixty years of more. Only in academic libraries has this responsibility been delegated beyond the library staff to any significant degree, and only in university libraries (and to a certain extent in large public libraries) has the pattern of this delegation been noticeably altered in recent years. In examining organizational models for collection development in various types of libraries, one should look at the changing picture in each individual type.

UNIVERSITY LIBRARIES

Faculty members have traditionally played a primary role in collection development in American university libraries. However, there has been a dramatic shift in the respective roles of faculty members and librarians as developers of these libraries' collections in the past twenty years. American graduate universities, as opposed to colleges, date back only to the end of the nineteenth century, and they were largely modeled after German universities (1). Even though at least one major university, the University of Göttingen, had a strong tradition of librarian selection (2), the prevailing pattern of collection development organization in German university libraries at that time was one which involved charging library faculty committees in the various departments with the responsibility for selecting materials and accordingly distributing the book funds to these various departments (3). This was the pattern which was adopted for American university libraries and which continued relatively unchanged until the second half of the twentieth century. It is ironic that German universities changed their approach to collection development very shortly after they had launched us in this direction, establishing a formal system of library bibliographers which was firmly in place in most universities in Germany by 1900 and which has continued to the present (4). That faculty selection was the dominant factor in collection development in American university libraries at least up until the late 1950s and early 1960s is clear when one examines the literature of that period on the subject.

In 1956, in the second edition of *The University Library*, Wilson and Tauber stated about selection that "In a university library . . . responsibility for the actual selection of materials is generally divided between . . . [the librarian] and the library staff on the one hand and the faculty on the other. . . . Members of the faculty are usually charged with the responsibility for selecting materials in support of courses and programs of research, whereas the librarian and the library staff are held responsible for selecting general reference books and bibliographical apparatus, noncurricular books, periodicals, and other materials intended for general and recreational reading" (5). In 1959, Carter and Bonk, in their book *Building Library Collections*, expressed a similar view: "The various departments of schools and colleges [within a university] are . . . responsible for selection in their subject areas, while the library staff remains responsible for the fields of general bibliography, for those areas not covered by departments, for special materials such as periodicals and documents, and for overseeing the general development of the collection" (6).

Both of these views recognized that the library had an important role to play in selection, but it was a subordinate and supplemental role, and Guy Lyle, in his 1963 book *The President, the Professor, and the College Library*, made it clear that this was as it should be: "The librarian has a job of leadership, but he should use his office to coordinate and inform and not to dominate book selection. If occasionally he becomes impatient with what appears to be the procrastinating and slipshod selection methods of his teaching colleagues he should not compound their faults by taking over their selection responsibilities" (7).

The impatience of which Mr. Lyle speaks has been widespread for a long time, and greater library involvement in selection has been suggested much earlier. In 1932, William Randall, in his book *The College Library*, said, "One possible escape from the difficulty [inherent in having control of the greater part of the funds for book purchases pass from the library to the academic departments] is for the college to refrain from a departmental budgeting of its book funds and, instead, to leave them, or a large portion of them in one sum under the control of the librarian and a library committee of the faculty . . . . It is certainly evident that some means must be found to correct the ordinary attitude of the faculty toward the library. . . . Too much influence is given at present to the individual tendencies of single members of the faculties. The result has been poorly balanced book collections with some subjects overdeveloped and some almost neglected" (8).

In 1940, Keyes Metcalf wrote: "I have already stated my belief that too much reliance on faculty initiative has been unfortunate, I might also say disastrous. What then can be done? It seems to me evident that the solution should be twofold. 1) While we should not expect faculty to do the work without aid or compulsion, full benefit of the special knowledge residing with its members should be taken advantage of and every effort made to persuade its members to suggest freely titles for purchase and also to cover systematically the fields in which they work. 2) I believe that at least in a large institution the subjects which the library tries to cover should be divided between members of the library staff. In these libraries it should be possible to find men and women who have a fair, even if somewhat simplified, knowledge of most of the broad fields. These assistants may do very little of the book selection themselves, but they should have the responsibility of seeing that there are called to the attention of the faculty members who are specialists the various lists of new books and old books that are available and that these specialists shall be almost forced to make recommendations. The staff members should then try to cover material that falls between the different lines cared for by the faculty and thus round out the work" (9).

In spite of these complaints and forward-looking suggestions, however, the pattern of faculty-dominated selection continued with little change until the early 1960s, when a number of factors combined to change it. J. Periam Danton summarized some of these factors well in an article in 1967: "The remarkable increment in the pace, intensity, and activities of modern academic life which leaves most faculty members with little time or inclination for book selection; the great growth in the size and complexity of library collections and of world publishing, to the bafflement of the 'old-fashioned' part-time book selector; and, if it is chiefly poverty that makes dedicated book selectors of faculty, he becomes disinterested and unconcerned when his library nears the million volume figure" (10).

Rutherford D. Rogers and David C. Weber pointed up the differences between the old and the new approaches in their book *University Library Administration* in 1971:

Book selection in the modern university library differs in two major respects from what it was a generation ago: it is much more a library responsibility, and it is infinitely more varied and complex. The two factors are not unrelated. As book selection has become bigger (in terms of numbers of items) and broader (in terms of number of countries, agencies, learned societies) and more varied (in terms of methods used to insure adequate coverage), the library has had to establish more elaborate machinery to carry out this basic mission. Other members of the university community, like the faculty, still play an important role, but it tends to be in the form of specialized consultation on major purchases or the recommendation of isolated titles (11).

A key factor in the development of "more elaborate machinery" was the emergence of the bibliographer, the librarian with a full-time or part-time assignment not simply to fill in where the faculty had missed or to call titles to the faculty's attention, as Mr. Metcalf had suggested, but to have primary responsibility for the development of certain areas of the collection. As early as 1956 Wilson and Tauber, in their book *The University Library*, mentioned that "a few university libraries have appointed staff bibliographers to select materials in special fields" (12), but it was not until the early 1960s, aided by the influx of federal funds to support area study centers on campuses all over the country, that bibliographers became an important factor in university library collection development. Between 1963 and 1966 the University of Indiana added ten bibliographers; between 1960 and 1964 UCLA added nine. This pattern was repeated in libraries throughout the country, so that by 1967 Robert Haro could include the following in his report on a survey of acquisition practices of seventy academic libraries: "Most of the larger academic libraries with firmly established area studies or medium-sized libraries with accelerated programs for collection development were utilizing bibliographers or subject specialists responsible for the selection of library materials" (13) and in a 1969 article he could say that Columbia, Cornell, Harvard, Indiana, Michigan, Stanford, UCLA, and Washington, among the major universities, had transferred considerable book-selection responsibilities to area or subject specialists and that, in addition to their selection responsibilities, these specialists were also engaged in advanced reference work, research, instruction, and liaison activities between academic departments and the library (14).

The greatly increased use of approval plans and blanket orders which also occurred in the early and middle 1960s was both a cause and a result of the increase in librarian selection. As books came in to the libraries which had been selected by a dealer, according to an agreed-on profile of needs, there was less reason for faculty members, even those faculty members who still had the time and the inclination, to pore over bibliographies and catalogs and make their individual selections. Also, the regular arrival of shipments of preselected books required that knowledgeable selectors be available on a regular basis, and faculty members could simply not be counted on for this kind of service.

An excellent profile of the organization of collection development in large universities in 1978 was provided by Wilmer Baatz in his report "Collection Development in Nineteen Libraries of the Association of Research Libraries" (15). With regard to the relationship between selection by faculty and librarians in the libraries studied, he indicated that in only three of the nineteen did the faculty actually have control of what is selected for the Main Library (largely humanities and social science collections), and that in these libraries at least 90 percent of the selection is done by the librarians. Most of the Main Library selectors, bibliographers, and curators reported to or worked very closely with a Chief Collection Development Officer, who was usually on the Assistant Director level, but all of them were also involved with technical services departments and several, particularly those who deal with the more exotic languages, were either supervising the acquisition and cataloging of their materials or actually doing some or all of the cataloging. Not surprisingly, bibliographers' assignments varied widely, but there were certain general areas of similarity. Geographical area bibliographers and curators were very common, particularly for the Slavic and East European countries, the Far East, the Middle or Near East, Latin America, Africa, and South and Southeast Asia, but responsibility for Western European languages and literatures, and general humanities and social sciences (usually limited to Western Europe and North America) was assigned in as many different patterns as there were libraries.

UNIVERSITY LIBRARY BRANCHES

If the American graduate university dates from the late nineteenth century, the present-day American university library system, with its pattern of a central library and a widely varying number of branch libraries, often not including the medical and law libraries, under the control of a single administrative head is considerably newer. The head of a university library in the early years of the twentieth century was concerned with building a library, not a system of libraries, for the campus, and multilibrary systems became a reality only when individual academic disciplines within the emerging universities became so large and specialized in their library needs and also, in many instances, so far removed physically from the central library, that their faculties forced the creation of special branch libraries to serve them, or alternatively, forced the central library administration to assume responsibility for departmental libraries which had been established with departmental funds to provide the special services which were required. This takeover of departmental libraries by the university library system is by no means complete, and virtually every university today, particularly privately supported ones, have a number of such departmental libraries or collections which are still outside the control of the university library head.

Given the history of the development of specialized branch libraries, then, it is not surprising that their ties to the faculty were even closer than those of the central library, which from the start had a tradition of some autonomy. Faculty members tend to view these branch libraries as their creation, which in many instances they were, and their property. This is particularly true in the area of collection development, with the result that faculty responsibility for selection in these libraries was and continues to be greater than in the central library. Nonetheless, a number of the same factors which brought about the increase in librarian selection in the central library have been at work in the branch libraries: the increasing demands on the faculty members' time, the increasing size and complexity of the collections, the development of approval plans and blanket orders for the subject areas covered by these libraries, and consequent recognition on the part of both faculty members and librarians of the need for more, and more regularized, involvement of the librarian in the development of the collections. The result is that selection by librarians in these libraries today is nearly as great as it is in the central library. Baatz reports that 75 percent of the selection in the science branches he studied and 76 percent of selection in the nonscience branches was done by librarians. Baatz, interestingly enough, reports that the branch libraries reporting the highest percentage of librarian selections were the undergraduate libraries. One hundred percent of these libraries reported that librarians did all the selection, except for reserve materials. Presumably this is because faculty members do not feel either that the undergraduate library is their special province or that it contains the research collection that they are most interested in developing.

While the percentage of the total selection that is done within branch libraries has changed significantly in recent years, the place of collection development in the organization of many of these libraries has not, simply because most of them are so small that all the selection done by the library staff, however much that may be, is done by the head librarian, who is also the only librarian. In the larger libraries, where a differentiation of function is possible and indeed necessary, collection development may still be the responsibility of the head librarian, or it may be assigned to the head of acquisitions, the head of serials, the head of reference, or any other staff member as an additional assignment. Rarely, if ever, does a branch library have a full-time selector.

The chief collection development officer in a university library system has a responsibility to coordinate the collection development policies and practices of all the libraries that make up that system, so the person or persons in each branch library with responsibility for collection development must also work closely with the chief collection development officer, whether or not the branch librarian reports to that officer in the administrative hierarchy. Collection developers in libraries within a single system which have similar or related collection responsibilities must also stay in close and constant communication.

COLLEGE LIBRARIES

American colleges go back much further in our history than American universities. Correspondingly, their dependence on faculty selection goes back further. While the factors that brought about changes in this dependence upon university central libraries and branch libraries have affected college libraries, they have done so to a lesser extent. Competing demands for faculty members' time have not increased as severely in colleges as in universities, much smaller and much less rapidly increasing book budgets have meant that selection could still be done reasonably by individual faculty members making individual selections, and approval plans and blanket orders do not work well when there is a relatively small book budget to cover a wide range of subject areas. In addition, college libraries were and are rarely in a position to hire additional staff specifically and exclusively for the development of their collections. The result has been a relatively unchanged pattern in college libraries, which is very similar to the university library pattern of twenty years ago, that of faculty selection in their subject areas with library staff selecting the general reference material and filling the gaps, although there has been a slight shift toward more selection by librarians in recent years. This slight shift has rarely resulted in any major organizational changes, however; for, as with university branch libraries, staffs are usually too small, when changes in collection development responsibilities occur, to allow for anything other than a reapportionment of these responsibilities as added duties to existing staff members.

LARGE PUBLIC LIBRARIES

While the primary perceived function and raison d'être of the American public library has changed in the past several hundred years from reform to education to recreation to research (16), there has never been any question as to who is responsible for developing the collections to perform these functions. It was, is, and almost certainly will continue to be the librarian and the library staff, for unlike academic libraries, public libraries have never had a body or group outside the library staff which was adequate to or consistently interested in the performance of this vital task. There have of course always been the self-appointed guardians of public morals who have from time to time shown a consuming interest in certain portions of one or another public library's collection, but their focus has been narrow, their interest inconstant, and their qualifications doubtful at best. Also, their interest has been less in selecting than in deselecting.

Nearly all professional staff members in public libraries of all sizes are usually involved in the selection process in one way or another. In large public library systems, however, with the large numbers and wide deployment of their staffs and the great variety of their organizational patterns, the manner of that involvement varies widely.

Large metropolitan library systems are usually made up of a central library with subject departments headed by subject specialists and a general collection for popular or home reading, together with branch libraries containing predominantly popular materials. The general collection in the central library and the branch libraries are usually headed by generalists. The subject specialists select for their departments, but selection for the general reading collections in the central and branch libraries may vary from highly centralized to widely dispersed. One pattern often followed is a selection committee in the central library, made up of both central and branch librarians, who may serve on a rotating basis. Review copies are distributed to the individual librarians in the central and branch libraries who prepare evaluations for the selecting committee based on an examination of the book and/or published reviews. The committee meets regularly to consider these evaluations, some of which are presented orally, and to prepare lists of those approved for purchase by central and branch librarians (17). In some systems these reviews are prepared by the central library department heads. It is by no means universal, however, that branches can only select books that have been approved by a higher, or another, authority, and, indeed, all the elements in the selection pattern described above are subject to almost infinite variation.

A librarian in a large public library system may be involved in selection in a wide variety of ways then, including reviewing assigned books for consideration by another individual or body, selecting from an approved list, and selecting from any source that is available, including written reviews, oral reviews, approval copies of the books themselves, etc. One thing which nearly all public librarians have in common with regard to selection responsibilities, however, is that they have only part-time responsibilities in this area. Few if any librarians in a public library of any size are full-time selectors. Even subject specialists in highly specialized departments of major metropolitan libraries usually have other service or administrative responsibilities.

While the organization of collection development in large public libraries varies widely, there are certain trends that are discernible. One is a decreasing emphasis on the central selection meeting with oral reviews and an increase in the authority of branch librarians to make selections without reference to an approved list. Another is the increase in the use of subject specialists. The educational function of the public library has been assuming increasingly greater importance in the past several years, and it has been predicted that by 1980 the central city libraries will be primarily research centers. Indeed, those in New York, Boston, Cleveland, Cincinnati, Detroit, Baltimore, Pittsburgh, and Los Angeles, to mention only a few, can be said to fit that description now (18). This of course means a greater reliance on subject specialists, librarians who are chosen for their subject expertise and whose primary, but not sole, responsibility is the development of the collection in that subject area.

COUNTY AND REGIONAL PUBLIC LIBRARY SYSTEMS

Book selection in county and regional systems is very similar to that in large public library systems that have a major central library with a large research component. Without the additional subject knowledge which is available from subject specialists in the central library of a large public library system, however, it would seem logical to assume that there is less centralized control of selection and more autonomy for the member or branch libraries in a county or regional system, but it is not clear whether or not this is in fact the case. The procedures of assigning reviews to individual librarians within the system and holding regular system-wide review meetings are still widespread. The individual librarian in such a system has as good a chance of being involved in selection and in as great a variety of ways as the individual librarian in a large public library system.

MEDIUM-SIZED PUBLIC LIBRARIES

The medium-sized public library, which is not part of a county or regional system, has fewer options in the use of its staff for collection development and less expertise overall to draw on. The selection is ordinarily coordinated by the head librarian or the assistant head, with help from the entire professional staff. The review of the major selection aids is often assigned to staff members, either by assigning certain aids to certain staff members or by assigning the responsibility for them by subject, according to the librarians' interests or educational background. Responsibility for reviewing individual titles is rarely assigned, however, since approval copies are rarely available to libraries of this size. Some librarians in medium-sized libraries attend the selection meetings of large public library or regional library systems and many of them receive the lists of reviewed books that are prepared by these systems (*19*).

SMALL PUBLIC LIBRARIES

In these libraries there is often only one full-time staff member and more often only one professional librarian, so there is no question as to how or to whom selection responsibility is assigned: it rests with the librarian, who may solicit help from other staff members, interested users, and trustees, and who often relies heavily on state library extension agency lists and a limited number of selection aids (*20*).

SCHOOL LIBRARIES

Like the librarian of a small public library, the school librarian is nearly always solely responsible for the development of the collection. However, the public served by the school librarian is more limited and more available, and so can be called on for more regular help. A faculty library committee may be appointed, or interested teachers may be enlisted to aid in selection. In larger school systems, evaluation centers have been established, where librarians may examine materials, and some school systems hold regular review and discussion meetings (21). Certain large schools have established departmentalized resource centers in place of the single school library. With several librarians involved in selecting materials for the various departments, there are the inevitable problems of overlap and duplication, and a coordinator may be needed (22).

The Grosse Pointe, Michigan, Public Library has developed a program in which librarians from local high schools and private schools are invited to attend the public library book-selection meetings. The school librarians can make recommendations at these meetings and comment on the recommendations of the public librarians, particularly with regard to the projected use of the recommended titles by students in their schools. The public librarians also of course give the school librarians valuable suggestions for additions to their collections. This interplay is important and productive for all concerned, for public and private schools often depend on public libraries.

SPECIAL LIBRARIES

Special libraries vary widely in their size, their subject matter, the forms and types of materials which they collect, and the clientele they serve. In the great majority of cases, however, they are so small that the development of the collection is the sole responsibility of the head librarian, who is often the only librarian. Special librarians have a special need, however, to work closely with their users in discharging this responsibility, for these users often require specific and detailed information very rapidly. It is essential, therefore, that the librarian have as clear an understanding as possible of the nature of the information which the library will be expected to provide. Usually special libraries collect in a relatively narrow subject area, but within that area they may collect in considerable depth. This often requires going beyond the regular selection tools employed by other librarians and discovering and developing other sources of information, which can include contacting individuals working in the field and institutions directly. This too can involve a special library's own users, who may well be not only requestors but also potential sources of information.

A formal library committee made up of the most interested and knowledgeable users is sometimes employed, to advise on selections and in certain instances to help present the library's case for adequate support (*23*).

CONCLUSION

Librarians have always been responsible for the content and therefore the development of their collections. Rarely, however, have they had libraries which were large enough or well-funded enough to allow them to assign that total responsibility to themselves or to other staff members in the same way they assign responsibility for acquisitions, cataloging, or circulation, without any thought of outside help. Assistance in collection development has always been available from outside sources, whether they be faculty members of other interested users, and the success of a library in serving its users is dependent to a very large extent on how effectively the librarian uses the total selection resources available, both inside and outside the library.

REFERENCES

1. J. Periam Danton, *Book Selection and Collections: A Comparison of German and American University Libraries.* (New York: Columbia University Press, 1963), pp. 12-13.

2. Ibid., pp. 14-19.

3. Ibid., p. 26.

4. Ibid., p. 47.

5. Louis Round Wilson and Maurice Tauber, *The University Library*, 2nd ed. (New York: Columbia University Press, 1956), pp. 349-359.

6. Mary Duncan Carter and Wallace John Bonk, *Building Library Collections*. (Metuchen, N.J.: Scarecrow Press, 1959), p. 82.

7. Guy Lyle, *The President, the Professor, and the College Library*. (New York: H.W. Wilson, 1963), p. 39.

8. William Randall, *The College Library*. (Chicago: ALA, 1932), p.p. 22-23, 105.

9. Keyes Metcalf, "The Essentials of an Acquisitions Program." In *The Acquisition and Cataloging of Books*, William M. Randall, ed. (Chicago: University of Chicago Press, 1940), pp. 82-83.

10. J. Periam Danton, "The Subject Specialist in National and University Libraries," *Libri* 17 (1967): 49.

11. Rutherford D. Rogers and David C. Weber, *University Library Administration*. (New York: H.W. Wilson, 1971), p. 119.

12. Wilson and Tauber, op. cit., p. 352.

13. Robert Haro, "Book Selection in Academic Libraries," *College and Research Libraries* 27 (March 1967): 104.

14. Robert Haro, "The Bibliographer in the Academic Library," *Library Resources and Technical Services* 13 (Spring 1969): 163-169.

15. Wilmer H. Baatz, "Collection Development in Nineteen Libraries of the Association of Research Libraries," *Library Acquisitions: Practice and Theory* 11, no. 2 (1978).

16. James Howard Wellard, "The History of the Public Library Movement as the Basis for a Social Theory of Book Selection." In *Background Readings in Building Library Collections*, Mary Virginia Gaver, ed. (Metuchen, N.J.: Scarecrow Press, 1969).

17. Mary Duncan Carter, Wallace John Bonk, and Rose Mary Magrill, *Building Library Collections*, 4th ed. (Metuchen, N.J.: Scarecrow Press, 1974), pp. 17-19.

18. Larry Earle Bone and Thomas A. Paines, "The Nature of the Urban Main Library: Its Relation to Selection and Collection Building," *Library Trends* 20 (April 1972): 627-628.

19. Carter, Bonk, and Magrill, op. cit., pp. 21-22.

20. Ibid., p. 23.

21. Ibid., p. 61.

22. Eleanor Ahlers and Mary Sypert, "The Case for Decentralization," *Library Journal* 94 (November 15, 1969): 4207-4210.

23. Carter, Bonk, and Magrill, op. cit., p. 67.

The Allocation of Money Within the Book Budget

Murray S. Martin

INTRODUCTION

It is the purpose of this chapter to discuss the reasons for budget planning, the kinds of things that must be considered and various ways of making the allocation. There is no pretense that there is any best way of handling money, just as there is no single best way of deciding on a collection development policy statement. The librarians in each library must determine what is best for that library. Inasmuch as the statements made are general, they apply equally to all types of libraries. Each type, however, has specific differences which must be taken into consideration. It is clearly impossible to offer three or four different solutions or sets of guidelines on every topic. The practice followed will therefore be to select examples from different kinds of libraries to illustrate specific points. Finally, it presumed that the concern here is with the distribution of funds within a given budget rather than the preparation of a request for funds.

THE PURPOSE OF AN ALLOCATION SYSTEM

The primary purpose of any allocation is to match funds with needs. Since the library budget itself "is a statement that identifies in monetary terms the ways in which an institution will seek to achieve its goals" (1), the amount of money allocated for books already has made to some extent a statement about the resource expectations of the library. Those who have further to subdivide this amount will have to live within the constraints it sets or revel in the indulgences it allows. It is important to remember that this statement of expectations may and usually does issue from a higher authority than the chief librarian. The total amount budgeted may thus express satisfaction with or concern about library activity in the recent past, and, whatever the message, it should be heeded as the total is subdivided.

Matching funds with needs appears simplistic as a basic rule for budgeting, but it is, in fact, as Schad has demonstrated (2), the only sound one. Determining those needs and then giving them a dollar value is, however, a far from simple process. Some guidance will be found from the library's collection development statement, some from the experience the year just past, and some from the reactions of administrators and patrons. Whatever the ways of determining these needs may be, the allocation system is an attempt to distribute funds in a way that will satisfy them.

The second purpose is to provide guidelines for personnel involved in selecting and ordering materials. The amount allocated for a subject, for a type of purchase, e.g., serials, or for a branch sets both limits and quotas: limits because a ceiling is set that represents only so many purchases, and quotas because that number of purchases must be seen in relation to the total potential number. The way in which such strictures are interpreted will depend on those upon whom responsibility devolves. It is important therefore that both the method of allocation and the resulting allocation be understood by those who must work to achieve the goals it represents. Unless this is so the important quidelines function will have been neglected.

Thirdly, any allocation should reflect priorities. Ideally, these will have been set forth in a policy statement, but policy statements, however detailed, can only be in general terms. Implementation of policy requires that priorities be set and values defined. Any budget is the "central expression" (3) of this process and, in effect, crystallizes and gives permanent form to earlier decisions. Sometimes indeed the simple matching of financial cost to previously unchallenged, because unmeasured, priorities will assist in their reassessment. This should occur during the process of allocation rather than become evident during the year when any change in priorities must result in shifts between funds with all the confusion that implies. The budget statement automatically establishes priorities. This is not because the book budget tells people what to do. It is because it is impossible to respend money differently. Once the bills are paid they are, unless refunds can be obtained, paid and the money that was paid to them is no longer available for any other purpose.

Finally, the allocation provides a plan against which to measure accomplishment. How rigidly the plan must be observed will depend on the various constraints under which the library must work. No plan should be so rigid that variation is impossible, yet it is clear that if it is so flexible as to accommodate indefinite degrees of change then there is truly no plan. A plan offers incentives toward responsible activity and provides ways in which individuals can measure their own sense of contribution to the goals of the whole library. The allocation must therefore be firm enough to support and maintain the general and specific goals of the library, but flexible enough to allow adjustment to match demonstrated need. It must also be able to be measured during the year in order to know whether goals are in fact being achieved and needs met.

It is seldom that any allocation will achieve all these purposes equally, but they need to be borne in mind during the allocation process in order to decide, if necessary, which is the more important to the library so that more stress can be given to it. This is particularly important when the library is undertaking a major new activity when it may be essential to divert funds temporarily to the activity. One instance might be stocking a new branch or book-mobile, another the development of a basic collection in a new discipline. Since it is seldom the case that adequate new money is supplied, it will usually be necessary to cut back in some degree in established programs. In such a case specific new goals and priorities would take precedence over the general ones relating to maintenance of past efforts. Nevertheless, the budget allocation would still respond to and provide for current goals.

FACTORS WHICH INFLUENCE THE ALLOCATION PROCEDURE

The provision of funds is basically a political process. This is so whatever the context, whether in institutions supported by public funds, or in private industry. Political in this sense means reflecting the realities of power and control, embodying the results of trade-offs between different groups, responsive to customer pressure. These are factors which many managers and professionals overlook. Many also disapprove of them as matters which distort the purity of an ideal pattern. Whatever the case, these factors are real and cannot be ignored unless to set other accomplishments at risk. They may be classified into three broad groups: internal, relating to the library itself; institutional, relating to the institution of which the library is part; and noninstitutional, relating to external factors such as legislation and economics.

Internal Factors

There are four kinds of internal factors that may be considered as operational, organizational, historical, and philosophical. Operational factors relate to the ways in which decisions will be implemented. Clearly the actual allocation of funds will be very different if records and assignments are to be kept by vendor rather than by subject.

Equally, if large segments of the budget are allocated to blanket orders or approval plans, the resulting fund distribution will be very different from one where no such plans are to be accounted for. A decentralized ordering process will result in an operating budget that is very different from one prepared for a single ordering department, even though both may reflect precisely the same institutional goals. The principal difference will lie in the numbers of funds and their organization. Similarly, where orders for monographs and serials, perhaps microform and other nonbook media, are handled in different departments this fact must be reflected in the structure of the budget. This might be reinforced by institutional arrangements for budgetary reimbursement to separate purchasing or processing agencies within the institution. Whatever the operational factors, the budget will need to be so constructed as to facilitate translation into operational terms.

The organization of the library will affect the shape of the budget considerably. The simplest organization—one librarian in a small, single-purpose library—can have a very simple budget, perhaps even one line representing total expenditure, but such simplicity is not available to a large university with several campuses, nor to a county library system with large numbers of branch libraries. The goal of any allocation should be to reflect the purpose underlying the structure of the organization. After all, branch libraries are set up to provide reading matter for a given community, whether it is the Department of Physics, or a suburban community, and each will have different interests and different needs. These should be provided for in the budget. It is important to realize that this system of allocation may intersect with others, for example, the need to be aware of total expenditures by type of purchase. The resulting allocation would therefore form a matrix by location and type of purchase. The mode of selection used will also have an effect. It has been common in academic libraries to distribute selection functions widely both inside and outside the library itself. If these are each to be treated as individual accounts then the budget will contain a large number of allocations. They may, however, be grouped together and the responsibility for further subdivision at the working level farmed out. This style of working reflects the lack of homogeneity on the academic community. On the other hand, where interests are likely to be held in common regardless of location, as in a public library system, accounts may be cast in broad terms, e.g., fiction, non-fiction, juvenile, and assignment to location achieved by review or policy committees or by inspection and ordering of titles from a central display. Similarly, the distinction may be made between reference and circulating collections. Reference in this case would mean a central consulting (noncirculating) collection of rather larger dimensions than a reference collection in a department or branch library and would range widely in subject matter. These examples could be multiplied many times, but the important point to remember is that the way a library is organized affects the allocation system used.

Organization is linked closely to history. Over time any institution will develop some kind of tradition, and libraries are no exception. Although the cry "we've always done it this way" may disguise inefficiency and be used to obstruct necessary change, it may also represent a sense of tradition which can be neglected only at your peril. In many academic libraries, for instance, no matter how rational the transfer of some subject responsibilities may be, faculty opposition may make it impossible or at best very slow to achieve. In such cases the librarian must decide how necessary the change is to the programs of the library and to be prepared to make and defend it only if it is essential. The same argument applies to the closing and reshaping of branch libraries where social, fiscal, and political forces come into play and may force a decision which is inefficient for the library but clearly effective for the group of interested users. When examining an existing budget for change it is therefore important to know the historical facts that lie behind it. Only with such knowledge at hand is it possible to work for necessary changes. Another way of defining this factor is as style of operation. Style is far harder to change than organization. Unlike fashion, it represents the deeply held beliefs and values by which the library is guided in its daily business. Changing a system of allocations cannot change style, at least not overnight, and may well simply result in confusion. This is not an argument for rigid traditionalism, merely a caution to be aware of the limits to which innovation can be effective. Alternative ways of achieving the same ends may be more in line with traditional ways and thus easier to accept. The history of approval plans and blanket orders in academic libraries provides many examples of ways to innovate and ways not to. In budget terms, it is frequently possible to maintain the desired control and to retrieve needed management information by manipulation of the financial records into various formats and thus avoid the problems caused by the alteration of an established system of fund responsibilities.

The intention behind any system of allocation is also important. Close supervision and generalized guidance are totally different objectives requiring totally different kinds of financial controls. To some extent the library's objectives are determined by outside considerations, notably those of the governing body, but some general attitude must be adopted. A budget is, for example, a tool used to ensure fiscal responsibility. Ford describes briefly an interesting application of this principle in the use of the "periodic release of funds—to assure that there will be sufficient funds to provide for purchases throughout the year" (4). Such quarterly disbursements of funds may also be used by institutions to control cash flow and to prevent the accumulation of unwanted encumbrances at the end of the year. This kind of fiscal control may be one of the objectives of the funding system. Another may be control of the proportions of expenditure by type of purchase. The needs of different kinds of libraries are different, but in each case a decision has to be made as to what kind of control will be exercised over what purchases, and the budget allocations structured to reflect that decision. The ability of the library to shift funds after the beginning of the year must also be considered. If no such possibility exists, then it becomes very important that selectors and purchasers adhere closely to the fiscal restraints expressed in the budget allocation. If some latitude is allowed, generally expressed in budget terms, by the existence of contingency or reserve funds or by statements concerning the degree of over- or underexpenditure permitted by category, the adherence to the fiscal restraints has less importance than a fulfillment of the general goals. In no case, however, can expenditure exceed the total made available to the library. Overexpenditure in one area must be balanced by underexpenditure in another. In such a case the decision as to what will be permitted is a political one based on perceptions of the best interests of the library, rather than a purely economic one.

Institutional Factors

There are four kinds of institutional influences. These derive from the general objectives of the parent institution, its organization, the locus of budgetary control, and the kinds of budgetary restraints exercised. The library, with the rare exception of those independent libraries whose services are their own raison d'être, is usually part of an institution or organization and its goals must therefore be in conformity with the goals and objectives of the larger whole. In the case of a university, its library's goals should be to support the institution's academic programs. Special libraries are required to support the research and service goals of the organization, which may, for example, require a great deal of information retrieval but have little use for stored resources. In fact, it is only a small minority of libraries, the great research libraries of the nation, which have as a resource goal the accumulation of resources. Most public and many smaller college libraries are much more interested in maintaining a strong collection of current interest because this corresponds more closely to their service goals. Differences of this kind require that the allocation of funds should aim at different mixes of incoming resources. In the same way, differences in the size and composition of the community served will affect the distribution of funds. The numbers of readers may be less important to an academic library than the numbers of academic disciplines they represent, but the absolute numbers of children, young people, and adults served by a public library may be the most important determinant of the way money should be allocated.

The way in which the parent institution is organized can also have an important effect. This is particularly so in an academic setting where the existence of separate colleges or professional schools may determine the initial gross division of expenditures, but the same is true of large public library systems and school units where the numbers of service points need to be taken into account. It is frequently difficult to reconcile such organizational patterns to the necessities of a library. In effect, academic departments or differing service points constitute a kind of arbitrary classification system which will almost certainly not correspond to the classification system used by the library. If the collection development policy has been worked out in terms of the classification system then these must be reinterpreted to match the organizational classification (5). Or, to look at it in reverse for a moment, the processing which is needed to locate materials in their eventual homes will be that much more complicated as organization is superimposed upon classification and cataloging requirements. The character of each unit within a library has to reflect the needs of its users. The users of a downtown business-reference library have needs totally different from those of readers in a branch serving mostly retirees. The costs of the resources, their numbers and upkeep will be different. Moreover, some units will undoubtedly have more political clout than others. A college or department that brings in a lot of research money, thus enhancing the prestige of the university, can expect far more attention to be paid to its demands than one with a low profile and little need for research resources. Moreover, in times of change, the administration may well be downgrading a department where there are no jobs for graduates, and it would be foolish for the library to increase its share of the resources.

The way in which an institution is governed and managed may have a great deal to say about how a library's funds should be allocated. Librarians tend to feel that they as professionals should be entrusted with the task but, particularly in public libraries, the general control may rest with the council, committee, or board of trustees, who may even specify in detail what must be done. This can be accomplished by use of line-item budgeting or by the mechanism of the bid process. Formulas, such as are used in many states, may set the general trend of the acquisitions budget. They are less likely to make positive requirements, than by inertia to have a negative effect, since they are based on numbers of programs, numbers of students and similar parameters which make it very hard to alter significantly the historical pattern of distribution. Where a faculty committee decides the distribution of funds it is very likely to be political in nature rather than programmatic. The librarian can persuade by argument or by demonstration of economic facts but will seldom be able to make much headway in getting a development plan adopted that does not in some way accommodate the prejudices and beliefs of the committee.

If the financial administration of the institution has specific rules for the handling and recording of purchases, these must be taken into account when establishing a budget allocation, since those rules may mandate certain kinds of groupings and it may not be worth the time and energy to maintain separate records within the library.

Budgetary sources themselves are an important factor in setting up any budget. In most cases there is one major source, the grant from the general funds of the institution, which may or may not be accompanied by restrictions. If, as is the case in some public or school libraries, this sum is already divided between general categories such as books, periodicals, and audiovisual materials, the main lines of the allocation have already been set and any variation may require a budget amendment on the part of the governing body. Frequently libraries receive special-purpose grants, such as those for setting up a new branch or buying basic materials in support of a new program. Such grants normally require the keeping of separate records to demonstrate that expenditures have been made in line with the purpose of the grant. Gifts and endowments may be general or specific and allocations must be made in order to ensure that the materials selected match the terms of the gifts. The same is true of federal funds, where the regulations may require certain emphases in line with the original proposal. The funds granted to libraries are intended to be used to further the intentions of the grantors and they will expect at least some congruence with these intentions to be demonstrated by the year-end reports. Melcher makes the very interesting point that "control of the details of public expenditure is critically important" (6). Although he is discussing broader categories of expenditure, it is necessary for librarians to remember that they are accountable to others for their acts as professionals. Allocations of expenditures should conform to budgetary restrictions and should be in line with the intentions of those who provided the money. If a pet program was not approved and not funded, money provided for other purposes should not be diverted to it.

Noninstitutional Factors

There are four kinds of noninstitutional factors which must be borne in mind. These are political, economic, social, and professional in nature. Although some political factors have been touched on already, there are others more general in nature and usually reflected in legislation. While libraries are for the most part not specifically mentioned, legislation on discrimination, urban renewal, the handicapped all carry with them messages to libraries that these are areas they should be concerned with. Sometimes indeed they are directly concerned since funds from these sources may be received by their institutions and the library may be asked to assist or required to meet standards or adhere to regulations required by the legislation. Sometimes library programs are directly funded by local, state, or federal legislatures. Such programs might include a state-wide, shared-resource network, specific allocations for collection-development, special responsibilities to the blind or other handicapped groups. Funding under an equalization system, or to forward public libraries in the state, may require the meeting of specific standards, including levels of expenditure on library materials. Such requirements might then in turn require accounting for matching funds or showing what funding sources were used for what kinds of material purchases.

Economic factors relate principally to inflation. It is very important to be aware of the differential rates of price increase shown by different types of publication and by different subject areas (7). Reference to the annual reports on price indexes (8) and to the historical summaries published in the Bowker Annual can be used to determine general trends which can be modified by the specific needs of the library's own resource mix. It is in this connection that the proportion of expenditures on periodicals is important to establish and control, since these expenditures are those most subject to inflationary increases. Significant shifts do, however, occur within such groupings. Close study of an article such as that by Brown on "Price Indexes: 1978" (9) will indicate just how diverse are the trends that may be incorporated within any one price index. Although we are accustomed to thinking of such matters principally in relation to periodical subscriptions, similar trends are visible in book prices, where, for example, the prices of fiction and children's books have increased substantially and where poetry books and books on music are no longer so low in relation to other categories.

The second kind of inflation that must be taken into account relates to the world economy. Devaluation of various currencies, floating dollars, strong and weak economies have all had their effects on library allocations. This is particularly noticeable in the case of hard-bound British books which have now almost entirely lost a once wide price advantage over books published in America. Almost any survey would show similar extensive differences in relationships over a period of two to five years. If a library, to fulfill its collection development goals, must buy extensively the publications of a country such as Germany, then provision will have to be made for a much higher proportion of the budget each year, unless the goals are to be modified by being scaled downward. Although frequently disregarded, postage and other shipping costs are a very important factor, particularly now that the U.S. Postal Service has decided to phase out over a period of years the postal advantages previously enjoyed by firms shipping to libraries. Unless more money is available this must mean that the numbers of units ordered will decrease or alternative methods of supply will be sought, both of which may cause changes in the system of allocation.

Social influences relate to the goals libraries will seek to achieve. These may include increased services to and awareness of minorities with resulting emphases on materials that previously were neither sought nor acquired. Such a change in goals will require the allocation of funds, most probably the reallocation from other programs. At different times society will stress different areas. A good example will be the stress on scientific research that followed Sputnik. These may be as dramatic as that episode or as subtle as the present disillusion with international affairs, one result of which has been decreased interest in foreign languages. The question here is how can and should libraries respond to such social changes. While no one would suggest that response to every fad should be immediate it is unlikely that libraries will be more immune than any other institution from the effects of long-term social trends. Another kind of change arises from society's ways of communication. Whereas the book reigned almost alone until the middle of this century, other forms of communication have now come to rival that preeminence. There are indications that we seem to have moved from a cognitive to an affective mode of learning (*10*). This would have long-range implications for libraries since they would be required to divert more and more resources to the audiovisual type of material including computer retrieval of information and transmission by television. Even without moving to such an extreme, libraries must respond to demands for a wider range of resources which require reconsideration of budgetary strategies.

The library profession, partly in response to social and economic influences but also in response to clearer analysis of its own capabilities, has come to regard ownership of materials as less important than it was. We have not yet come to substitute access to information entirely for ownership, but all libraries now design their programs to encompass both. Such a change requires that we rethink the setting of previously unquestioned fund boundaries. Some libraries have already decided to pay for individual access to information (*11*) as being simply an extension of buying materials, albeit on a temporary, personal basis. As it becomes increasingly more efficient to use computer-based searches and to obtain the necessary materials either from a distant sole-source or through a consortium or network (*12*), then it would be appropriate to allocate a portion of the library materials budget to the cost of that process. Even now, in the interests of equal access, careful consideration should be given by all libraries to absorbing the cost of borrowing materials by interlibrary loan, that is, transaction costs or photocopy costs imposed by lending libraries. A parallel movement can be found in the extension of consortia goals to include cooperative acquisition and other forms of cost-sharing. For a long time memberships in such consortia as the Centre for Research Libraries have been regarded as legitimate charges against library materials budgets and it is to be expected that such instances will multiply in the future. Whether the sum in question is a specific amount or a percentage or variable is less important than the concept that a certain amount of the library's budget will be dedicated to resource-sharing.

In summary, all the factors enumerated above will affect to some degree that final allocation of funds. Sometimes the effect will be in terms of the influence on general goals, sometimes in small, specific areas, but the most important effect may be termed *environmental*. These influences may best be compared to climatic variations and their effects on agriculture, industrial location, social behavior and therefore ultimately politics and culture in general. While they may not control specific allocations they provide guidelines which are no less powerful from being unstated.

PREPARATORY INFORMATION

There are two kinds of information needed when planning an allocation of funds: historical and current. Both contain objective and subjective statements, each of which must be evaluated and placed in relation to the others so that an appropriate weighting can be given to it.

Historical information includes long-term trend analyses. These can usually be derived from the library's own budget reports, supplemented by the various price-index analyses and by the library's annual statistics. Items to look for include changes in total budget, changes in the relationships between the various parts, and patterns of expenditure. The latter, in particular, should be compared with such matters as numbers of items purchased. Have there been any significant variations or changes that suggest that item prices have forced a redistribution of effort?

The results of examining budgets and statistical reports should then be compared with the goals and objectives of the collection development program. This comparison will reveal whether budget allocations or changes in prices have caused significant deviations from the original plan. These deviations can then be examined for their causes and their effects. Some will require budgetary correction, either by providing more money in order to obtain more materials, or by reductions in allocations to bring expenditures more in line with general goals. Persistent deviations revealed by such a survey may require more study by other administrators in order to develop recommendations that can be incorporated in the budget allocation system. They may also suggest that the system of allocation used is unresponsive to current needs and that it should be changed. Naturally, such a change is easiest to prepare before the beginning of the fiscal year and it may be necessary to provide a temporary solution, e.g., the provision of contingency funds, while a longer-term solution is being developed.

Most libraries have some planning documents, even if they are not so labeled. Frequently, for example, an annual report will make some statements about future needs and future goals. Budget requests reflect and are founded upon goals for the period under consideration. Even if they are not explicitly stated, the amounts of money requested make implicit statements about the library's plans and expectations. These documents should be examined for their implications. If, for example, one goal is to bring a branch up to a level equal with certain others, or to expand specified services, then it is necessary to know how far these objectives have been achieved, and what remains to be done and what it will cost.

Current information refers essentially to the state of the library as it enters the new fiscal year. The most important information can be found from the records of last year's library materials budget. It will provide information as to how great a proportion of the budget is precommitted to standing orders of one kind or another. The year-end statement will also indicate how many outstanding orders there were and their value. How these are treated will be determined by the institution's financial policies. If they are carried forward as encumbrances, then they represent a further portion of the total that is precommitted. If they must be canceled and reordered, then that proportion still likely to be wanted must be allowed for. In the latter case, their existence may also suggest a more rigorous approach to control of ordering and expenditure during the next year.

The latest information on price trends, whether from the library's own records or from external sources, is of great importance. Unless such information can be incorporated in budget planning, price increases are likely to overthrow any collection development goals. Although this is specially true of increases in the price of periodicals, it is also true, as suggested earlier, of books from other countries and special subject fields. If there is no way of adjusting for differential price increases, then the adjustment will be made in terms of numbers of items bought which will almost certainly not be in conformity with the library's goals.

Although it may seem unnecessary since the budget has already been provided, it is essential to determine what money is actually likely to be available. This implies careful examination of predicated funds, of balances in special funds carried forward, and of conditions attached to any or all funds. It is also important to be aware of when funds will be made available since in some cases cash flow must be related to income flow (e.g., taxes which are collectible only late in the year), and this may in turn affect buying patterns and possible expenditures. In cases where an institution allows the reallocation of salary savings or other lapsed funds, it is highly desirable to begin the year with an estimate of what amount of such funds may become available. This management style has become increasingly necessary in academic institutions where reduced income expectations require that all funds be subject to contingency planning (12). Such estimates must, for safety, be conservative but the earlier they can be built into the budget the easier it is to incorporate them into planned expenditures. This is, incidentally, why rigid formulas are very difficult to apply in periods of fiscal uncertainty.

Information about program changes is essential. This kind of information extends from changes in population served to the addition of new academic programs. It will also incorporate stated changes in policies and priorities. If, for example, certain services such as quick provision of best-sellers in multiple copies are to be financed by rental charges or by any of several variations on lease plans rather than by regular purchase, this must be allowed for. Similarly, changes in the number of books that may be ordered for reserve use will cause changes in the corresponding allocations. Too often changes in library procedures or policies are introduced without thought to their budgetary effects and as a result the budget officer is criticized as obstructive. It may, for instance, make good sense to buy paperbacks for certain collections but, if the intention is to have them bound or stiffened, money has to be made available for that purpose. If the original allocation was made in terms of hard-bound units and instead double the number of paperbacks were purchased, not only will there be insufficient binding money, but the goals of collection development policy may be significantly changed. The examples could be extended indefinitely, but simply serve to remind librarians that budget allocations can respond only to known changes in policies and practices.

Frequently special needs exist which require specific budget provisions. Contracts may be up for review or cyclical renewals of periodical subscriptions may be at a higher level than last year. Even, perhaps, the purchase of a five-year index to *Chemical Abstracts* has come due. Sometimes also a special purchase has been agreed to on a kind of installment plan and must be regarded as something "off the top" of the budget. Equally in a good year savings may have been used to pay in advance on subscriptions, series or sets, so that the annual cost has been lost sight of but must now be met. All such needs must be investigated, their importance and priority determined and sufficient money set aside to meet their cost. Sometimes this means they must supersede other routine needs and sometimes the special program itself will have to be discontinued if enough money is not available to meet all needs.

METHODS OF ALLOCATION

The methods used for allocating funds vary all the way from simple impulse to carefully calibrated formulas. There is no particular evidence that the long-term results of the one are any better or worse than the other. All things being equal, however, it is more likely that a library will be better able to meet its collection development objectives, if allocation is undertaken in a systematic fashion.

The specific method used should be that which is most responsive to the individual library's needs and capacities. The guidelines currently under discussion by the Collection Development Committee of the Resources Section of the Resources and Technical Services Division of the American Library Association (*13*) make this plain and set out many of the questions and considerations applicable to any method. These guidelines, when published, will be a useful tool but like any other tool will need to be used with care and precision.

No existing method will meet all the needs of any library, and it is likely that elements of two or more methods will have to be used. Which method is stressed will depend partly on the type of library, partly on its size, and partly on the institutional approach to budgeting.

There are four basic approaches: the historical/political, the planned, the flexible responsible, and the organizational. The author's preference is for a matrix based on planning and organization with adjustments to recognize the need for flexible response to historical patterns (14). If that sounds like having your cake and eating it too, there are quite definite similarities, but its main defense is that it works. Nevertheless, no specific advocacy is being advanced in this section. Instead, the principal elements of each approach, its advantages and disadvantages will be reviewed briefly.

The Historical/Political Approach

No matter what approach is taken, history will play a part in its development. This type of allocation usually follows a political distribution, by academic department in a university, by branch or member library in a public library system. It is usually traditional and will reinforce what already exists by continuing the same pattern of expenditure. It is usually couched in broad terms such as Reference and Lending, Humanities and Science, but may also be allocated on a basis which bears little relation to library concepts, e.g., the College of Human Development, or in divisions of incredible minuteness, e.g., Comparative Oceanic Linguistics. In this it reflects the organization of the parent or controlling organization. Some element of this approach will always remain whenever a library has some special organizational unit that is relatively independent and not easily amenable to classification. A standard example would be a Rare Books Room or an endowed children's collection.

The advantages of such a system are that it responds to the sense of individuality and autonomy held by units with their own history. This allows and encourages such units to develop appropriate collections in close harmony with their user's needs. It also encourages careful selection and high standards but only if the budget is not so generous as to encourage slackness. This can be countered by the ease with which accountability can be enforced.

The disadvantages include the serious one of wide duplication and overlapping of collections. In a public library system this is, of course, necessary but in a university it can lead to serious wastage of funds. It may also lead to competition for funds or even for subjects which are thought to attract further funding, and except with the most dedicated group of specialists it is unlikely to lead to any cohesive development of collections since so many areas will inevitably be overlooked as being no one's responsibility. It is therefore most appropriate in an institution which consists of loosely linked units each of which has a specific area of responsibility which is clearly separated from all the others. It is inappropriate in any institution which is unitary in nature.

The Planned Approach

This approach regards the budget allocation as a means of reaching the goals of the institution. It reaches its apogee in the formula budget, but may in fact range from very simple to very complex allocations. The element common to all is that it expresses in fiscal terms the results of a number of statements about the library's resource and service goals. The effectiveness of the allocation does not need to depend on the elaboration of the variables used. In fact, too elaborate an analysis would be counterproductive in the case of a small general library or of a single-purpose special one.

A basic requirement for planned allocation is the division of the library (or the collection; the two are not necessarily synonymous) into units each of which can be assigned as specific developmental areas. These areas can then be analyzed for variables such as numbers of published books and average prices on the one hand, and numbers of readers or students, circulations or credit hours on the other. By comparison of the variables a sense of priority or a series of weightings can be developed which will enable budgetary allocations to be made reflecting these conclusions. The various elements can be refined and their numbers increased or decreased depending on the fineness with which the eventual division of funds has to be made.

Such an approach is frequently characterized as using a formula. This is not necessarily so. A formula implies that no exercise of intuitive sense is desirable or that deviations from its results are improper. If indeed it is applied so insensitively it does the library a disservice. As an example, at the author's institution all students are required to take three credits of Physical Education which results in a credit-hour production greater than that of the French Department. Rigid application of a formula based on credit hours would require that more money be spent on basic books on sports than on all the riches of the French language. Formulas, that is to say, must be interpreted with sensitivity and discretion. They are useful guides but tyrannous masters.

The best-known formula approach is that of McGrath (*15*) where the principal service element measured is circulation. This has the advantage of being common to all types of libraries, but the severe disadvantage of eliminating consideration of all noncirculating use, usually of periodicals. Proposals developed by Kohut (*16*) do take periodicals into consideration. From a rather different point of view Gore in *Farewell to Alexandria* (*17*) uses the formula approach to destroy belief in the effectiveness of the accumulation of riches in favor of strict utilitarianism. Such a brief note of several careful and elaborate allocation proposals is somewhat unfair but the reader is better served by reading the articles than by the best of synopses.

The difficulties of any formulaic approach lie in determining the elements to be measured and then in measuring them adequately. The fewer the factors the easier they are to count and to manipulate, but the coarser will be the results. It is, however, questionable whether a fine division is necessary, particularly if there are not enough people to assign to the eventual divisions made. Conversely, of course, there may be plenty of people and the assignments could be so small as to resemble a book-of-the-month lottery. Practicality, which in this instance frequently has historical or organizational overtones, must be the touchstone in deciding what kinds of factors should be used and what divisions made.

Relating one factor to another can be difficult. The use of library classification systems to sort out academic course offerings may be useful in small schools without wide variety and overlap, but a catalog of 6,000 courses in 100 departmental arrangements is simply too unwieldy (*18*). Besides, how do you organize the resulting profile? It may quite successfully define the range of subjects or highlight areas of concentration, but there is no way in which it can suggest a grouping of selection assignments that can be used to designate library or faculty selectors. In the same way circulation figures are a simplistic measure of use and do not, moreover, indicate how this measure is to be extended into allocation or selection in any practical way.

The advantages of a planned approach, whether or not a recognized "formula" is used, stem from the word *planned*. Analysis of present success, analysis of available information on use, the development of techniques to define a clientele, which are planning elements, are all necessary parts of the allocation process. Whether or not collection use is taken to be a critical factor throughout, if records *and inspection* show that one or more portions of the collections are not being used then it is clear either that there is no interest in those materials or that the wrong selections have been made (*19*). In either case the allocation and selection mechanism must be used to correct a serious defect. A planned allocation sets collection goals that reflect the goals and activities of the institution. To this extent, at the least, planned allocation must be a feature of all allocation systems.

Disadvantages are many, but they are mostly the results of specific applications rather than of principle. Rigidity is a danger. It can only be avoided if every factor of the analysis is reworked each year. The difficulty of doing this is a serious drawback, as is the difficulty of obtaining values for all the necessary variables in the first place. Most systems have difficulty with nonstandard areas such as noncirculating reference, replacement needs, duplicates or reserves. Moreover, nearly all formulas are couched in terms that apply to academic and research libraries. Work on this method of allocation will continue and refinement will improve its acceptability. In the meantime its major lesson—that allocation should in some measure reflect user activity—should be learned and incorporated into the planning of all libraries.

The Flexible/Responsive Approach

The principal element of this approach is the view that each budget allocation is a new endeavor. Its purpose is to respond to demonstrated need, regardless of past practices. Need is defined principally as the ability to define what is required to forward the goals and objectives of the unit making the request. This may be stated in such terms as proportions of standard bibliographies not held, or proportions of current publications not able to be obtained. It may also be stated in terms of unsatisfied user needs, e.g., how many personal reserves per title and how long they had to wait, or changed needs reflecting population changes in a branch library area (20). Whatever the factor being considered it is considered as objectively as possible. If no one is carrying on advanced research in classics it is probably immaterial whether the library holds 20 percent or 80 percent of the titles in Migne, but only 20 percent of the nineteenth-century titles cited in the *Cambridge Bibliography of English Literature* is almost certainly inadequate to support a major doctoral program in nineteenth-century English literature.

The statement of need should also contain a specific suggestion on how that need can be met to enable the different statements to be melded together. In addition there are more general statements relating to a current purchasing profile (21), to maintenance of subscriptions, and the like. These general or continuing needs account for the major portion of the allocation, and special needs are fitted into the budget in a variable fashion. In one year specific programs may be given higher priority with funds allocated to achieve specific goals during the year and in the next year some of these will be deemphasized while new ones are given more prominence. This may be called a symphonic approach, with the collection development officer as conductor calling forth particular instruments at particular times in order to achieve an overall pattern.

The principal advantage of this method is that it can respond to particular need, even to crises, because the distribution pattern is not firmly set. Another advantage is that it can respond more readily to change. It also requires the proponents of specific proposals to provide evidence to justify an allocation.

Its disadvantage lies in the necessary element of subjectivity involved. Evaluation can include prejudice and the whole process places a heavy strain on whomever is adjudicating the allocation. It is therefore open to abuse and to charges of favoritism, and to combat these charges it is very likely that the degree of flexibility will be diminished as time goes on. Nevertheless some such element of flexibility is essential. At a minimum, this should be represented by an unallocated reserve. A more sophisticated use is the provision of enrichment funds for special collection development projects.

The Organizational Approach

This distribution is based on the ways in which purchases and expenditures will take place. The questions asked are what kinds of things will be bought and who will buy them. What is being sought is a way to monitor allocations once they are made without having to maintain several parallel methods of fiscal control. Allocations are therefore made primarily by type of material, e.g., periodicals, books, microforms, records. Secondary divisions are usually made by subject, department or branch, but primary accountability is reserved for the major division. Certain types of library budget where separate lines are used for each type of expenditure mandate this approach. Various combinations have been made such as using a formula for allocations for books but leaving periodical expenditures in a lump sum. None of these methods are adequate as the sole basis for an allocation. It is, however, essential because of differential price increases to know what proportion of the budget is allocated to each type of purchase and to maintain some kind of control over these proportions.

The principal advantage of this distribution is simplicity. It is probably adequate for a small single-purpose library and may also provide an appropriate basis for general allocations to units where unit activities are decentralized. In the latter case other methods of allocation can be used to determine the distribution within the unit. It is also easier to monitor and to control. Adjustments resulting from increased or decreased budgets can be made by changing the numbers of purchases to be made in each area. Needless to say, increments are more readily handled than decrements since the latter will mean canceling subscriptions as well as simply reducing book purchases. It does place responsibility and accountability squarely in a few places thus simplifying the decision-making process. It can be expanded by increasing the numbers of types of expenditure. Thus "books" can be subdivided into current and retrospective purchases and current subscriptions can be separated from the purchase of back issues. Although these differentiations appear mechanistic they may relate very directly to the mission of the library. Where, for example, the need is for current information, very strict limitations may be imposed on older purchases and borrowing encouraged as a substitute. A category such as replacements may also be used, temporarily or permanently, simply to keep track of the cost of losses or as part of the costing of a collection preservation program.

The disadvantage is also its simplicity. Broad categories require subdivision to allow for the rational allocation of activity to selectors. In that case other allocations will be made, and it is better that they be made with official sanction. It can also become hidebound and may become an instrument for deterioration, since one of the major categories, periodicals, is at once the most difficult to reduce and the one most susceptible to superinflation. If the periodical proportion cannot be adjusted in the case of declining revenues, then all others will automatically be curtailed. Advance knowledge of the distribution can help to forestall such a situation. In combination with other allocation methods allocation by type of expenditure can help provide an essential element of control.

ALLOCATION PROBLEMS

Regardless of the system of allocation used, there are several problem areas none of which can easily be resolved. This intractability is in part historical, in part the result of the inertial forces within libraries. It also reflects the nature of library collections. It is relatively easy to control the purchasing arrangements needed for most raw materials. Suppliers are few in number and the materials themselves are relatively uniform; the process is more or less standardized and the market is established. Libraries, however, must purchase (or otherwise obtain) nonstandard individualized items in numerous formats from wholesalers, retailers *or* producers in large numbers throughout the world, for a market whose specific needs and interests can only be uncertainly described. It is not, in the circumstances, surprising that libraries have problems in deciding how to spend their money. What is surprising is that, by and large, they succeed so well. There are, however, important areas where there is neither theory nor guideline to go by. These include various proportions, ratios or balances, alternative expenditures and the need to harmonize the dynamic and conservative forces within the library and its community.

THE SERIALS/MONOGRAPHS RATIO

No single recommendation can be made as to the proportions of a book budget that should be spent on the two major types of publication. This is a question that must be decided by each library after due consideration of the needs of its users. Special libraries and science-technology collections are likely to need a higher proportionate expenditure on periodicals than general libraries or collections in the humanities. Some studies have, however, called into question this now traditional view that science and technology are journal-dependent and other areas are not. Baughman has at least suggested that it is true of the social sciences (22), which on balance are monograph-dependent. Such variations must be taken into account when analyzing expenditures and making allocations based on those analyses. Nevertheless, regardless of variations within a library's collections, attention must be paid to the overall balance. As shown by Martin (23) if nothing is done to adjust the proportion committed to periodical expenditures differential inflation rates will ensure an inexorable reduction in the amount that can be dedicated to other kinds of purchases. There is no general agreement on the desirable ratio, but collection-development officers seem to feel uneasy when periodical expenditure rises far above 60 percent. Even in the most serial-dependent library, it is necessary to have sufficient funds for reference materials, basic monographs, replacements or even back runs of journals. Because there is a tendency to maintain journal subscriptions (24) it is always other purchases that are reduced. It is, therefore, necessary at allocation time to pay particular attention to this aspect of collection development. It may be necessary to recommend a reduction in periodical expenditures in order to retain any flexibility at all (25). At the very least it is necessary to understand what are likely to be the effects of leaving things as they are. In such circumstances studies of user need are invaluable, one example being the use of weighted criteria as described by Johnson and Trueswell (26), not only as a method for carrying out actual reductions but for determining what assessments can be levied.

SCIENCE, TECHNOLOGY, AND THE HUMANITIES

Although it is frequently misused, the "two cultures" concept seems applicable to libraries whether in the matter of use of periodicals and monographs as discussed above or in the often used description of the humanities as book-dependent. While this may reflect the humane education of most librarians as much as anything else, the differential needs of these major subject areas are matters of lasting budgetary concern. This concern arises from the fact that the sciences tend to need expensive serials whereas the humanities tend to need and retain large numbers of cheaper items. The areas of science and technology also tend to be less interested than the humanities in older material and consequently to feel less need for retrospective purchases.

These differences in need must be reflected in differences in total budget allocation. They may also result in differences in detail because the selection mechanism is likely to be more diffuse in the humanities. Into the distribution will also enter an external factor—the publisher. Current acquisitions, at least, will reflect the current book-publishing pattern where both by number and by price the humanities and social sciences far outweigh the sci-tech areas (27). Even in a university where purchases of fiction and children's books are likely to be small, this still holds true. For public libraries, where multiple copies of popular books are likely to be bought, this imbalance may be intensified, since fewer serious works on science achieve a high level of popularity. Similarly, replacement of worn-out copies is more likely to be an important budget factor in literature than, say, in physics.

REFERENCE AND GENERAL FUNDS

One of the most difficult problems in any allocation is the handling of general funds. Analysis of circulation, of courses, or of reader population does little to help determine what amounts of money should be set aside for works of bibliography, for dictionaries, and encyclopedias or, in a university context, for a browsing collection. Nor can they do more than suggest what funds may be needed for replacement or binding.

Library organization will also play a significant role since the amount required to support reference collections will depend on how many collections there are and what their purposes are. Should each branch in a library system, for example, have the same capacity for answering reference questions or should everything above a certain level be referred to a central reference service? Separation by format (as periodicals or microforms) may also require that funds be set aside to provide at least some reference and information materials.

In large libraries the bibliographical support of the library's own technical operations may become budgetarily significant since it may be cheaper to subscribe to a second set of the *National Union Catalog* than to pay for the time consumed in walking to and from the Reference Room.

Where large documents collections have been developed, provision must be made for their support. Although allied to low, politics, etc., it is not truly possible to assign a subject to such a collection. This may cause difficulties if one objective is to align expenditures with academic department or subject areas, but any attempt to force such an alignment would distort even the best formula.

Blanket orders and approval plans represent a totally different way of allocation from any subject-based approach since such a distribution can be made only after the fact. Many agents will undertake an analysis for their clients, and it is useful to have; but the only way of setting up a budget allocation in advance is to estimate the total likely expenditure under the plan.

No attempt can be made in this brief summary to include every kind of exception—Rare Book collections in themselves would require a chapter—but these samples indicate the kinds of special cases that must be allowed for in any budget allocation if it is in any way to represent actual activity.

CURRENT AND RETROSPECTIVE PURCHASES

In addition to points touched on elsewhere it is important here to note the alternatives offered by different media. Allocation formulas seldom provide specifically for the purchase of microforms, leaving the choice of format to the professional judgment of selectors. Yet the decision to embark on a long-range microform acquisition program can have dramatic effects on the allocation of funds. A case in point would be the decision to convert back runs of serials to microform, where, despite ultimate savings, the immediate need is for a substantial expenditure even if this may be partly offset by the sale of superseded volumes. A second kind of special need arises from the commitment to long-term purchases, such as the *Short Title Catalog*, which take on quasi-subscription form and should be budgeted for in the same manner as journals. More generally the decision will have to be made whether such purchases are to be allocated by subject or by format or in both ways. For planning purposes it is necessary to have both kinds of information even though the microforms themselves may be located in one place.

When funds are tight it is generally better to give preference to current publications since most books appear to be used most actively soon after publication. It must also be remembered that the antiquarian purchases of the year 2000 are the unpurchased current publications of 1978. Naturally this is not an immutable law. Needed older books must be budgeted for and purchased but the financial provision made for this process should not be such as to crowd out current publications. This is one of the areas where reserve funds can be used judiciously to supplement allocations in response to demonstrated need.

RESPONSE TO CHANGE

Budgets and allocations have an inertial force which is hard to redirect. Libraries of their nature tend to be conservative, that is, they conserve what is past and absorb the new only slowly. The alteration of an allocation structure will therefore take time to effect. Selectors are very jealous of their rights and catalog departments will talk about needing to change procedures. While these may be thought of simply as resistance to change they do reflect the difficulty of changing library procedures. The difficulty is made even clearer if physical changes are taken into account. A shift in collection emphases may over a relatively short period of time require the literal shifting of most of the library's collections with all the patron and staff dislocations this entails. This is not an argument against change which is necessary, only a warning that change cannot be effected simply by altering allocations. Change should be introduced carefully with as full support and understanding as possible.

The kinds of change which result from changes in budgetary support are equally disruptive and require careful advance planning if for no other reason than that periodical subscriptions are usually paid a year in advance and the decision to reduce them should therefore be taken before payments are due and made. Advance warning also allows those affected time to plan and to develop the new selection strategies needed.

SUMMARY

The allocation of funds for the purchase of library materials is a complex process. No simple set of rules exists. The general intention is to distribute funds in such a way as to support the collection development goals of the library. It must also be easily administered and responsive to the structure of the library. While not to be seen as a rigid control mechanism, the allocation process is a means of encouraging a sense of accountability. It also sets measurable goals. Care must, however, be taken to forestall the rigidity that always develops over time. Formulas in particular must be reconsidered periodically. If one method does not work well try another, but always remember that the ultimate measure is the satisfaction of the user, not the exaltation of the librarian.

REFERENCES AND NOTES

1. Murray S. Martin, *Budgetary Control in Academic Libraries.* (Greenwich, Conn.: JAI Press, 1978), p. 14.

2. Jasper C. Schad, "Allocating Book Funds: Control or Planning?" *College and Research Libraries* 31 (May 1970): 155-159.

3. Virginia Held, "PPBS Comes to Washington." In *Programming, Budgeting: A Systems Approach to Management*, Fremon J. Lyden and Ernest G. Miller, eds. (Chicago: Markham, 1965), p. 13.

4. Stephen Ford, *The Acquisition of Library Materials.* (Chicago: ALA, 1973), p. 14.

5. William E. McGrath, "The Significance of Books Used According to a Classified Profile of Academic Departments." *College and Research Libraries* 33 (May 1972): 212-219. In this article the suggestion is made that the higher the correlation between the classified profile of the courses taught and the classified distribution of circulation, the better the selection process must be.

6. Daniel Melcher, *Melcher on Acquisitions.* (Chicago: ALA, 1971), p. 39.

7. Gary S. Sampson, "Allocating the Book Budget: Measuring for Inflation." *College and Research Libraries* 39 (September 1978): 381-383. This article suggests using a unit approach giving values which can be corrected for inflation.

8. Price indexes are available from various sources and should be consulted regularly. *Publishers Weekly* contains a great deal of information on books. Each year *Library Journal* carries an article on periodical prices. *The Bowker Annual of Library and Book Trade Information* includes an entire section, "Publishing Industry Trends and Statistics," which should be studied carefully.

9. Norman B. Brown, "Price Indexes, 1978: U.S. Periodicals and Serial

Services." *Library Journal* 103 (July 1978): 1356-1361.

10. From personal discussions with Helen Snyder, Director of the Basic Skills Program at The Pennsylvania State University following discussion within the University Faculty Senate.

11. Richard De Gennaro, "Copyright, Resource Sharing, and Hard Times." *American Libraries* 9 (September 1977): 430-435.

12. Harold T. Shapiro, "Resource Planning and Flexibility." *Business Officer*, (September 1978): 20-23.

13. "Guidelines for the Allocation of Library Materials Budgets." These are presently being circulated in draft form and contain very useful summaries of factors to be considered. They also contain summaries of the strengths and weaknesses of various formulas and a handy bibliography.

14. Martin, op. cit., pp. 113-128.

15. William E. McGrath, "An Allocation Formula Derived from a Factor Analysis of Academic Departments." *College and Research Libraries* 30 (January 1969): 51-62; "A Pragmatic Book Allocation Formula for Academic and Public Libraries with a Test for Its Effectiveness." *Library Resources and Technical Services* 19 (Fall 1975): 356-369.

16. Joseph J. Kohut, "Allocating the Book Budget: A Model." *College and Research Libraries* 35 (May 1974): 192-199; "Allocating the Book Budget: Equity and Economic Efficiency." *College and Research Libraries* 36 (September 1975): 403-410.

17. Daniel Gore, ed., *Farewell to Alexandria.* (Westport, Conn.: Greenwood, 1976).

18. William E. McGrath and Norma Durand, "Classifying Courses in the University Catalog." *College and Research Libraries* 30 (November 1969): 533-539.

19. William E. McGrath, "Correlating the Subjects of Books Taken Out of and Books Used within an Open-Stack Library." *College and Research Libraries* 32 (July 1971): 280-285. This study, which makes clear the high correlation between use in and out of a library, also unintentionally highlights the problem of locating selection in the right place since its purpose is to measure usage of what is in the collections rather then of methods of getting those materials to where they can be used. Further studies would be required to determine how closely use by specific user group related to selection by representatives of that group.

20. George Schlukbier, "Transgressing the System: Performance Measurement and Library Development." *Canadian Library Journal* 35 (August 1978): 303-306. Although this article is about more general questions such as measurement of services, it should be read as a salutary reminder of the need

for care in determining user needs in order to avoid projecting on to the public the librarian's own preconceptions.

21. Virgil F. Massman and Kelly Patterson, "A Minimum Budget for Current Acquisitions." *College and Research Libraries* 31 (March 1970): 83-88. This is a very useful example of a way of determining the minimum budget requirements, including a sample profile by subject.

22. James C. Baughman, "Toward a Structural Approach to Collection Development." *College and Research Libraries* 38 (May 1977): 241-248.

23. Murray S. Martin, "Budgetary Strategies: Coping with a Changing Fiscal Environment." *Journal of Academic Librarianship* 2 (January 1977): 297-302.

24. Harry M. Kriz, "Subscriptions vs. Books in a Constant Dollar Budget." *College and Research Libraries* 39 (March 1978): 105-109.

25. A.M. Woodward, *Factors Affecting the Renewal of Periodical Subscriptions.* (London: Aslib, 1978.) This very useful report on British library practice indicates that shortage of funds is more important than the availability of alternative access as an incentive for trimming the numbers of subscriptions, but that user need ranks even higher in deciding whether to retain or cancel.

26. Carol A. Johnson and Richard W. Trueswell, "The Weighted Criteria Statistic Score: An Approach to Journal Selection." *College and Research Libraries* 39 (July 1978): 287-292.

27. Reference to the table "American Book Titles Output—1975" on p. 179 of the *Bowker Annual* for 1976 will illustrate this. Of 30,004 new books, 26,985 were in nontechnical fields. Even the elimination of juveniles (2,098 books) and undeterminable portions of fiction (2,407 books) and religion (1,414 books) will not greatly affect this ratio. In fact, Sociology and Economics as a category is more than twice as large as any other category. Publishing distribution of this sort cannot but affect library allocations.

The Formulation of a Collection Development Policy Statement

Sheila T. Dowd

THE NEED FOR A
COLLECTION DEVELOPMENT POLICY STATEMENT

It is an undeniable fact that the great libraries of the world have not been shaped from their beginnings in accordance with carefully detailed statements of collection policy. It is a further fact that many of them today continue to grow apace without a written and coordinated policy statement. The early builders of research libraries were typically individuals who brought, perhaps a breadth of scholarly vision, perhaps expert knowledge of a limited range of subjects, perhaps a degree of eccentricity, and almost always a passion for certain fields of learning, and a sublime confidence in their own abilities to identify the best. The work of such a collection builder was sometimes supplemented by the acquisition of a private collector's library, again bearing the stamp of its begetter's broad learning, special knowledge, or idiosyncrasies. As a result of these highly personalized origins, the collections of great libraries are full of surprises. The viewer might recall a Henry James character's reflection on the Soane Museum: " . . . it would be a very good place to find a thing you couldn't find anywhere else—it illustrated the prudent virtue of keeping." Yet a study of a great library will generally reveal some consistency of philosophy and of values in its formation; some evidence, that is, that its builders were in fact pursuing a policy. A continuing emphasis on particular subjects of special interest to the user group; a regular effort to acquire the publications of certain learned institutions; a conscious determination to assemble the works of a literary school, or to support an extensive list of journals, or to alert antiquarian dealers to the library's permanent interest in a defined area—all such activities give evidence of the existence of policies, however limited the understanding of those policies may be.

The selector with broad or special knowledge, scholarly passion and self-confidence is still vitally important to the development of strong collections. But the heroic figure whose judgments governed the growth of the whole collection has been replaced in most libraries by a group of selectors, each with more limited responsibilities. No one or two or three librarians can determine what should be acquired for a large general library or library system in an era when both the volume of published materials available and the range of information demanded by users has so dramatically expanded. With the division of collection development responsibility, the need for a formal articulation of policies governing selection becomes increasingly urgent.

Users no longer see even a large library's catalog as the profile of what it is. The widespread availability of such information sources as the National Union Catalog, published library catalogs, indexes to government publications and technical reports, on-line bibliographic data bases, and innumerable other access routes to the universe of publication create for public, academic and research libraries a clientele capable of sophisticated and unpredictable demands. A clear understanding of acquisition policy is necessary for all who attempt to interpret the library's collections to users, not merely for those persons charged with responsibility for selection decisions.

In accepting the fact that no collection can be comprehensive enough to meet all its clients' needs, a library acknowledges dependence on other resources. Mutually understood statements of policy can foster this interreliance and increase its effectiveness.

Finally, in determining how to divide the limited book funds available to a library, the budget planner must make hard choices. A collection development policy statement which defines the library's goals for each subject field can assist the administrator in establishing priorities for fund allocation.

DESIGN REQUIREMENTS FOR THE POLICY STATEMENT

Policies relating to collections, like policies in other areas, are formulated at various levels to address specific problems. Decisions as to which contemporary authors shall be collected exhaustively, which areas of social change shall be documented in collections of ephemeral materials, what kind of scholarly institutions or government agencies should be courted for exchange or depository agreement are frequently made by the librarian responsible for the collection involved, without further administrative review. Often the policy implications of such decisions are not even recognized. A library- or system-wide statement of collection development policy should embody a degree of specificity sufficient to bring to light these ad hoc policy decisions, and permit them to be reviewed in relation to the total institutional policy.

The first problem, then, is to determine a structure for the review which will assure that all areas of concern are considered. For certain special collections a scrutiny arranged by form, provenance, imprint date, or other perspective might be practical; but the policy statement of the broad or general collection will most usefully be organized according to some kind of subject structure.

The second problem for the policy statement designer is the

determination of the kinds of judgments which must be made regarding the collections. In addition to defining the subject scope of the collection, the statement should indicate the level or quality of collection desired for each subject field. Other limitations of objective to be considered are language coverage, and emphases or exclusions of period, place or form. Each library must design a framework for its inquiry which will best promote a clear enunciation of the institutional collecting goals.

The third problem to be addressed in the structuring of the policy statement is the problem of definition of terms and the establishment of a standard language. All persons working on the statement must have a common understanding of the subject terms used, the qualitative terms employed to express collection level, and the descriptive terms used to define such aspects of scope as language coverage and chronological or other inclusions or exclusions.

THE SUBJECT STRUCTURE

Many libraries have chosen to analyze their collecting activity under broad subject rubrics and subdivisions, usually outlined by the individual directing the analysis. The collection development policy statements of Stanford University and the University of Texas at Austin (1) are impressive examples of policies so organized. Other statements parallel in subject structure the academic departments served, like that of the Northwestern University Library (2).

The broad subject structure has the advantage of appearing to be readily intelligible to readers, without taint of jargon or "libraryese." As the examples cited indicate, the entire document can be readable, and even urbane in tone. The problem with such organization is that the apparently common language cannot be defined with enough precision to insure that its meaning is in fact standard among its readers, or even among the selectors contributing to the document. Particularly in a situation where many units are contributing to an overall policy statement, there is a strong possibility that activity in certain subject areas will be overlooked because the selector is viewing his collection in a special light, and ignores the fact that it is an aspect of a related discipline. For example, many of the titles added to an urban planning collection might be appropriate for consideration in the sociology section of the policy statement, but may not be so recognized by the urban planning librarian. Thus, a policy organized by broad subject language can lead to an analysis which reflects the existing habits of thought in a library, and so does not serve to illuminate omissions and duplications.

Policy statements which are simply composites of existing units' policies, or which in academic libraries are structured to conform to the academic departments served, reinforce to an even greater degree the status quo of collecting policy and responsibility, with a concomitant difficulty in identifying interdisciplinary interests and areas of overlap and omission.

It was these considerations which led to the Collection Development Committee of the Resources Section, Resources and Technical Services Division, American Library Association, to recommend that the detailed analysis of collection development policy for subject fields be organized by classification scheme (3). The classification scheme chosen would normally be that used for the arrangement of the library's collections; though if a locally originated classification lacks universality or comparability with other collections, it might be advisable to shape the analysis around Library of Congress or Dewey Decimal classification elements. The organization by class assures an objectivity in the library's survey of its practice and policies. Each person conducting a portion of the examination will consider the span of human knowledge from A to Z—or from 000 to 999. (It is frequently pointed out in this context that the Library of Congress classification scheme was developed to organize a particular library collection, not to create a theoretical structure for all knowledge; but its approach to universality is surely sufficient to provide a frame for most general libraries' collection analyses.) When the classification scheme employed in the project is that used by the library for its collections, the shelf list can serve to point up anomalies, interdisciplinary aspects, and variations in past and present practice. The entire library or library system's activity in a discipline can be identified, and areas of duplication or neglect revealed. Also, the classed structure provides the closest approach to a linga franca, a truly common language for library staff in their internal discussions and their cooperative collection development with other libraries. If the precision and clarity of the classed language are purchased at the price of the immediate readability characterizing subject terms, this disadvantage can be reduced by attaching a subject descriptor to each classification block, as is done in the classification tables themselves. Indexes which relate class to subject descriptor, and possibly to library unit, academic department or other service concept, can facilitate use of the document.

The inscrutableness of classification schemes to users should not be exaggerated. The library user, and the librarian too, may find it difficult to lodge securely in his memory the notation of the Library of Congress or Dewey classifications; but the notation is only the outward sign of an inward order which is readily perceived when a sequence of classes is reviewed. The structured organization provided by a good subject classification may be more comprehensible and satisfying to a scholar than freer use of language, for the purposes of a comprehensive analysis of collections and collecting practice. However, for greatest effectiveness, it may be well to view the information assembled by class as a data base from which statements can be specially prepared for particular audiences as needed.

The collection development policy statements of the National Agricultural Library and the Columbia University Libraries (4) are interesting examples of policy statements organized by Library of Congress classification.

ELEMENTS OF THE POLICY STATEMENT

In identifying the elements of a policy statement, a distinction can be made between those judgments or discriminations which can be summarized in an introductory statement of general institutional objectives and limitations, and those which must be made for each subject class analyzed.

Certain very important elements must be treated in the general introduction. These include a statement of the mission of the library as a whole; identification of the programs and clienteles it is established to serve; and definition of the kinds of user needs—instructional, research, recreational, etc.—for which its collections are being developed. Most libraries experience continuing demands for materials which they consider to be inappropriate, or out of scope for their collection goals. If funds are not to be dissipated in unplanned and uncoordinated purchases, it is necessary that these pressures be resisted. Thus, if a university library has determined that its primary mission is the support of the university's instructional and research programs, it may decline to spend its funds for publications in disciplines not included in the academic programs, or for popular materials without academic value. Yet it may receive frequent requests for such materials from members of a broader general public which looks to the university library as a resource, or from members of its own academic community pursuing personal interests. In responding to such requests it is essential to recognize that the collection development goals and the service goals of a library may not be identical. A collection developed with carefully defined perimeters to meet specific objectives will, as it grows in quality and strength, be viewed as a resource by a wider clientele than its primary one. The library can accept with enthusiasm the challenges of this broader usefulness, and endeavor to create service mechanisms to accommodate the demand for its strong collections; but it should not in the process alter the nature of the collections, or be deflected from its defined mission, to meet these pressures (unless, of course, its mission is redefined in the light of the changing environment, and its funding accordingly reviewed). This analysis of mission, clientele and programmatic objectives is a vital prelude to the detailed subject analysis of collection policy. It presents the library's philosophy of collection development as a frame for the more precise definitions to follow.

A statement of the implications of cooperative collecting agreements, local, regional or national, for the development of the library's collections should be included in the introductory statement. The impact of cooperative agreements may also be indicated in appropriate places in the detailed subject analysis.

The detailed subject analysis will require, at a minimum, an indication of the level of acquisition determined to be desirable for the continuing development of the library's collections in each subject or class, and an indication of the selector or unit with primary responsibility for the field. The RTSD Collection Development Committee "Guidelines" (previously cited) recommend that two other related judgments be made regarding collecting level by classed breakdown: an indication of the strength or level of the existing collections in that class; and an indication of the current level of collecting for the class. These elements will be discussed later, in relation to a consideration of standard language.

Where the library's activity with regard to a subject or class is affected by a formal cooperative agreement, it is well to indicate this cooperative reliance in the detailed subject analysis, expanding on the more general treatment of the cooperative program in the introductory statement. Other elements which may require detailed subject analysis include languages collected (or excluded); chronological periods or geographic areas which represent strengths or exclusions; and forms of material collected or excluded. The decision as to whether these elements should be analyzed by subject, or treated in a general introductory statement, will depend on the degree to which the library's practice varies from subject to subject. If, for instance, the library collects in all applicable languages or in English only in all disciplines, this fact can be stated in an introductory statement. If, on the other hand, works in mathematics are collected in Western European and Slavic languages only, philosophy in all applicable languages, and sociology in yet another configuration, it will be necessary to indicate policy regarding language for each subject classification.

In the final coordinated and edited statement, anything which can be generalized regarding the library's collecting aims should be included in the introduction, and only those elements which are variable in the detailed analysis by subject. However, it may not be possible to know in advance which elements reflect standard practice, or where variations in collecting activity actually lie. Therefore it may be wise to ask selectors to incorporate all the elements identified above—languages, time periods, geographical areas, forms—in their detailed subject responses, relying on editing to distinguish the uniform from the variable policies.

IN SEARCH OF A STANDARD LANGUAGE

If a policy is to be applied by many people, read intelligently by many more, and used to guide the hard practical judgments of fund allocation and cooperative agreements, it is essential that all using it have a common understanding of its meaning. Accurate use of the English language (which Max Beerbohm terms "beautifully vague . . . with its meanings merging into one another as softly as the facts of landscape in the moist English climate . . . ") does not in itself insure this universal comprehension. The *HEGIS* (5) effort to define academic programs, and the responsive efforts of institutions to fit their data into the *HEGIS* mold, have demonstrated the range of meanings which can be encompassed in the name of a discipline. A qualitative term frequently reflects the personal goals or standards of the person applying it. For example, the term *research level* might be used to describe a collection which supports doctoral and post-doctoral investigations at one institution, one adequate for upper-division course work at another. Without clear definition of language, comparisons between subjects and between libraries become, if not odious, at least invalid.

It has already been suggested that the use of a classification scheme, and particularly of the widely used Library of Congress or Dewey Decimal schemes, provides the closest possible approach to a lingua franca for a consistent and accurate identification of subject fields. A classification scheme demonstrates the interrelationships of concepts, and lessens the "beautiful vagueness" of free language.

Two problems impede the establishment of a standard language to express qualitative judgments regarding the level of collections and collecting activity in a given class. The Collection Development Committee "Guidelines" attempt to address both. The first difficulty is the definition of collecting levels in terms sufficiently concrete to be applied in a comparable way by all institutions using them. The terms which the group produced were revised as a result of work accomplished at a Preconference Institute on Collection Development sponsored by the Committee at the Detroit American Library Association Conference of June 1977. They are as follows:

A.   *Comprehensive level.* A collection in which a library en-
      deavors, so far as is reasonably possible, to include all
      significant works of recorded knowledge (publications, manu-
      scripts, other forms) for a necessarily defined and limited
      field. This level of collecting intensity is that which maintains
      a "special collection"; the aim, if not the achievement, is
      exhaustiveness.

B.   *Research level.* A collection which includes the major pub-
      lished source materials required for dissertations and inde-
      pendent research, including materials containing research
      reporting, new findings, scientific experimental results, and
      other information useful to researchers. It also includes all
      important reference works and a wide selection of specialized
      monographs, as well as an extensive collection of journals and
      major indexing and abstracting services in the field.

C.   *Study level.* A collection which supports undergraduate or
      graduate course work, or sustained independent study; that
      is, which is adequate to maintain knowledge of a subject
      required for limited or generalized purposes, of less than
      research intensity. It includes a wide range of basic mono-
      graphs, complete collections of the works of important
      writers, selections from the works of secondary writers, a
      selection of representative journals, and the reference tools
      and fundamental bibliographical apparatus pertaining to the
      subject.

      Note: Some college librarians have expressed a need for
      further refinement of the "C—Study Level" code for use by
      libraries without comprehensive or research level collections,
      to enable them to define their collecting policies explicitly
      enough to meet the needs of network resource planning. We
      include the following optional sub-codes for such institu-
      tions.

      C (1).   *Advanced study level.* A collection which is adequate
               to support the course work of advanced under-
               graduate and master's degree programs, or sustained
               independent study; that is, which is adequate to
               maintain knowledge of a subject required for limited

or generalized purposes, of less than research intensity. It includes a wide range of basic monographs both current and retrospective, complete collections of the works of more important writers, selections from the works of secondary writers, a selection of representative journals and the reference tools and fundamental bibliographical apparatus pertaining to the subject.

C (2). *Initial study level.* A collection which is adequate to support undergraduate courses. It includes a judicious selection from currently published basic monographs (as are represented by *Choice* selections) supported by seminal retrospective monographs (as are represented by *Books for College Libraries*); a broad selection of the works of more important writers; a selection of the most significant works of secondary writers; a selection of the major review journals; and current editions of the most significant reference tools and bibliographies pertaining to the subject.

D.   *Basic level.* A highly selective collection which serves to introduce and define the subject and to indicate the varieties of information available elsewhere. It includes major dictionaries and encyclopedias, selected editions of important works, historical surveys, important bibliographies, and a few major periodicals in the field.

E.   *Minimal level.* A subject area in which few selections are made beyond very basic works.

Note: Some subject fields may be completely out of scope for a library's collections. These class numbers can be lined out in the analysis, or "O" can be used to indicate "not collected."

The language of these definitions is certainly capable of further refinement; but it may be questioned whether continuing efforts to refine the terminology can contribute as much to comparable and widely understood statements of collection development as can general adoption of the collecting level codes and definitions. It is intended that judgments as to level of collection be made objectively, based on the actual materials collected, rather than relatively, based on the comparative worth of collections within a library or group of libraries. The five collection-level code definitions and two optional sub-codes attempt to describe recognizable groups of materials, with the explicit understanding that not every institution will have collections at every level.

The definition of collecting levels in concrete and comparable terms, then, is one problem in the creation of a standard language for qualitative judgments. The other problem recognized and addressed in the "Guidelines" is the problem of getting people to talk about the same thing while applying the collection-level codes. Distinctions between what always has been, what is today, and what ought to be often merge, in discussions of library collections, into a twilight of blurred judgments, where the richness of existing collections obscures the view of current collecting inadequacies, or an aggrieved recognition of current underfunding colors the assessment of the total collection. To insure that all of a library's selectors consider the same aspects of collecting and collections, the Collection Development Committee has recommended that three distinct evaluative judgments be made for each classification under analysis. One collection-level code should be applied to describe the strength of the existing collections; another to represent the actual level of collection development being sustained in the current budgetary year; and a third to represent the level of collection development deemed appropriate for the support of the institution's goals. This third judgment is, of course, the policy judgment. It can be arrived at consistently and rationally only if the other two factors, the strength of existing collections and the current level of activity, are consciously considered and distinguished from the policy judgment. In the happiest of all library worlds, the three collection-level codes assigned to a class would be the same, indicating a steady and serene growth. However, it is sometimes necessary to add a wing to the House of Intellect, or to convert the servants' quarters to a workshop. In the real world of library service new scholarly or popular interests require support, old disciplines take new turnings or even lapse into inactivity, and budgets fluctuate erratically, all making what has been, what is and what ought to be three distinct considerations.

The terms in which subject analysis and qualitative judgments are to be couched represent the most important and perhaps the most debatable decisions to be made regarding standard language. However, other aspects of collecting should be coded, or expressed in clear terms, if they are to be analyzed as variables in the collection policy statement. One such aspect is the languages in which a library collects. The "Guidelines" include a set of recommended language codes, and the suggestion that some libraries might usefully analyze their language-collecting policy further by use of MARC language codes. MARC codes will in fact amount to linguistic overkill for most libraries' collection policy statement requirements. Each library should assess the variations in collecting practice with regard to language which must be expressed for accurate internal and inter-library understanding, and adjust the suggested codes to accommodate those needs. The important thing is that the codes be clearly understood by all selectors applying them. It will also be useful to establish standard terms or codes for forms collected or excluded, if these are to be analyzed by subject.

Information and communications specialists have accepted as a truism the statement that "there is no perfect message." The approaches to standard language which are described above are essential to the success of the collection development policy statement effort, if it is to produce a widely comprehensible and comparable document. But even the most impeccably defined terms will be understood in surprisingly disparate ways by a large group of readers or hearers. (Humpty Dumpty was not unique in his attitude toward words: "When *I* use a word, it means just what I choose it to mean—neither more, nor less. . . . The question is, which is to be master—that's all.") Workshops to discuss the established terminology form an important element in the preliminary organization of the collection policy statement project. Further thought will be given to this need in the section on procedures below.

ASPECTS OF THE COLLECTION DEVELOPMENT POLICY
NOT ENCOMPASSED IN THE SUBJECT ANALYSIS

There is no perfect message; and there is no perfect structure wherein a library's complex collections and collecting practices can be effortlessly described. The analysis by class provides for a detached and rather Olympian scan of the library's relation to the whole world of knowledge. Where selection responsibilities are assigned by geographic area rather than by subject, careful coordination of the selectors' responses will be necessary to arrive at a decision as to institutional policy for a class. In cases where form or provenance of publications dictate the collection development responsibility, as for instance with newspapers, maps or government publications, it may not be possible to define practice and policy entirely in terms of subject. In these cases an alternative structure should be designed, and a supplementary statement appended to the policy document. For example, a map librarian might respond to the G classification with regard to subject and area spread but wish to append a supplementary statement regarding the forms of maps collected or excluded. The curator of a newspaper collection may have to eschew subject analysis entirely and append a statement organized by geographic area. No such appendix should be resorted to until analysis in the subject framework has been seriously considered; but important information which cannot fit into the subject mold must be expressed as effectively and succinctly as possible and appended without apology.

The elements thus far prescribed for the policy statement have been designed to measure the breadth and depth of coverage which the library's subject or form collections provide. The level of collection density (existing collections) and collecting intensity (current and desirable activity) relate to the range of titles acquired; the question of the number of copies available is explicitly excluded from consideration in forming the collection-level judgments. Yet the problem of necessary duplication of materials is distinctly a concern for book budget allocation; and user satisfaction with a collection depends finally on accessibility of works, and not simply on their theoretical availability. ("Stand and deliver!" was the cry of the highwayman of old. Modern library users sometimes approach the same degree of desperation.) Hence a library's policies governing duplication of materials form a necessary element of the collection development policy. In some cases it may be possible to incorporate these policies in the introductory statement; in others it will be necessary to make them separate appendices to the final document. Resources-sharing agreements have been discussed in relation to the general introductory statement and the detailed subject analysis. It might be well also to append the texts of formal agreements, as a further indication of the library's concern for access to information.

FORMULATING THE POLICY STATEMENT: SOME PROCEDURAL SUGGESTIONS

Counsel is most effective when reinforced with a *vade mecum*. A few practical suggestions can be offered to assist in the actual organization and implementation of the policy statement project.

The first question to consider is that of staffing for the project. The person charged with overall responsibility for collection development in the library will ordinarily be responsible for directing the policy statement project and assuring its regular progress; but much additional staff time must also be dedicated to the effort if it is to be successfully completed. The nature of the project requires participation by all who have selection responsibility within the library. On the other hand, the scale of the enterprise demands that special provision be made for the massive work of gathering, coordinating and editing selectors' responses, and drafting the actual policy document. Depending on the size of the library, the complexity of its organization, and the time frame set for the policy project, this data gathering, analysis and editorial function may represent a full-, half-, or quarter-time commitment of an able librarian's time. Each selector will also invest significant time in the initial survey and in follow-up meetings to reconcile differences of opinion. In his summary of workshop discussions at the 1977 Collection Development Preconference, Norman Dudley stated, "Developing a collection development statement takes more time than you think it will,

no matter how much time you think it will take. By far the most
effective way to go about it is to have a part-time or full-time person
who has full responsibility for at least the gathering and organization
of the basic data" (6). The effect of his warning should not be to
deter a library from undertaking this important work, but rather to
insure that it is undertaken with a serious commitment which can
promise results.

In creating a policy document which will have so direct an effect
on the library's essence, the head of collection development and the
editor will need continuing and constantly available advice. This can
be provided by appointing a special committee to review the work as
it proceeds, or by assigning responsibility for such review to an
existing committee.

The planning group's first duty will be the design of the form or
questionnaire on which the data is to be gathered. Elements to be
included in the policy statement have been discussed at some length
above; but each library must decide which of the various elements is
to be analyzed by class and which summarized in general statements.
Table 1 provides an example of a possible form for soliciting
selectors' responses. It has columns for coded responses regarding
collecting level, language, forms, primary responsibility, and areas of
cooperative reliance. It also includes a column for explanatory notes
in free language. These might include geographical or chronological
strengths or exclusions, special aspects of a subject, or other
limitations perceived by the individual selector with regard to the
particular subject class under scrutiny. Much stress has been laid on
the value of standard and codifiable language. Nonetheless, there is
also a value, at this early stage of the effort, in giving respondents a
chance to say in free language what they cannot fit into the formal
scheme. An inevitable restlessness in the face of forms will be
allayed, a good deal of preliminary and in-process debate stilled; and
the coordinator/editor will be able to reflect in tranquillity on the
significance of the variations in practice which emerge. Some of the
refinements expressed will be minor and of no importance for the
policy draft; but others will have relevance to the collection development policy and can be included in an explanatory note field in the
final draft.

TABLE 1.

COLLECTION DEVELOPMENT POLICY DATA FORM
(Example)

UNIT _____   SELECTOR _____

L.C. Class	Descriptor	Collecting Level Codes			Language Codes			Forms	Primary Responsibility	Coop. Re-liance	Notes
		X	Y	Z	X	Y	Z				
D1-50	History (General)										
D51-95	History, Ancient										
D111-203	History, Medieval										

NOTE:
Columns X, Y, and Z are provided under collection-level codes and language codes to permit the selector to record three evaluative judgments: X = strength of existing collections; Y = current level of collecting activity; Z = level of collecting appropriate to institutional goals (i.e., collection development policy).

A very important decision for the project planners is the degree of classification detail to be used for the subject analysis. The Collection Development Committee "Guidelines" have this to say:

> Libraries will differ in the degree of detail they will require for the analysis of their collection development policy by class. A suggested minimum of refinement of the Library of Congress classification on which to structure the analysis is the breakdown into approximately 500 subdivisions used in: *Titles Classified by the Library of Congress Classification: National Shelflist Count, 1975*. Berkeley, General Library, University of California, 1975. . . . For Dewey or other classification schemes a comparably refined breakdown should be attempted (7). It must be stressed that this recommendation indicates a minimal refinement or classification analysis needed for interinstitutional comparisons. Many libraries will prefer to analyse their collections in greater detail.

Large libraries will almost certainly require greater detail of subject analysis than that used for the *Titles Classified . . . National Shelflist Count*. The degree of expansion which will be needed depends on the amount of variation in policy and practice selectors must express within each large class. The planning group should be reconciled to the fact that the most painstakingly developed outline of classification will probably not be considered adequate by everyone in a large group of selectors. (Most selectors will find the outline to be excellent, except in their own fields of interest, where more detail is needed.) The goal in developing the outline should be to provide only those breakdowns of classification needed to express variations in collecting activity in the library. But since no single person or planning group will be able to predict accurately all of the areas in which practice varies, it is probably advisable to allow librarians to expand their own statements to include any further refinements they deem necessary. The compiler's work will be complicated by this freedom; but again preliminary haggling will be reduced, and information of possible importance to the project will be recorded for the editorial eye.

When the design of the form and the outline of classification are completed, workshops should be held to acquaint selectors with the procedures of the survey, its language and assumptions. Of primary urgency is the development of common understanding with regard to the five collection-level codes, and the separate discriminations to be made about existing collections, the current year's collecting activity, and the level of collecting activity appropriate to the library's goals. Also on the agenda should be a consideration of the degree of objectivity possible, or perhaps the degree of subjectivity inevitable, in judging existing collections. Relatively objective measures for the evaluation of collections are certainly possible and desirable; but they are costly and time-consuming, and must be applied to limited and carefully defined parts of the collections. So vast an undertaking as a survey, from the Library of Congress's A through Z (or equivalent), of the quality of a library's existing collections must depend on the indisputably subjective judgments of those people who know them best, the librarians who develop them and the faculty or other clients who use them heavily. For the purposes of this project, excellence or inadequacy must, like beauty, be in the eye of the beholder. The librarians formulating the qualitative judgments should, as far as time and opportunity permit, consult with the most knowledgeable users of the collections; and should then record their assessments with a calm awareness that the library will have the rest of its existence to test those judgments by more scientific measures.

It is indispensable that each selector respond to the entire outline of classification provided, indicating his policy and practice for every class or block of classes specified. Each individual will of course indicate that many classes are not collected, or are out of scope from the point of view of his responsibility; but it is nonetheless important that everyone contemplate every line, at least briefly. This universal scan by all participants is the mechanism through which inter-disciplinary interests, overlapping responsibilities, and omissions in the library's total collecting activity can be identified. Consultation of the shelf-list at this point will alert selectors to some of the questions to be studied.

The editor, having collected the individual statements, must compile them by class. At this point policy discussions can be held among all concerned selectors, to reconcile conflicting judgments and refine the data into a statement of proposed library policy. These meetings to establish consensus can contribute greatly to the education of the library staff. Even before the policy statement is finished, selectors broaden their understanding and clarify their views of collecting goals and responsibility by examining library-wide practice in a subject field.

The draft statement of proposed collection-development policy will usually be reviewed by the library director, and perhaps by other advisory groups, faculty or user committees, or governing boards before it becomes formal library policy. But it is important to remember that, even after it is formalized, a policy cannot be viewed as fixed. Collections are living things, growing and developing in response to real needs. As those needs change, the collections and the policies which govern them must also change and adapt. Therefore sections of the policy statement should be continually subject to re-evaluation as institutional goals, environmental considerations, or knowledge of the existing collections alter and develop. At regular intervals a formal review of the entire policy should be conducted, to insure a balanced and rational pursuit of objectives in changing circumstances.

A word might be added as to the desirability of recording the collection development policy statement data in machine-readable form. Review and revision will be facilitated if the data can be so converted. It will also be more easily manipulated to provide information for special audiences and purposes. These considerations lend added weight to the importance of the arguments for standard codifiable language.

CONCLUSION

Libraries have existed and even flourished in many times and climes without formal statements of collection development policy. Today the dispersal of responsibility for collection development, the complexities of the publishing universe from which books and other materials are selected, and the need for cooperation among libraries to meet increasingly sophisticated user demands require that the building and management of collections be carefully organized and planned. The library which undertakes to formulate a detailed statement of its collection development policy embarks upon a costly and difficult task. It is, nevertheless, a task that is becoming recognized as essential for effective accomplishment of the library's first and fundamental work, the creation of the information resource on which all library service depends.

ANNOTATED REFERENCES

1. E.M. Grieder, ed., *Book Selection Policies of the Libraries of Stanford University.* (Stanford, Calif.: Stanford University Libraries, December 1970.) University at Austin, Texas Library. *Collection Development Policy; The University of Texas at Austin; The General Libraries.* (Austin: The Library, 1976.)

2. Richard L. Press, *An Acquisition Policy for the Northwestern University Library, Evanston Campus.* Rev. ed. (Evanston, Ill.: Northwestern University Library, January 1972.)

3. American Library Association, Resources and Technical Services Division, "Guidelines for the Formulation of Collection Development Policies." *Library Resources and Technical Services* 21 (Winter 1977): 40. A revised edition of these "Guidelines" is currently in preparation. Quotations throughout this chapter are taken from the final draft of the revised text.

4. U.S. National Agricultural Library. *Library Collection Development Policy.* Beltsville, Md.: The Library, 1977.) For a description of the Columbia project, see: Jerome Yavarkovsky, Ellis Mount, and Heike Kordish, "Computer-based Collection Development Statements for a University Library," *ASIS Proceedings* 10 (1973): 240-241.

5. *Higher Education General Information Survey*, U.S. Office of Education.

6. Norman Dudley, "Collection Development: A Summary of Workshop Discussions." *Library Resources & Technical Services* 23 (Winter 1979): 53.

7. The Council on Library Resources is currently sponsoring an effort by LeRoy Ortopan, University of California, Berkeley, to create equivalency tables relating the Library of Congress and Dewey Decimal classifications.

A Survey of Attitudes Toward Collection Development in College Libraries

James Baughman, Andrea Hoffman,
Linda Rambler, Donald Ungarelli and
Harvey Varnet

INTRODUCTION

Collection development is an effort to improve the quality of choices open to library users, just as education is an effort to improve the quality of choices open to man. Professor Robinson, Librarian of the University of Rochester, in an 1876 report wrote: "For the purposes of general education, teachers, students, and books are together. Any department of the library filled for any other purpose is filled amiss" (1). The professional literature is amply supplied with testimonials about the relationship between quality teaching/learning and quality library collections.

During the past several decades, while money flowed relatively freely, librarians endeavored to build quality library collections by

concentrating on acquiring materials at an exponential rate, expanding staffs to control the information explosion, and building larger
facilities. This modus operandi is changing.

As colleges experience financial exigencies created by a host of
problems (e.g., recurring recessions, rapid inflation, lack of growth in
the stock market, energy problems, decreased federal aid in terms of
real dollars, and declining student enrollments), budget outlays are
necessarily being cut back. While small private colleges with high
costs and limited endowments are suffering the most, some of the
largest state-supported universities also have had to cut programs. As
rising costs mount, tuition will be higher and cuts in faculty and
programs may continue year after year. Many individuals fear that
the resulting austerity will seriously undermine the quality and
diversity of education. Even colleges that manage to maintain
enrollments at a comfortable level will still have to contend with
soaring costs (2).

President Kemeny of Dartmouth College addressed this problem in
relation to libraries and other new facilities. He wrote:

> As long as enrollments (and therefore revenues) increased, institutions
> could justify the building of new facilities such as computer centers,
> libraries, art centers, or audiovisual centers. But it is difficult to see how
> they will pay for new facilities when enrollments and income level off. For
> example, growth of libraries is dictated more by the expansion of human
> knowledge than by enrollments on campus. In steady state, how will
> institutions keep their university libraries up to date, add tens of
> thousands of new volumes annually, and build new buildings to store the
> books, without having the library budget become disproportionately
> large (3)?

While President Kemeny has posed the central question, it is the
librarians' responsibility to find the best possible solutions, not just
answers. Most assuredly, libraries will not be exempt from cost
reductions in the steady-state institutional environment.

Many of the budget difficulties that beset academic librarians in
the steady-state situation relate directly to collection development.
Once documents are acquired, they must be organized, housed,
preserved, and made available for use. Each of these activities

requires a budget allocation. It becomes axiomatic that the larger the library collection, the more funds one needs to maintain and service it. A smaller number of annual acquisitions poses a logical solution to the cost reduction problem, both from the standpoint of capital outlay and of maintenance expenditures.

As the realities of the current fiscal situation and the necessity of reductions in the quantity of acquisitions persist, librarians will be expected to develop "growth" policies that continue to offer an excellent library collection for use by the students and faculty. "Growth" used here means quality, not quantity. Quality growth is not a new idea in the library environment. Again, citing Professor Robinson, the 1876 report states:

> In managing its growth an active librarian and purchasing committee can do much, but they cannot be expected to know the whole library thoroughly, and, so to speak, also to read ahead of its growth, so as to know which of all the books published each department needs. *Outside of what they happen to be familiar with, they will be apt to trust too much to numbers.* But every teacher knows that the number of books in an alcove has very little to do with their educational value. . . . Ten good books may be worth more than a whole case twenty-five years old. . . . So far as the administration of the library relates to its growth, it is clear, then, that it must be directed in its different parts by masters of those parts, men who shall know perfectly its true relation to the progress of thought. Fortunately, in a college library such men are always at hand. The officers of instruction are in general the only persons capable of determining what books their several departments need (4).

To maintain a high degree of quality in library collections, librarians must act in cooperation with other significant individuals, particularly the faculty, who determine not only the content and structure of the educational program but also in large part the use made of the library.

Keyes Metcalf once wrote: "I have believed that . . . the most important single task that any librarian can perform is to build up the collection in his library" (5). In today's environment the phrase "in order to . . . " could easily be added to Mr. Metcalf's statement since the "in order to" operator connotes purposeful, goal-directed activity. Thus, the academic librarian's current task of implementing quality growth must be accomplished in relation to specific goals within a particular academic environment.

Identifying appropriate goals for a specific library in a specific college or university requires an understanding of both the social function of librarianship and the basic concepts of collection development. In characterizing the librarian's mission Jesse Shera wrote: "Despite the popular image of the librarian, he is not, or at least should not be, a drudge whose only purpose is to fetch and carry in a bibliographic lumberyard" (6). Instead, the aim of librarianship is to maximize the social utility of recorded knowledge.

The following interaction model suggests that there is an intellectual, a sociological, and a psychological dimension to the social responsibility of librarianship—intellectual (knowledge) in that librarians acquire knowledge records; sociological (transmission) to the extent that librarians perform specified social tasks in order to provide effective access to recorded knowledge, and psychological (use) since librarians disseminate information for use by individuals.

FIGURE 1.
Social Responsibility (Function) of Librarianship.

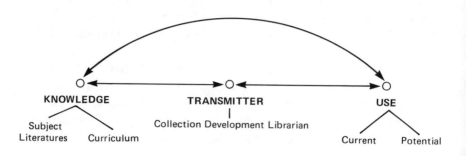

Stiffler noted that "in the dynamic terms of process, a book collection may be thought of . . . as a social mind whose effectiveness depends upon a balanced relationship between the special capacities of a librarian and the unique requirements of a scholar" (7). It should be realized that librarianship and its primary associated activity of collection development are a social responsibility formed at the various interacting points, as illustrated in Figure 1. While the relationship between the librarian and the user has long been established, the emerging issue in this context is the interaction among the structures of 1) curriculum, 2) subject literature, and 3) use (8). "Structure" is to see how things are related (9). "Curriculum" is a plan for the education of students. "Subject literatures" represents the extant body of knowledge (10). "Use" relates to a phenomenon (11), and it is crucial to understand that there is not only "current use" but also "use potential." In terms of the academic program of studies, relevancy will be determined by the degree to which the interaction among these structures is determined, mapped, and implemented.

A clear distinction must be drawn between the "library collection" and "collection development." The library collection represents the *result* of the collection development process; i.e., the collection consists of the knowledge records that have been made available for use, while collection development relates to the processes used in acquiring those records.

Effective collection development in a quality growth situation depends not only upon an understanding of the social functions of librarianship, but also upon a concept of the basic elements inherent to the collection development process. Baughman (12) suggested that collection development is the intertwining of three basic concepts: 1) collection planning, 2) collection implementation, and 3) collection evaluation. He defined the terms as follows:

Collection planning is the schema for accumulating documents that belong together as determined by the needs, goals, objectives, and priorities of the library.

Collection implementation refers to the process of making documents accessible for use.

Collection evaluation involves examining and judging with respect to goals and objectives.

Thus, collection development is a plan which can be implemented and evaluated and may be represented as follows:

Collection planning	+	Collection implementation	+	Collection evaluation	=	COLLECTION DEVELOPMENT

The theoretical issues associated with the concept of library collection development as expressed in a written policy fall under the heading of collection design. It is the design characteristics that make one library collection similar to or different from another. Hence, the policy statement becomes the design. There are two fundamental dimensions to collection design. These are breadth and depth, i.e., how widely one collects and how much one collects in each subject, discipline, topic, or area of study.

The process of collection development may be considered to be the single most important problem, the *locus problem (13)* of librarianship. It is somewhat of a bleak fact that the profession has been unable to come to terms with its locus problem. If it had, there would be adequate, demonstrable, scientific knowledge that would form the base for engaging in description, explanation, and prediction with respect to collection development. At present such scientific knowledge is lacking.

Without an adequate collection development knowledge base it is important to realize that effective collection building requires, in the main, good judgment. Good judgment comes from the special activities associates with experience, which is ideally enriched with intelligent hypothesizing and creative decision-making through discerning and comparing. How formalized that judgmental process is differs among colleges. It can range from selections made at random by a single librarian to those made according to highly specific written policy.

STRUCTURAL ASPECTS OF THE STUDY

The primary assumption of this study is that if the significant groups concerned with educational planning are involved in collection development policy formation from positions of commitment, dedication, and excitement, then responses to library collection development will be one of dynamic positiveness. In terms of a general approach, it is believed that the library, through its collection development program, can serve as a powerful generating force by coordinating all the relevant factors in the college environment that pertain to documents and their use. This, of course, requires direct involvement of the responsible people concerned, who should be included from the beginning as well as on a continuing basis.

A library collection, which is the end product of collection development, is an integral part of the educational program of a college. The collection can be built by facilty, administrators, and librarians working cooperatively and constructively toward a common set of goals. While the effectiveness of the educational program rests with the articulation of human, social, and intellectual structures, it is the existence of an appropriate attitudinal complex that determines the altitude of the collection development task. If educators and librarians do not agree on role relations, orientations, and factors in the collection development process, then it may be concluded that before an effective collection development schema can be formulated and implemented, serious attention would have to be given to conflict resolution. On the other hand, if there is strong agreement on roles and responsibilities, then collection development planning could begin from a mutually agreeable position.

Regardless of the situation in any individual college, the library staff would be wise to consider the atmosphere of the college and to do whatever they can to engender continuing positive attitudes toward the library, its collection, and the use of the collection, since the college library can be as important to effective learning as actual classroom work.

Attitudes represent a tendency or predisposition to respond in a specific manner to people, objects, and situations; hence, they play a central role in human activity. Since attitudes are learned and are

reasonably long-lasting, the investigators felt that a survey of attitudes would reveal specific points of view and that identified
postures, taken as a whole, could provide relevant information to
library managers in terms of collection development policy.

The purpose of this study is to determine the extent of agreement
that exists among the most influential academic personnel concerning the fundamental issues entailed in collection development policy
formation. The personnel whose roles involve the most influential
decision-making and the strongest input into policy formulation are
faculty, college administrators, and library directors. To determine
the present status of faculty-administrator-library director attitudes
concerning significant aspects of collection development is to pave
the road for serious policy statement initiation.

In formulating a collection development policy statement there
are a number of issues to be grasped and resolved. Since policy
formulation at any level requires not compromise but integration, it
is imperative that those involved seek a common point of departure (14). Questions such as the following should be asked and
answered:

1. Should there be a formal written collection development policy
   statement?
2. Who should be involved in developing the policy statement?
3. How much say should each party have?
4. What factors should be considered in drafting collection development policy?
5. To whom should collection development policy issues be directed?
6. Through which channel should policy matters be presented?

In recent years a variety of issues relating to policy for collection
development have been explored in the literature. Included are
arguments on who should be accountable for collection development (15), what should be contained in the document, and how the
policy should be formulated and implemented (16). Arguments for
and against the desirability of a formal collection development policy
have also been expounded (17). The literature indicates that there
has not always been a consensus on the guiding principles which
American academic libraries should adopt in developing their collections. For example, faculty, administrations, and librarians have

often held different views about which persons are responsible for the control of funds and the selection of materials, as well as issues relating to cooperative collection building.

The question now raised is: Do college faculty, academic administrators, and library directors hold similar views on the issues involved in the formulation of collection development policy? It is to this particular question that the present study is directed.

The major research hypothesis for this investigation is that the three respondent groups do not differ significantly in their attitudes toward the principal issues centrally related to collection development policy. Several sub-hypotheses were formulated to test the general conjecture:

1. The three respondent educational groups (faculty, college administrators, and library directors) will strongly favor a formal written collection development policy statement.
2. The educational groups will not differ among themselves in their attitude that a collection development policy statement would strengthen their library collection.
3. The three respondent educational groups will hold similar views as to who should have how much say in collection development policy.
4. Choice of optimal channel through which individuals and/or groups may represent their input to collection development policy does not depend upon educational position.
5. The proportion of responses with respect to attitude toward a collection development librarian is the same in all educational positions.
6. There is no difference among the weights assigned by the educators to collection development factors that should be used in building library collections.
7. There is no difference among the respondent groups in the proportion of responses in each attitude category with respect to a formal library materials needs assessment survey.
8. Attitude toward commitment to cooperative collection building with other institutions does not depend upon educational position.
9. Attitude toward an allocation formula for the library budget does

not depend upon educational position.

In keeping with the thrust of the study, a survey instrument was prepared and pretested to elicit attitudes from faculty members, general college administrators, and library directors about issues surrounding collection development policy formulation. The questionnaire was designed to be brief, objective, and easy to answer.

Since there are more faculty members in any one college than administrators or library directors, the investigators decided that the best way to eliminate any possible bias in the selection of representative faculty members would be to take a direct random sample of faculty. One hundred faculty members, representing 100 different four-year colleges throughout the United States were randomly sampled from *The National Faculty Directory, 1978* (*18*). In the event that a faculty member was sampled from a college already selected, the name was discarded and another immediately following was chosen. Community college, junior college, and university faculty members were excluded from the sample. College with full-time enrollments of less than 500 and more than 12,000 were also excluded from the study.

After the initial 100 faculty members were selected, the names of the corresponding general college administrators and library directors were obtained from *The World of Learning, 1977-78* (*19*) or *The U.S. Education Directory, 1977-78* (*20*). In some instances, library directors were not listed in either source, so the names were obtained from *The American Library Directory, 1976-1977* (*21*). Thus, one faculty member, one administrator, and one library director from each college received a survey instrument.

RESULTS

Out of the 300 questionnaires mailed to 100 different colleges, 158 were returned, representing a 53 percent return rate. Table 1 gives the number of respondents, with the percentage for each respondent group.

Information from separately returned postal cards was used to determine the academic departments represented in the sample.

TABLE 1.

NUMBER AND PERCENT OF RESPONDENTS
BY EDUCATIONAL POSITION

Educational Position	Number of Respondents	Percent of Total Respondents
Facilty	36	23
General College Administrators	52	33
Library Directors	70	44
Total	158	100

Table 2 lists the 19 different academic departments represented by the faculty respondents.

In addition to educational position, the respondents were asked to indicate their years of experience and their highest earned degree. Table 3 displays information about the number of years of experience by educational position, and Table 4 summarizes data on highest earned degree.

Should there be a collection development policy statement and would it strengthen a library's collection? Question 1 on the survey instrument reads: "Do you think there should be a formal written collection development policy statement for your institution's library?" Given the operational definition of a collection development policy statement as a written guide which considers all the necessary components and levels of collecting materials for a college library, the respondents agree that there should be such a guide. Table 5 gives the compilation of responses to this question.

These data strongly indicate that faculty, administrators, and library directors agree on the concept that there should be a formal written collection development policy statement for their respective libraries. Of those responding to the survey question, 86 percent indicated "yes" to the question, while 7 percent indicated "no" and

TABLE 2.

ACADEMIC DEPARTMENTS FOR
FACULTY MEMBERS

Department	Number of Returns
Biology	4
English	3
History	3
Business	2
Education	2
Math	2
Religion	2
Speech and Drama	2
Accounting	1
Chemistry	1
German	1
Home Economics	1
Marketing	1
Physical Education	1
Physics	1
Political Science	1
Psychology	1
Social Sciences	1
Theater	1
Total	31[a]

NOTE:

[a]The difference between the 36 faculty member returns given in Table 1 and the 31 listed here is accounted for by the fact that five faculty member postal cards were not received.

TABLE 3.

YEARS OF EXPERIENCE

Educational Position	Years											
	1-5		6-10		11-15		16-20		21+		Total	
	N	%	N	%	N	%	N	%	N	%	N	%
Faculty	3	8	8	22	5	14	9	25	11	31	36	100
Administrators	0	0	7	13	17	33	17	33	11	21	52	100
Library Directors	3	4	15	21	21	30	13	19	18	26	70	100
Total	6	4	30	19	43	27	39	25	40	25	158	100

TABLE 4.

HIGHEST DEGREE EARNED

Educational Position	Bachelor		Master		Doctoral		Total	
	N	%	N	%	N	%	N	%
Faculty	0	0	17	47	19	53	36	100
Administrators	0	0	14	27	38	73	52	100
Library Directors	2	3	58	83	10	14	70	100
Total	2	1	89	56	67	42	158	100

TABLE 5.

RESPONSE DATA ON COLLECTION DEVELOPMENT POLICY STATEMENT
ACCORDING TO EDUCATIONAL POSITION

Educational Position	Yes		No		No Opinion		Total	
	N	%	N	%	N	%	N	%
Faculty	30	83	3	8	3	8	36	100
Administrators	41	85	3	6	4	8	48	100
Library Directors	61	88	4	6	4	6	69	100
Total	132	86	10	7	11	7	153	100

another 7 percent indicated "no opinion." One may infer that opinion concerning a collection development policy statement is not evenly divided and that the largest proportion of responses is in the direction hypothesized; i.e., the educational groups strongly favor a formal written collection development policy.

This strong response to the advisability of a formal written collection development statement correlates with recommendations made in the literature. The ALA "Guidelines for the Formulation of Collection Development Policies" states:

> Libraries should identify the long- and short-range needs of their clientele, and establish priorities for the allocation of funds to meet those needs. A collection development policy statement is an orderly expression of those priorities as they relate to the development of library resources (22).

Bach declared that "an acquisition policy, at least a broad acquisition policy is . . . becoming more and more a necessity" (23).

While the investigators were interested in determining the extent to which the respondents thought there should be a collection development policy, it seemed advisable to seek a rationale for this belief. Therefore another question asked the respondents to check the intensity of their agreement with the statement: "A collection development policy would strengthen your library's collection."

The data for that question were analyzed using the chi-square test (24) (See Table 6.) Since the null hypothesis could not be rejected at the .05 level, it may be concluded that attitude toward the belief that a collection development policy would strengthen a library's collection does not depend upon educational position. Therefore, in interpreting the data one needs to be concerned only with categorizing the data by the classifications of "agreement." Table 6 gives the number and percent on the five-point scale of agreement.

Visual inspection of the data suggests that the total responses are not evenly divided among the agreement categories. Thus, one may infer that agreement with respect to a policy strengthening a library's collection is not evenly divided. The overwhelming majority feel that a collection development policy will strengthen a library's collection,

TABLE 6.

INTENSITY OF AGREEMENT ON COLLECTION DEVELOPMENT POLICY STRENGTHENING LIBRARY COLLECTION

Educational Position	Strongly Agree		Agree		Undecided		Disagree[a]		Strongly Disagree[a]		Total	
	N	%	N	%	N	%	N	%	N	%	N	%
Faculty	15	43	14	40	6	17	0	0	0	0	35	100
Administrators	18	35	25	48	8	15	1	2	0	0	52	100
Library Directors	23	33	36	51	7	10	3	4	1	2	70	100
Total	56	36	75	48	21	13	4	2	1	1	157	100

$X^2 = 5.22$, df = 6 (N.S.)

NOTE:

[a]The categories "Disagree" and "Strongly Disagree" were combined into one before performing the chi-square test.

with 84 percent either "strongly agreeing" or "agreeing," and only 3 percent "disagreeing" or "strongly disagreeing."

It may be said that a collection development policy statement is a planning tool. It represents a course of action selected from among alternatives to guide decision making. Collection development is, in effect, a series of decisions. By virtue of acquiring even one book or journal, the librarian has engaged in a decision-making process relative to collection building. If this decision, and the many others to follow, is made with some aim or objective in mind, then some sort of collection building plan is being followed. How systematically this plan was formulated and how effectively its objectives are fulfilled may well determine the eventual quality of the library collection.

If the librarian's main concern is the development of quality collections; if quality collection building directly relates to an effective plan; and if the collection development policy statement is a planning tool (25); then it follows that the formulation of a collection development statement should be of primary concern to librarians.

It is important to understand the fundamental relationship between policy and collection building. The crux of quality collection development rests upon policy. The respondents to the survey feel that the policy process should result in a formal written statement. Writing on acquisition policies in American academic libraries, Bach noted that policies "put direction and purpose to buying," and that without a policy demand may guide the potentially uneven development of the library collection (26).

Referring again to the ALA "Guidelines," "a written collection development statement . . . enables selectors to work with greater consistency toward defined goals, thus shaping stronger collections and using limited funds more wisely" (27). While the policy is the means to a strong collection, it should be realized that the formation of the policy is a shared academic responsibility and that its ultimate success rests primarily with how implementable it is. As one administrator respondent so aptly stated: "I believe a policy statement should be formulated; I believe that it is in the implementation of this policy that the quality of the collection is insured." This same respondent specifically identified several groups who should be deeply involved in implementing policy; they are director of the library, librarians, department chairpersons, faculty, and college administrators.

Following this rationale, the policy statement becomes a management tool; hence, careful consideration must be given to communications. The policy statement must communicate a definite plan of action toward reaching the goal of excellence in library collection building. The word *communicate* is emphasized because the lifeblood of a policy statement is its ability to communicate to others what the library intends to do to develop its resources. Failure to create a collection development policy statement along the lines of a management communication tool severely limits not only its usefulness and its effectiveness, but also the ultimate quality of the collection.

Who should be involved in collection development policy formulation? Responsibility for collection planning and selection has long been a sensitive issue in the academic library. Well into the 1900s book selection was primarily the responsibility of the faculty. By the 1960s selection began to be recognized as an activity belonging to the library (*28, 29*). Changes in higher education, along with a growth and sophistication of the subject literatures, constitute underlying factors in the more recent sentiment that a cooperative effort results in the most effective collection building. In addition to librarians and faculty, other groups—including students, department chairpersons, college administrators, college staff, alumni, and friends groups—might offer valuable input.

Question two on the survey tests attitudes concerning who should be involved in formulating collection development policy, and how much say each should have. The respondents were asked to check one of five categories ranging from "complete say" to "no say at all" regarding the amount of influence each individual group should have in determining collection development policy.

It was hypothesized that the three respondent educational groups hold similar views as to who should have how much say in collection development policy. Table 7 presents, by number and percent, how much say each group of individuals should have in determining collection development policy. Examination of the percentage data

TABLE 7.

RESPONDENT GROUPS RESPONSES FOR SAY CATEGORIES

	Complete Say		Quite a Bit of Say		Some Say		Little Say		No Say at All		Total	
	N	%	N	%	N	%	N	%	N	%	N	%
Students												
Faculty	0	0	3	8	27	(75)	5	14	1	3	36	100
Administrators	0	0	2	4	43	(83)	5	9	2	4	52	100
Library Directors	0	0	10	15	44	(65)	14	20	0	0	68	100
Total	0	0	15	10	114	(73)	24	15	3	2	156	100
Director of Library												
Faculty	4	11	23	(64)	9	25	0	0	0	0	36	100
Administrators	2	4	46	(88)	4	8	0	0	0	0	52	100
Library Directors	13	18	53	(76)	4	6	0	0	0	0	70	100
Total	19	12	122	(77)	17	11	0	0	0	0	158	100
Librarians												
Faculty	1	3	25	(69)	10	28	0	0	0	0	36	100
Administrators	0	0	39	(78)	11	22	0	0	0	0	50	100
Library Directors	3	4	62	(89)	5	7	0	0	0	0	70	100
Total	4	2	126	(81)	26	17	0	0	0	0	156	100
Faculty												
Faculty	1	3	32	(89)	3	8	0	0	0	0	36	100
Administrators	0	0	45	(87)	7	13	0	0	0	0	52	100
Library Directors	0	0	61	(88)	8	12	0	0	0	0	69	100
Total	1	1	138	(88)	18	11	0	0	0	0	157	100

Department

Chairpersons											
Faculty	0	22	(61)	11	30	2	6	1	3	36	100
Administrators	0	39	(75)	13	25	0	0	0	0	52	100
Library Directors	0	54	(82)	12	18	0	0	0	0	66	100
Total	0	115	(75)	36	23	2	1	1	1	154	100
General College Administrators											
Faculty	0	8	23	19	(54)	7	20	1	3	35	100
Administrators	0	13	25	32	(62)	7	13	0	0	52	100
Library Directors	0	7	10	41	(60)	20	30	0	0	68	100
Total	0	28	18	92	(59)	34	22	1	1	155	100
College Staff											
Faculty	0	2	6	12	34	16	(46)	5	14	35	100
Administrators	0	1	2	16	31	28	(54)	7	13	52	100
Library Directors	0	3	5	23	35	30	(46)	9	14	65	100
Total	0	6	4	51	33	74	(49)	21	14	152	100
Alumni											
Faculty	0	1	3	13	36	18	(50)	4	11	36	100
Administrators	0	0	0	11	21	33	(65)	7	14	51	100
Library Directors	0	1	2	15	22	41	(60)	11	16	68	100
Total	0	2	1	39	25	92	(59)	22	14	155	100
Friends' Group											
Faculty	0	0	0	11	37	15	(50)	4	13	30	100
Administrators	0	0	0	16	33	21	(44)	11	23	48	100
Library Directors	0	1	2	16	26	32	(52)	12	20	61	100
Total	0	1	1	43	31	68	(49)	27	19	139	100

109

NOTE:
All percent is by row. The highest percent in each row appears in parentheses.

TABLE 8.

RESPONSES FOR SAY CATEGORY

Group	Complete Say W=8		Quite a Bit of Say W=7		Some Say W=5		Little Say W=3		No Say at All W=2		Total		Mean for Weighted Scores
	N	W	N	W	N	W	N	W	N	W	N	W	
Director of Library	19	152	122	854	17	85	0	0	0	0	158	1091	6.91
Faculty	1	8	138	966	18	90	0	0	0	0	157	1064	6.78
Librarians	4	32	126	882	26	130	0	0	0	0	156	1044	6.69
Department Chairpersons	0	0	115	805	36	180	2	6	1	2	154	933	6.45
General College													
Administrators	0	0	28	196	92	460	34	102	1	2	155	760	4.90
Students	0	0	15	105	114	570	24	72	3	6	156	753	4.83
College Staff	0	0	6	42	51	255	74	222	21	42	152	561	3.69
Friends Group	0	0	1	7	43	215	68	204	27	54	139	480	3.45
Alumni	0	0	2	14	39	195	92	276	22	44	155	529	3.41

KEY:
N = Number of responses
W = Weight

110

compiled according to separate respondent groups reveals basic agreement on the categorization of the various college input groups for purposes of collection development. The results of this question support the hypothesis that respondent groups hold similar views as to who should have how much say in collection development policy.

While the percentage data in Table 7 could be utilized to establish a rank for the groups of individuals, means of weighted responses perhaps offer the best method of analysis. The weighted responses determine the intensity of opinion that the respondents hold on how much say the respective individuals or groups should have in collection development policy. The responses were weighted according to procedures described by Backstrom (30). In effect, the weighted scale responses add more exactness to measures of importance on a given factor because the weights yield information about how much difference there is among structured responses. Table 8 gives not only the results on how much say individual groups should have in determining collection development policy by weighted scores but also the scale of weight values.

Using the data compiled in Table 8, collection development policy say groups may be categorized according to means as illustrated in Table 9.

These data indicate that the survey respondents in toto believe that the librarian, in conjunction with faculty, should play a major decision-making role in the formulation of the policy statement. Apparently the respondents agree with Danton (31) that in any event faculty/librarian cooperation to the fullest is recommended. Osburn (32) believes that such cooperation serves as the foundation of validity of a collection development policy.

Upon the foundation of librarian/faculty cooperation, further cooperation among significant college community groups is considered by the respondents to be advantageous in effective collection building. Students and general college administrators would be involved in defining the parameters of the library's collection, and to a lesser extent even alumni, college staff, and friends groups. Some respondents suggested additional groups who should have say. They include the Board of Trustees; contributors of manuscripts and rare books; the community at large in the local area; expert consultants; and consortia groups.

TABLE 9.

CATEGORIES BY AMOUNT OF SAY INDIVIDUALS AND GROUPS SHOULD HAVE
IN DETERMINING COLLECTION DEVELOPMENT POLICY

Greatest Amount of Say		Medium Amount of Say		Least Amount of Say	
Position	Mean	Position	Mean	Position	Mean
Director of Library	6.9	General College Administrators	4.9	College Staff	3.7
Faculty	6.8	Students	4.8	Alumni	3.4
Librarians	6.7			Friends' Group	3.5
Department Chairpersons	6.5				

How can individual or group input best be conveyed for collection development policy purposes? While identification of those groups or persons who should have input into policy formulation is essential, determining the best way to represent that input is also necessary. There are various ways in which such communication can be established between the library and the academic community. They range from the more formal written report to the less formal individual recommendations or suggestions.

To determine the attitudes of the respondents with respect to preferred methods of conveying input for collection development policy purposes, the respondents were asked to indicate their first choice of four suggested channels and one "write-in" blank. This was followed by an opportunity to suggest combinations of input methods.

To test the null hypothesis that choice of optimal channel through which individuals and/or groups may represent their input to collection development policy does not depend upon educational position, the chi-square test was employed. The obtained X^2 = 11.15, df = 8, was not significant at the .05 level. The null hypothesis could not be rejected; therefore, it may be concluded that choice of optimal channel for input into collection development does not depend upon educational position. Accordingly, one may consider the variable "choice of channel" irrespective of educational position. Table 10 gives the results of the best channel for input to collection development policy by the respondent groups.

Table 11 gives the results of the total respondents on choice of channel through which individuals or groups in the college community can best represent their input for collection development policy purposes. Employing the chi-square one-sample test to the hypothesis that the frequency of responses differs significantly among the input categories, the obtained X^2 = 11.92, df = 3, is significant at the .01 level. (The "Other" category was excluded in this test.) Since the null hypothesis was rejected, it may be concluded that opinion concerning channel of input to collection development is not evenly divided in the population from which the sample was drawn; therefore, one may infer that the dispersion of responses among the input methods is unequal.

TABLE 10.

CHANNEL FOR INPUT TO COLLECTION DEVELOPMENT POLICY

Educational Position	A		B		C		D		E		Total	
	N	%	N	%	N	%	N	%	N	%	N	%
Faculty	10	29	8	25	7	20	8	24	1	3	34	100
Administrators	23	45	15	29	4	8	9	18	0	0	51	100
Library Directors	21	31	12	18	15	22	15	22	4	6	67	100
Total	54	36	35	23	26	17	32	21	5	3	152	100

$X^2 = 11.15$, df = 8 (N.S.)

KEY:

A = A college-wide library committee
B = A collection development policy committee
C = Individual recommendations, either written or spoken
D = Primarily written academic department recommendations
E = Other

TABLE 11.

CHANNEL FOR INPUT TO COLLECTION DEVELOPMENT POLICY
BY OPINION CATEGORY PROPORTION

Channel	Number	Percent
A college-wide library committee	54	36
A collection development policy committee	35	23
Primarily written academic department recommendations	32	21
Individual recommendations, either written or spoken	26	17
Other	5	3
Total	152	100

$X^2 = 11.92$, df = 3 (p < .01)[a]

NOTE:
[a]The "Other" category was excluded from the chi-square test.

The literature indicates that college-wide library committees, the respondents' first choice, play an important role in the college community, serving as an excellent vehicle for faculty/librarian interaction on resource development (*33*). One administrator respondent reported: "We currently have a college-wide committee with students and it works well." A faculty respondent stated that the channel "would depend on the setting and that one would have to vary techniques as listed depending on local college needs at the time."

While five respondents checked the "Other" category for input, four specified the methods. They are as follows:

Library Director respondents
  1. Subject bibliographer who is in touch with college community
  2. Library committee
  3. Collection development committee (to formulate)
     A college-wide library committee (to examine)

Faculty respondent
  4. Library director who is knowledgeable of strengths and weaknesses of collection

Regarding combination of ways to represent input for collection development purposes, 118 respondents (75 percent) indicated that they favored various combinations of channels for input to collection development (see Table 12).

Whatever mode or combination of alternatives is adopted by an individual college, the most effective way may well depend upon the climate of the institution, its traditions, and its governance pattern.

Should there be a collection development librarian? A great deal of time can be spent on drafting a collection development policy. The responsibility of implementing the efforts and coordinating the project might conceivably rest with a librarian whose activities are specifically directed toward collection building. One question on the survey addresses the issue of whether or not a collection development librarian is advisable in the college setting.

This question was one of two in the survey for which the null hypothesis could be rejected. Response, in this case, depends upon

TABLE 12.

COMBINATION OF CHANNELS FOR COLLECTION DEVELOPMENT INPUT

Rank	Channel for Input	Number	Percent
1	College-wide library committee Individual recommendations, either written or spoken	23	19.5
2	College-wide library committee Primarily written academic department recommendations	21	17.8
3	Collection development policy committee Primarily written academic department recommendations	18	15.3
4	Collection development policy committee Individual recommendations, either written or spoken	13	11.0
5	College-wide library committee Collection development policy committee	11	9.3
6	Individual recommendations, either written or spoken Primarily written academic department recommendations	10	8.5
	Nine other combinations	22	18.6
	Total	118	100.

117

TABLE 13.

RESULTS OF RESPONSES ON A COLLECTION DEVELOPMENT LIBRARIAN

Educational Position	Strongly Agree			Agree			Undecided			Disagree			Strongly Disagree			Total	
	N	E	%	N	E	%	N	E	%	N	E	%	N	E	%	N	%
Faculty	5	(5)	14	11	(10)	31	12	(8)	34	6	(10)	17	1	(3)	3	35	100
Administrators	2	(7)	4	8	(14)	16	16	(12)	31	21	(14)	41	4	(4)	8	51	100
Library Directors	14	(9)	20	24	(19)	35	8	(16)	12	16	(19)	23	7	(5)	10	69	100
Total	21		13	43		28	36		23	43		28	12		.8	155	100

$X^2 = 24.06$, df = 8 (p $<$ .01)

KEY:
N = Number of observed frequencies
E = Expected frequencies

educational position; i.e., when you categorize by agreement classifi-cations ("strongly agree," "agree," etc.), you must also categorize by educational position (faculty, administrator, library director). The null hypothesis for this question is: "The proportion of responses with respect to attitude toward a collection development librarian is the same in all educational positions." Using the data given in Table 13, the obtained X^2 = 24.06, df = 8, is statistically significant at the .05 level. Therefore, the null hypothesis is rejected. It may be concluded that attitude on the need for a collection development librarian is not independent of educational position among the college personnel sampled. Table 14 presents information on the two respondent groups that contributed most to the chi-square value. Statistically, these discrepancy figures reveal that administrators tended to disagree in greater numbers than expected and that library directors were more strongly in agreement than expected.

The polarization of attitudes about this issue may perhaps be explained through differing interpretations of the survey statement. The written comments by respondents indicate that some interpreted the question only in terms of hiring new staff or assigning the collection development function as the sole responsibility of a particular librarian. For a small library this would, indeed, be impractical. The economics of additional staff may have been a major consideration by administrators, who more strongly expressed disagreement with the idea.

Given the option of assigning collection development activities to an existing staff member, either as his/her sole or partial function, it is theoretically possible that administrators might have tended to concur with the attitudes of library directors on this question. Librarians, who were more solidly in favor of a single collection development librarian, may have viewed this proposal as a manage-ment issue. Perhaps librarians consider the formulation of an ef-fective collection development policy to be dependent upon compe-tent leadership by a collection development librarian who would have both authority and responsibility in library collection develop-ment activities. Clearly, the library director would expect the collection development officer to get the right things done, and this is simply that he/she is expected to be effective. Regardless of the

TABLE 14.

RESPONDENT GROUPS CONTRIBUTING MOST TO CHI-SQUARE VALUE

	Respondent Group	Agreement Category	Expected	Observed	Rank by X^2 cell value
1	Library Directors	Undecided	16	8	4.01
2	Administrators	Strongly Agree	7	2	3.45
3	Administrators	Disagree	14	21	3.32
4	Administrators	Agree	14	8	2.67
5	Library Directors	Strongly Agree	9	14	2.31

line and staff arrangement that is worked out, library collection development activity will need to conform to the general principles of management as outlined by Allen (*34*), those being management planning, management organizing, management leading, and management controlling.

Which factors are the most important in determining collection development policy? For the purposes of this survey, five factors were identified from the literature as key elements in collection development that should be considered in designing a collection development policy statement, according to the individual philosophy of each college. They are as follows:

1. General college goals
2. College curriculum
3. Use of library materials
4. Content value of books, periodicals, etc.
5. Faculty research interest

These factors, in the broadest sense, may be viewed as basic referents, i.e., orientations possible to consider in the construction of distinctive collection development patterns. These referents provide not only the sources from which collection development and theorizing grow but also the base for making many pivotal collection development decisions. A library collection differs from others basically in the priorities (order of referents) used to develop the specifics of a given library collection-building program.

A question on the survey instrument was designed to ascertain the degree of importance that the five selected factors should have in determining which materials should be collected by the library. The hypothesis for that question is that there is no difference among the weights assigned by the educators to collection development factors that should be used in building library collections.

The respondents were asked to assign degrees of importance on a scale of from 1 to 4. To analyze these scaled responses, each level of intensity was assigned weights as Table 15 shows.

After weighting the responses, the data were analyzed using the Kruskal-Wallis one-way analysis of variance test (ANOVA) (Siegel, 1956, pp. 184-189). The result of the test was not statistically significant at the .05 level (X^2 = .14, df = 2). It may be concluded that the three respondent groups come from the same population,

TABLE 15.

WEIGHTS ASSIGNED TO
INTENSITY LEVELS

Intensity	Weight
1. Very important	8
2. Somewhat important	7
3. Of little importance	3
4. Not important	2

The rationale for weight assignment on scaled response questions was provided by Backstrom (*35*).

i.e., faculty, administrators, and library directors weigh collection development factors in the same way.

Since the result of the Kruskal-Wallis ANOVA was not statistically significant, it is of interest to observe the rank of the factors by means of the weighted intensity levels, which are given in Table 16. The data in Table 16 reveal that the means fall within a small range, with the exception of "Faculty research interests."

The lower degree of importance ascribed to the factor on "Faculty

TABLE 16.

COLLECTION DEVELOPMENT FACTORS RANKED BY
MEAN OF WEIGHTED INTENSITY LEVELS

Factor	Mean	Rank by Mean
College curriculum	7.95	1
General college goals	7.48	2
Content value of books, periodicals, etc.	7.35	3
Use of library materials	7.12	4
Faculty research interests	5.71	5

research interests" for determining which materials should be collected by the library to enrich the overall educational program correlates with the Ladd and Lipset survey. They wrote:

> American academics constitute a teaching profession, not a scholarly one. There is a small scholarly subgroup located disproportionately at a small number of research-oriented universities (*36*).

From their data Ladd and Lipset drew four conclusions about faculty research and publication, which are as follows:

1. Over half of all full-time faculty members have never written or edited any sort of book alone or in collaboration with others. The proportion involved in scholarship becomes much lower when part-time faculty members are included.
2. More than one-third have never published an article.
3. Half of the professoriate have not published anything, or had anything accepted for publication, in the last two years.
4. More than one quarter of all full-time academics have never published a scholarly word.

Having identified the referents central to collection development policy and having found that there is no significant difference between the educational groups and weighting, it is possible to utilize the referents in collection building with confidence that discussion can begin from a common point of departure for establishing policy.

The *Standards* states: "The primary purpose of college library service is to promote the academic program of the parent institution" (*37*). Thus, it is imperative to relate the nature and scope of the collection to the program of studies of the college. Collection development policy is crucial in realizing this ambition.

With respect to the four highly rated factors, their priority for collection development at each college would need to be considered within the aims and constraints of the particular college. Osburn notes that "the history and the goals of the parent university set the context in which any principles of collection building must be established and implemented" (*38*).

In addition to the college goals and the college curriculum, collection development policy should take into account use and use potential. "Use" relates to documents called for in the library and "use potential" refers to documents that will potentially be requested. Use patterns are relatively easy to survey; however, projections on use potential become more complex. Relevant collection building in use potential requires an understanding of the structure of subject literatures in terms of their behavior and properties (39).

Are formal library needs assessment surveys advisable? As has been discussed, the function of librarianship is to provide effective access to recorded knowledge for use by individuals (40). The librarian may be conceptualized as a filter between the mass of recorded knowledge and the needs of a specific body of users (41). Particularly in a quality growth situation, this filtering process would logically have to be directed toward isolating and making readily available the highest possible percentage of materials needed by the library patrons. Obviously, these needs must be reflected in the collection development policy, which serves as the guideline for the filtering process—selection, retention, duplication, and weeding of materials.

How does one determine the needs of the college library's patrons? Several developmental concepts have been surveyed earlier in this study. One important question tests the respondents' attitudes concerning the advisability of regular formal library assessment surveys. Table 17 presents the results of this question.

The null hypothesis tested here is that there is no difference among the respondent groups in the proportion of responses in each attitude category with respect to a formal library materials needs assessment survey. The observed X^2 = 11.18, df = 6 was not significant at the .05 level. It may be concluded that attitude toward needs assessment surveys does not depend upon education position. Faculty, administrators, and library directors do not differ among themselves with respect to attitude toward needs assessment surveys. Thus, one may consider the variable of agreement without regard for educational position.

The data results indicate that 89 percent of the total respondents either "strongly agree" or "agree," and only 3 percent "disagree." Accordingly, it can be stated that a significant number of re-

TABLE 17.

FORMAL LIBRARY ASSESSMENT SURVEYS

Educational Position	Strongly Agree		Agree		Undecided		Disagree		Strongly Disagree		Total	
	N	%	N	%	N	%	N	%	N	%	N	%
Faculty	10	29	22	63	3	8	0	0	0	0	35	100
Administrators	8	16	41	80	2	4	0	0	0	0	51	100
Library Directors	15	22	42	61	7	10	5	7	0	0	69	100
Total	33	21	105	68	12	8	5	3	0	0	155	100

$X^2 = 11.18$, df = 6 (N.S.)

spondents feel that materials assessments of library collections should be conducted.

Apparently the respondents agree with the *Standards* statement: "College library collections should be evaluated continuously against standard bibliographies and against records of their use, for purposes both of adding to the collections and identifying titles for prompt withdrawal once they have outlived their usefulness to the college program" (*42*). The ARL's interest in collection assessment was expressed in a recent *SPEC Flyer*. In support of building user or client-centered assessment into the regular operations of the library, it states: "On one level this collection assessment improves the library's accountability system by measuring the success of the collection. On another level this process identifies needed changes and supports decisions to implement them" (*43*). Thus, a needs assessment survey may be defined as an instrument for identifying, in terms of users' needs, the real, the ideal, and the gap between the two. It assists immeasurably in the planning process of collection development policy. In the academic library, the relationship between the librarian and the user achieves its relevancy through the interaction of curriculum, subject literatures, and use—both current and projected. User needs center around all these structures. Thus, needs assessment surveys can vary in scope and interest. Some common methods are: 1) a questionnaire about users' perceptions of the library and its services; 2) a detailed description and/or count of the collection; 3) studies of actual library use patterns; 4) citation studies; 5) comparisons of the collection or parts of it with published library standards, bibliographies, and catalogs. Bonn (*44*) discusses five methods of evaluating library collections, and Broadus (*45*) treats the applications of citation analyses to library collection building.

Further variations have also been developed. For example, Golden (*46*) utilized a quantitative evaluation method to assess the library's collection in relation to the institution's course offerings. Her approach was to assign pertinent Library of Congress class numbers to each of the courses (subject content) and to check the number of times each course had been offered, along with the number of students. The library's shelf-list holdings were matched against the enrollment figures and the subject contents of the courses. Evans (47) also has been investigating the relationships among course offerings, Library of Congress classification, and book production in a U.S. Department of Health, Education and Welfare project.

Although the specific content and process of needs assessment surveys would be determined locally, the respondents of this nation-wide survey feel that library assessment surveys should be conducted on a regular basis.

Should a commitment to cooperative collection building with other institutions be included in the policy statement? Resource sharing through interlibrary loan, consortia, and cooperative access plans among neighboring institutions for faculty and students of most colleges is not a new concept. To a large extent these arrangements have been informal, much like gentlemen's agreements, among the librarians of the institutions. Some formal resource-sharing plans have been established among libraries, with interlibrary loan as the most common.

With the availability of fairly ample amounts of funds for purchasing resource materials, the need to create austerity mechanisms such as cooperative collection development policies has not been acute. Hiding under the umbrella of deep-seated collection development myths about self-sufficiency in collection adequacy and selection, as well as about size and quality correlation (48) librarians have traditionally indulged in building collections individually, without concern for coordinated acquisitions programs. National economic changes and the related shrinking of appropriations for higher education, along with the assertion from the National Commission on Libraries and Information Science that information is a national resource, are now putting the question of cooperation and planned sharing of collections in a new light.

Since in steady-state effective access to recorded knowledge may involve collection policies with both internal and external considerations, the investigators decided that it would be important to determine the current state of thinking by the academic community with respect to cooperative collection building. The respondents were asked to check the appropriate agreement category to the

TABLE 18.

COMMITMENT TO COOPERATIVE COLLECTION BUILDING

Educational Position	Strongly Agree		Agree		Undecided		Disagree		Strongly Disagree		Total	
	N	%	N	%	N	%	N	%	N	%	N	%
Faculty	11	31	16	46	7	20	1	3	0	0	35	100
Administrators	15	28	16	30	15	28	6	12	1	2	53	100
Library Directors	17	25	31	46	17	25	1	1	2	3	68	100
Total	43	28	63	40	39	25	8	5	3	2	156	100

$X^2 = 10.14$, df - 8 (N.S.)

statement: "The library's collection development policy statement should include a commitment to cooperative collection building with other institutions." The results are shown in Table 18.

The null hypothesis to be tested is that attitude toward commitment to cooperative collection building with other institutions does not depend upon educational position. Although there is a relatively high disparity level, the result of the chi-square test ($X^2 = 10.14$, df = 8) is not significant at the .05 level. One must accept the null hypothesis. Therefore, it may be concluded that the proportion of responses by agreement categories on cooperative collection building is the same in each educational position.

A perusal of this chart reveals that 77 percent of the faculty members, 71 percent of the library directors, and 58 percent of the administrators are in agreement with the survey statement. The disparity of the administrator group versus the faculty and library director groups is substantiated at the other end of the spectrum. Administrators were 14 percent strong in disagreement, while library directors and faculty members were only 4 percent and 3 percent unfavorably disposed toward including cooperative commitment as part of a collection development policy statement. This difference in attitude could reflect self-interest, professional awareness, newness of interinstitutional cooperation and pragmatic difficulties involved in cooperative policy-making.

Should the collection development policy include a library budget allocation formula? Through the allocation and expenditure of available funds the collection development policy is implemented. How funds are allocated for library materials has long been a controversial issue in academia.

At the end of the nineteenth century, the growth of research caused considerable competition for available book funds among academic departments. To restrain overly aggressive faculty members and to prevent monopolization of resources, institutions tended to allocate a definite sum of money to each academic department. This system placed responsibility for collection building directly on the faculty (*49, 50, 51*). Difficulties encountered in this procedure included lack of coordination, misspent monies, purchase of materials of value to only a single individual, and resultant unbalanced library collecitons. In the 1960s, the pattern of collection development authority began to change from the academic departments to the library. The rationale was that the librarian could better allocate funds and build collections since the librarian would have more objective insights into user needs and collection strengths and weaknesses. As indicated by the literature, responsibility for collection building in most academic institutions presently rests on the library.

The librarian, however, has since been faced with the problem of how best to distribute funds to departments or subject areas in order to insure adequate and balanced coverage. All too often pure intuition and political pressures prevail. To guard against impressionism and the like, the tool of formula budgeting became popular in the 1970s after the publication of the papers by McGrath et al. (*52, 53*). Beginning with William Randall (*54*) various formulas based on quantitative information have been developed. Measures such as the number of students and faculty, course offerings, graduate programs, use, etc., have been proposed as "objective" guidelines by which to distribute limited funds. The basis for the proposed figures contained in some of the formulas, such as the Clapp-Jordan one (*55*), can also be viewed as a product of subjectivity. In essence, the formula is the product of many desired subjective decisions on what is believed to be objective.

While quantitative information can provide some essential marking stones in allocation, matters of quality and judgment cannot and should not be avoided. A number of formulas, stemming from both qualitative and quantitative information, have been proposed, though their practicality is often questionable. They are based on such factors as economic efficiency (*56, 57*), number and importance of academic departments (*58*), and factor analysis of academic departments (*59*).

There is no accepted or fundamental theory or formula for allocating funds, although the recent ALA/RTSD "Guidelines for the Allocation of Library Materials Budgets" (*60*) does offer some helpful considerations. As stated by Schad (*61*), there is no real choice of whether or not to allocate. All libraries do so. The question of interest to this study is whether or not such allocation should be

TABLE 19.

ATTITUDE TOWARD BUDGET ALLOCATION FORMULA

Educational Position	Strongly Agree			Agree			Undecided			Disagree			Strongly Disagree			Total	
	N	E	%	N	E	%	N	E	%	N	E	%	N	E	%	N	%
Faculty	12	(8)	34	20	(15)	57	1	(4)	3	2	(5)	6	0	(2)	0	35	100
Administrators	11	(11)	21	27	(23)	52	6	(6)	11	4	(8)	8	4	(4)	8	52	100
Library Directors	11	(15)	16	22	(31)	32	12	(8)	17	17	(10)	25	7	(5)	10	69	100
Total	34		22	69		44	19		12	23		15	11		7	156	100

$X^2 = 23.75$, df = 8 (p < .01)

KEY:
N = Number of observed frequencies
E = Expected frequencies

131

done informally or formally with specific allocation criteria.

For the purpose of this survey, it was hypothesized that attitude toward an allocation formula for the library budget does not depend upon educational position. The results, summarized in Table 19, indicate that the null hypothesis must be rejected and the alternative hypothesis accepted; i.e., attitude on formula budgeting depends upon educational position. We conclude that the respondents' educational position is not independent of attitude.

While the data suggests that faculty and general college administrators tend to favor the allocation formula, librarians are not as much in agreement. One may conclude that administrators and faculty members envision the allocation formula as an aid to creating budgets based on the institution's priorities and goals, with an inherent equitable base for resource distribution among departments or subject areas. Perhaps they believe a model would, in fact, clearly and objectively articulate priorities, extricating the collection development budget from dispute and political disparagement.

The librarians' caution on this matter may reflect their awareness of inescapable problems. They would be faced with the dilemma of determining which formula or type of formula to adopt. Any formula will have embedded within itself a certain degree of subjectivity and inflexibility. How does one calculate mathematically the true value of one program to another in the spectrum of knowledge and its use? How does one escape being locked into a commitment which may not be adaptable to changing demands or publication patterns? One "undecided" respondent noted that the formula "would have to change yearly."

The library's adoption of a formula, which undoubtedly would not please everyone, could place the librarian in an untenable position. The very attempt to remove the budgeting process from the political arena through an allocation formula could create even more poignant and bitter disagreement. The use of a formula in itself does not solve the political problem. Pressure and criticism could arise from any group that believed itself to be slighted by any objective or subjective factor included in the formula.

SUMMARY

The results of this survey show that there is considerable agreement among four-year college faculty, librarian directors, and administrators regarding most of the issues related to collection development policy formulation. These groups agree that there should be a written collection development policy statement and that such a statement will serve to strengthen the library's collection. The groups agree on who should be involved in the formulating of such a policy, including to what extent their level of involvement should be. The primary developers of a collection development policy statement should be librarians, library directors, faculty and department chairpersons. The groups agree that college-wide library committees and collection development policy committees are the best ways to have input to a collection development policy. The groups also agree that a formal materials assessment survey should be regularly conducted and that cooperative collection building should be included as an element of a collection development policy. Also, the groups agree on the important question of which factors are important in determining which materials are to be collected by the library. In rank order, the factors are the college curriculum, general college goals, the content value of documents, use of library materials and faculty research interests.

The survey reveals that there are at present two areas of disagreement. The first is the issue of a collection development librarian. Librarians are generally in favor of having a collection development librarian, while administrators and faculty are undecided or in disagreement. Again, the question may have been interpreted by administrators and faculty as requiring additional staff; at four-year colleges, additional staff for this activity alone may be too expensive. Finally, there is disagreement on the issue of an allocation formula for materials acquisition, with faculty and administrators being pro and librarians being con. There is much in the literature on this problem. Basically, this is an issue of accountability versus responsibility. Library literature repeatedly points out that the allocation of funds to departments and the librarians' responsibility for collection development are in conflict. Danton stated: "Allocation tends to remove the responsibility for book selection from the library, where it administratively, philosophically, and usually legally belongs, and places it on the faculty, who cannot be held responsible or accountable" (62).

CONCLUSIONS

This survey reveals that general agreement exists regarding collection development policy formulation. Faculty, librarians, and administrators agree on the value of a collection development policy and on most of its elements. Given this agreement, the formulation process can begin on each campus. Those difficulties that may exist can be ironed out in committee.

Thus, the interactive process of developing the management tool known as a collection development policy should be an almost universal library activity. Needed from administrators will be a clear statement of the college's goals and objectives. Needed from the faculty will be information regarding the structure of the curriculum, as well as a profile of their research interests. And needed from librarians will be an ability to synthesize the various issues relating to collection development, including the ability to mold these factors into a workable statement that will serve as a communications document which is understandable, comprehensive, and flexible. This places the library and the activity of collection development centrally as part of the formal communications model. Demands are made by users on the subject disciplines (knowledge); and these demands, including user's needs, are facilitated by the library's collection.

For the purposes of education, the effectiveness of the book collection, as a social record, is dependent upon a balanced relationship among the distinctive qualities of a librarian, the unique requirements of a scholar, and the determinate dynamics of subject literatures. The very concept of *balance* is one that implies a rational and orderly plan for the library collection's *quality growth* during steady state. In an era of fiscal restraints, a well-conceived collection development policy will react to decreases in funds for materials as one of the variables included in the collection-building process. Better this consistent and rational approach than having the sporadic availability of funds determine the ups and downs of materials growth.

REFERENCES

1. Otis H. Robinson, "College Library Administration." In U.S. Bureau of Education, *Public Libraries in the United States of America; Their History, Condition and Management*, reprint ed. (Urbana, Ill.: University of Illinois, Graduate School of Library Science, n.d.), p. 508.
2. "U.S. Colleges: Life and Death Struggle." *U.S. News & World Report* (May 29, 1978): 65.
3. John G. Kemeny, "The University in Steady State." *Daedalus* 104 (Winter 1975): 88.
4. Robinson, op. cit., p. 508.
5. Keyes D. Metcalf, "The Essentials of an Acquisition Program." In *The Acquisition and Cataloging of Books*, William M. Randall, ed. (Chicago: University of Chicago Press, 1940), p. 77.
6. Jesse H. Shera, *Libraries and the Organization of Knowledge*. (Hamden, Conn.: Archon Books, 1965), p. 16.
7. Stuart A. Stiffler, "The Librarian, the Scholar, and the Book Collection," *The Library-College Journal* 3 (Summer 1970): 40.
8. James C. Baughman, "A Model for Establishing a Curriculum and Its Core Literature Source." (Unpublished Ph.D. dissertation, Case Western Reserve University, Cleveland, 1971.)
9. Jerome S. Bruner, *The Process of Education*. (New York: Random House, Vintage Books, 1960.)
10. Conrad H. Rawski, "Subject Literatures." (Cleveland, Ohio: Case Western Reserve University, 1971. Mimeographed.)
11. Conrad H. Rawski, "The Phenomenon of Use." (Cleveland, Ohio: Case Western Reserve University, 1972. Mimeographed.)
12. James C. Baughman, "Toward a Structural Approach to Collection Development." *College and Research Libraries* 38 (May 1977): 241-248.
13. Abraham Kaplan, *The Conduct of Inquiry: Methodology for Behavioral Science*. (San Francisco: Chandler Publishing Co., 1964), pp. 78-80.
14. Douglas McGregor, *The Human Side of Enterprise*. (New York: McGraw-Hill, 1960.)

15. J. Periam Danton, *Book Selection and Collection: A Comparison of German and American University Libraries*. (New York: Columbia University Press, 1963.)
16. Charles B. Osburn, "Planning for a University Library Policy on Collection Development." *International Library Review* 9 (April 1977): 209-224.
17. Harry Bach, "Acquisition Policy in the American Academic Library." *College and Research Libraries* 18 (November 1957): 441-451.
18. *The National Faculty Directory, 1978*. (Detroit, Mich.: Gale Research Co., 1977.)
19. *The World of Learning, 1977-78*. (London: Europa Publications, 1977.)
20. U.S. Office of Education, *Education Directory: Colleges and Universities, 1977-78*. (Washington, D.C.: Government Printing Office, 1978.)
21. *American Library Directory, 1976-77*. (New York: R. R. Bowker, 1976.)
22. American Library Association, Resources and Technical Services Division, Resources Section, Collection Development Committee, "Guidelines for the Formulation of Collection Development Policies." *Library Resources and Technical Services* 21 (Winter 1977): 43.
23. Bach, op. cit., p. 442.
24. Sidney Siegel, *Nonparametric Statistics for the Behavioral Sciences*. (New York: McGraw-Hill, 1956), pp. 174-179.
25. James C. Baughman, "The Library Ecology Problem." In *LJ Special Reports No. 1: Library Space Planning*, Karl Nyren, ed. (New York: Library Journal, R.R. Bowker, 1976), pp. 45-47.
26. Bach, op. cit., p. 442.
27. American Library Association, "Guidelines," op. cit., p. 41.
28. G.A. Kosa, "Book Selection Trends in American Academic Libraries." *The Australian Library Journal* 21 (November 1972): 416-424.
29. David O. Lane, "The Selection of Academic Library Materials, A Literature Survey." *College and Research Libraries* 29 (September 1968): 364-372.
30. Charles H. Backstrom and Gerald D. Hursh, *Survey Research*. (Chicago: Northwestern University Press, 1963.)
31. Danton, op. cit.
32. Osburn, op. cit.
33. Henry Scherer, "The Faculty and the Librarian." *The Library-College Journal* 3 (Fall 1970): 37-43.
34. Louis A. Allen, *The Management Profession*. (New York: McGraw-Hill, 1964.)
35. Backstrom, op. cit., pp. 76-77.
36. Everett Carll Ladd and Seymour Martin Lipset, "How Professors Spend Their Time." *The Chronicle of Higher Education* 11 (October 14, 1975): 2.

37. American Library Association, Association of College and Research Libraries, "Standards for College Libraries." *College and Research Libraries News*, no. 9 (October 1975): 292.
38. Osburn, op. cit.
39. Rawski, "Subject Literature," op. cit.
40. Shera, op. cit., p. 161.
41. José Ortega y Gasset, *The Mission of the Librarian*. (Boston: G.K. Hall, 1961), p. 22.
42. American Library Association, "Standards for College Libraries," op. cit., p. 290.
43. Association of Research Libraries, Office of University Library Management Studies, "Collection Assessment in ARL Libraries." *SPEC Flyer No. 4* (February 1978): 2.
44. George S. Bonn, "Evaluation of the Collection." *Library Trends* 22 (January 1974): 265-304.
45. Robert N. Broadus, "The Applications of Citation Analyses to Library Collection Building." In *Advances in Librarianship*, Melvin J. Voigt and Michael H. Harris, eds. (New York: Academic Press, 1977), pp. 299-335.
46. Barbara Golden, "A Method for Quantitatively Evaluating a University Library Collection." *Library Resources and Technical Services* 18 (Summer 1974): 268-274.
47. U.S. Department of Health, Education and Welfare; Office of Education, Office of Libraries and Learning Resources, *Collection Development Analysis Using OCLC Archival Tapes*. Final Report, Project No. 475AH60088, Glyn T. Evans, Project Director, November 1977.
48. Baughman, "The Library Ecology Problem," op. cit.
49. Bach, op. cit.
50. Danton, op. cit.
51. Jasper G. Schad. "Allocating Materials Budgets in Institutions of Higher Education." *The Journal of Academic Librarianship* 3 (January 1978): 328-332.
52. William E. McGrath, Ralph C. Huntsinger, and Gary R. Barber, "An Allocation Formula Derived from a Factor Analysis of Academic Departments." *College and Research Libraries* 30 (January 1969): 51-62.
53. William E. McGrath, "A Pragmatic Book Allocating Formula for Academic and Public Libraries with a Test for its Effectiveness." *Library Resources and Technical Services* 19 (Fall 1975): 356-369.
54. William M. Randall, "The College Library Budget." *Library Quarterly* 1 (October 1931): 421-435.
55. Verner W. Clapp and Robert T. Jordan, "Quantitative Criteria for Adequacy

of Academic Library Collections." *College and Research Libraries* 26 (September 1965): 371-380.

56. Joseph J. Kohut and John F. Walker, "Allocating the Book Budget: Equality and Economic Efficiency." *College and Research Libraries* 36 (September 1975): 403-410.

57. Steven D. Gold, "Allocating the Book Budget: An Economic Model." *College and Research Libraries* 36 (September 1975): 397-402.

58. S.K. Goyal, "Allocation of Library Funds to Different Departments of a University—An Operational Research Approach." *College and Research Libraries* 34 (May 1973): 219-222.

59. McGrath, et al., "An Allocation Formula," op. cit.

60. American Library Association, Resources and Technical Services Division, Resources Section, Collection Development Committee, "Guidelines for the Allocation of Library Materials Budgets." (Mimeographed, 1977.)

61. Schad, op. cit.

62. Danton, op. cit., p. 69.

Resource Sharing in Collection Development

John R. Kaiser

INTRODUCTION

The concept of library cooperation is not a new one: "From the turn
of the century to date, the topic of cooperation between libraries in
the development of their collections has been on the minds of
university administrators and librarians" (1). However, the need for
resource sharing has never been more apparent than today: "Powerful inflationary trends on the one hand, coupled with increasingly
effective technological and resource-sharing capabilities on the other
hand, are causing all academic research libraries to undergo a
fundamental reassessment and reorientation of their traditional
collection development goals and service strategies as they make the

painful transition from the affluent sixties to the austere seventies and eighties" (2). This same need has been expressed on an international level by UNESCO: "The international community is now fully committed to the establishment of a new economic order in which mechanisms for international exchange of knowledge and experience are recognized as a priority" (3). It is certain that the need for resource sharing has been felt to some degree by all public, college, university, school and special libraries and that the "concept of interinstitutional sharing of book, journal and other library resources in the context of consortia and networks has become a central focus of interest and activity . . . if those whom librarians seek to serve, are to realize the full promise of networking in the form of significantly enhanced access to information" (4).

DEFINITION OF RESOURCE SHARING

The concept of resource sharing has been commented on by many, but Allen Kent's definition expresses its specific relation to collection development in an admirably precise manner: " 'Resource sharing' in its most positive aspects entails reciprocity, implying a partnership in which each member has something useful to contribute to others [possession of sharable resources], and which each is willing and able to make available when needed [a willingness to make a commitment to sharing] . . . and having a plan for accomplishing resource sharing [a planned mechanism for collaborative use] " (5). In order to make resource sharing work, Kent points out four requirements: "(1) precise understanding of the use of the collection(s); (2) bibliographic apparatus to permit appropriate access; (3) an efficient system for delivering materials; and (4) influence on the purchasing of materials in a coordinated manner and on administrative functions which assure consistent service. In addition, and most important, there must be the development in the patron-community of an understanding of the philosophy of remote access in relation to local holdings" (6). Despite the establishment of philosophical concepts very little has been done to work out the practical mechanics of sharing. The Farmington Plan and other similar plans have been based on assumptions rather than facts and have had no machinery for the measurement of success or for enforcement of collective goals.

THE PROCESS OF RESOURCE SHARING

Before entering into any arrangement for resource sharing, a library should first survey its holdings (collection assessment) to ascertain what it indeed has to share; second, it should determine by use studies (collection use) exactly what it can afford to share; and third, it should examine its policies concerning acquisitions (collection development policies), formulating a statement of what it must collect and what materials it will depend upon a resource sharing partner to supply. Finally, it should decide with whom a consortium, network or cooperative should be formed bearing in mind what the technological requirements are and if they are possible in order to make a resource-sharing scheme work.

As mentioned above, a first step toward resource sharing is collection assessment. Whatever way a library determines to survey or assess its collections, some recognized standard technique should be used so that when the results are tabulated, they can be compared with the results of collection evaluations made by other like institutions. Once the strengths and weaknesses of the collections are thus determined, a suitable resource sharing partner can be sought. Most collection assessments are made only to determine if the collection patterns are in line with the collection development policy and if the acquisitions are meeting the teaching, research and service needs of the institution. But collection assessment, be it quantitative or qualitative, is also fundamental for any development of a resource-sharing effort and must be made with this additional objective in mind.

Although the effort was not made primarily from a resource sharing point of view, a Library of Congress shelf-list count by a group of American academic libraries stands out as one example of how collections might be compared on a quantitative basis. Realizing that there was a need to compile statistics on the subject distribution of their collections, the Chief Collection Development Officers which compose the Large Research Libraries Discussion Group of the American Library Association have undertaken a survey of their holdings. The purpose of the shelf-list count was "to enable individual libraries to analyze their own collection and collecting strengths in each subject area, as they relate both to other subject areas within their own collections and to the same areas in other libraries. The project, in addition, permits an analysis of national and regional collection strengths and weaknesses, and collecting trends" (7). This shelf-list measurement project, done by some 27 academic libraries throughout the country, is just the beginning for what could become a national program in terms of the evaluation and coordination of research library collections. The project does indeed have some practical shortcomings since not all the participating libraries have all of their holdings classified according to the Library of Congress classification; furthermore, there could be variations in any count since conversion to number of titles held was accomplished by measuring the thickness of catalog cards in shelf lists.

In spite of such drawbacks, the information obtained from this process could be very useful in any resource-sharing project. The data given includes a breakdown of the Library of Congress classification schedule into about 490 subgroups. In addition, the number of classified titles is given, the percent of the total collection this number represents, and a set of growth figures. By comparing one year with another, one can tell how many titles by Library of Congress classification were added to the collection, a relative percentage indicating growth in a particular classification as compared to the total growth of the whole collection and relative holdings percentage as compared to the holdings reported by all the libraries reporting, the Library of Congress and the group (all the libraries are grouped into three sections according to size) to which each institution belongs. Since one can determine from this process relative strengths and weaknesses, it can be used as a preliminary means of determining resource-sharing possibilities. In addition, the data from the shelf-list counts can serve as the analytical basis for assigning collection responsibilities among libraries in any resource sharing system. From a qualitative point of view, a set list of catalogs, bibliographies and other checklists could be established, a search made to ascertain holdings and those compared interinstitutionally to pinpoint areas in which resource sharing may be most effective. In principle, the two methods of collection assessment mentioned above would seem to work best for a combination of several libraries seeking resource-sharing partners since the responsibilities for collection would be spread more widely and thus be more economically feasible. Practically it must be remembered that the technological wherewithal for resource sharing is assumed as prerequisite for any such undertaking.

During the past few years there have been definite steps taken toward collection assessment or collection analysis. Developed by the Office of University Library Management of the Association of Research Libraries and funded by the Andrew Mellon Foundation, a number of Collection Analysis Projects (CAP) has been undertaken. Basically a guided self-study, the CAP programs seek to help libraries analyze and improve their collection development policies and procedures. Pilot study projects were conducted first in 1977 at the Massachusetts Institute of Technology and later at the Arizona State University Library and the University of California at Berkeley. The intention of CAP is "to review, describe, assess, and change the collection process at participating libraries. CAP assumes that collection funds can be used effectively by focusing on institutional needs, collection strengths and weaknesses, and user needs. CAP maintains that effective collection management requires that librarians be attuned to changes in institutional programs, promote realistic expectations from faculty and administrators, be aware of political factors, measure the needs and behavior of users, produce collection development policies, and be involved in resource sharing" (8).

At the Massachusetts Institute of Technology Libraries, the Task Force on Resource Sharing concentrated on the effectiveness of resource-sharing programs: "The analysis of existing and potential resource-sharing programs involving the M.I.T. Libraries and influencing the Libraries' collection development program had as its focus the effectiveness of these resource sharing programs in improving user access to available collection resources that complement and/or supplement the collections of the M.I.T. Libraries" (9). The following recommendations were made by the Study Team: 1) investigate possible resource sharing program with another university library; 2) increase effective participation in a local consortium by initiating a productive delivery system (materials and personnel), screening closely consortium privileges, making greater use of consortium facilities already in existence, producing greater publicity of consortium for library staff in order to promote a higher use rate; 3) promoting at large greater awareness of other formal and informal resource-sharing activities of the libraries and 4) ascertaining if a telefacsimile system can be set up whereby interlibrary loan could borrow materials not available in the local consortium (10).

Some of the same concerns and recommendations of the CAP program were voiced at the Arizona State University; among the charges to the Resource Sharing Task Force, the following are of interest: 1) improving structures for "sharing decisions, information and acquisitions; 2) providing remote bibliographic access to both staff and patrons; 3) providing a fast means of retrieving the actual publication"; and 4) determining "effective methods of communicating the advantages of resource sharing to the University community" (11).

In whatever way the library manages in its individual setting to increase resource sharing, all seem to be concerned with the following basic requirements: 1) determining what resources one has; 2) determining what resources one can share; 3) providing bibliographic access to the collections and 4) implementing an efficient document delivery system.

If any phenomenon has led to a serious consideration of resource sharing, a "systematic investigation into patterns of use of library collections has also contributed significantly to the creation of a climate in which it becomes increasingly possible to contemplate alternatives to exclusive local ownership" (12). Since 1961, the year that Fussler and Simon published their findings on *Patterns of Use of Books in Large Research Libraries* (13), numerous studies have attempted to determine exactly what is and what is not used in library collections. However, to date, the studies undertaken have been limited in scope and fragmentary in nature so that the whole question as to what is actually essential to any library collection is yet unanswered. This particular concern has been voiced in the Resources Section of the Resources and Technical Services Division of the American Library Association, and plans are underway to investigate the question of use of library materials on a broad scale.

While the question of what materials are needed in any given library is far from being answered to the satisfaction of all, it is already apparent that a comparatively small number of titles are used by clients and that books and journals in specific subject disciplines very rapidly tend to lose significance as valuable library holdings the older they get (14). However, since no extensive use studies have been made which prove conclusively what actual core materials are essential to the successful operation of any given type of library, no recommendations concerning any wholesale discarding of materials is possible at this time.

There is always the question of what kinds of libraries and collections fit together best. It stands to reason that libraries considering resource-sharing partners cannot be too different or there will be no common interest served, or too similar else there will be no incentive to share resources. Whether the collections of libraries bound by a network or consortia are complementary or supplementary to one other in nature, it is obvious that only little-used, or less frequently used materials can be shared. In a multi-type library consortia including perhaps a public, a school or a college library, this problem may not often arise, but in a single-type library consortia, say of three university libraries with almost identical missions, all may want to share more frequently used materials. Whatever the case may be, each library will indeed have to determine for itself those materials which must be kept on hand and those which can be lent without damaging the library's mission to supply its clients, on demand, with the materials needed.

Given the type of library—be it public, college, university, school or special—any acquisitions policy or collection development policy will undoubtedly vary greatly in its organization, its content and its length. However, a model for such a policy has been prepared by the Collection Development Committee (Resources Section, Resources and Technical Services Division, American Library Association) and has as its title, "Guidelines for the Formulation of Collection Development Policies" (15). Should these guidelines be adopted on a national basis, the process of developing coordinated collection development policy statements would be facilitated greatly. There are, of course, those who do not have written collection development documents, but if resource sharing is to be contemplated at all, some sort of cooperative collection agreements are mandatory if collection responsibilities are to be assigned and if there is to be some sort of relationship defined for the libraries in any given network, consortium or cooperative. Of the assumptions given by the Collection Development Committee for having a collection development statement, the most important for resource-sharing considerations is that such a document "informs library staff, users, administrators, trustees and others as to the scope and nature of existing collections, and the plans for continuing development of resources" (16).

Of the "Elements of a collection development policy statement" recommended by the Collection Development Committee, the one of greatest concern to resource-sharing partners is "Regional, national, or local cooperative collection agreements which complement or otherwise affect the institution's policy" (17). It is absolutely essential that this section of any collection development statement be given in the greatest possible detail. Thus it will not only be crystal clear to the institution acquiring library materials, but to those who wish to borrow materials, exactly where books and journals might be expected to be located. If several university libraries decided to divide collection responsibilities for, say, twentieth-century French literature, it might be possible for one to collect extensively in Surrealism, while another would be responsible for Symbolism. All would have to have some works on these subjects, but in-depth collections could be housed in one location. This should be based, where possible, on existing strengths. During the past years the subject "Cinema" has been added to the contents of the *French XX Bibliography*; this might be a subject area for one library to build large collections in. Such a collection may be complementary to a library with an emphasis on cinema as well as to one collecting French literature in general.

Again, it must be emphasized that the materials to be shared in a resource-sharing scheme must essentially be little used or less frequently used materials and the emphasis is on *used* and not little or less frequently.

In its attempt to formalize its collection development function, the Research Libraries Group has developed what it terms as the *RLG Coordinated Collection Development Program Manual, Coordinated Collection Development Policy Statement* (*18*). This document attempts to formalize a methodology for recording or describing current collection policy and retrospective collection strength and provides for assignments of primary collection responsibility for materials to be collected by each member of the consortium. The term " 'primary collection responsibility' refers to a subject, geographic area or form of material for which one member library has agreed to accept collection responsibility for the consortium" (*19*). By giving primary collection responsibilities to each library, it allows other consortia members to continue collecting in a specific area or to modify or discontinue completely their efforts to collect a certain subject.

Following closely the "Guidelines for the Formulation of Collection Development Policies," the Research Libraries Group has adopted the following codes which define the levels of the current collection policy and retrospective collection strengths: "(1) Minimal Collection; (2) Basic Information Collection; (3) Instructional Support Collection; (4) Research Collection and (5) Exhaustive Collection" (*20*). Various conditions have been set up for each consortium member to meet; for example, a primary collection responsibility for a subject, geographic area or form of material will not be assigned to a member unless it already collects on the Research Collection level and agrees to continue collecting at that level. All materials collected must be maintained in good condition. Serial runs and sets should be as complete as possible. As required by any resource-sharing system, bibliographical access to the collections must be provided and materials are available to all in the Research Libraries Group. Any failure to comply with the various conditions must be reported to the head of the Research Libraries Group. In all cases it is understood that the members of this consortium will comply with the various conditions to the extent that the member is financially able to meet them. Of course the Research Libraries Group has other documents pertaining to the administration of the consortium, but the previous comments are important in that they give just one example of how resource sharing and collection development work hand in hand, and of how they require explicit statement in policy documents.

DEVELOPING THE CLIMATE FOR RESOURCE SHARING

As indicated above, the collection development policy is just one instrument that can be used for developing a positive climate for resource sharing. Much has been written on why resource sharing is not working as it should. Among the many reasons for this failure are "the prior importance of local programs, an unwillingness or inability to support cooperative programs with sufficient funds, and procedural and policy incompatibility; lethargy and lack of interest on the part of the librarians and senior clerical or technical personnel who staff the public service desks; the absence of reciprocity; and the attitude that assigns cooperative activity a low priority" (21).

However, somehow the message must be got out that there is no such thing as a self-sufficient library and that resource sharing facilitates access to information and thereby realizes a library's main function, which is to serve the public. Even though there will inevitably be delays in document delivery time, the positive benefits of resource sharing must be made known; the user must understand that the library will indeed strive to purchase those materials which are most needed and heavily used and will rely on resource-sharing partners for other publications. By shifting the emphasis from building collections to serving library users, a positive climate for resource sharing is created and the base of materials which can be available to users is greatly expanded. Not only librarians but the public as well must be made to understand the opportunities that resource sharing offers. "Growth and fragmentation of conventional printed knowledge records, rising user expectations, and alternatives to print in storing and transmitting data, all have exerted their influence in altering the character both of traditional measures of library effectiveness and the traditional philosophical bases of library service" (22). To adjust to this change, to exploit new technology the collection development process must be organized among various types of libraries so that the greatest number of user demands can be served. Again, any attempt to serve the user well must take into consideration an understanding of the nature and use of the collections to be shared, a mode to provide access to the collections, an efficient workable document delivery system and a coordinated method for adding to the collections so that real resource sharing takes place. John P. McDonald considers the library patrons to be the most difficult problem as far as resource sharing is concerned: "But the problem may be not so much with librarians, with network participants or network managers as with library users" (23).

RESOURCE-SHARING ORGANIZATION

When one thinks of the organizational arrangements by which resource sharing might be accomplished, the terms *networks, consortia,* and *cooperatives* come to mind. There are "these cooperative structures which cross jurisdictional, institutional, and often political boundaries to join in a common enterprise, several types of libraries, academic, school, special and public. The intertype Library Network is commonly an interface between more or less highly articulated single type of library cooperatives" (24). More specifically, "a network, therefore, is defined as a formal organization of three or more autonomous organizations interconnected to achieve their common purposes through the joint use of communications and computer technology" (25). For our purposes, we shall be discussing the various organizational structures of networks for the purpose of resource sharing and shall deal later on with communications and computer technology.

According to Kent, there are five types of networks (26) when one considers resources and their use: "equally distributed networks" in which all hold about the same number of materials which are shared by network members; "star networks" where one member holds the greatest number of resources and shares its materials with members; "star networks with overlapping collections" whereby several members hold large quantities of library materials, their collections overlap and all is shared by network members and others; "hierarchical networks" whereby requests for materials are passed from a smaller library to a larger one until the requests can be filled, and lastly the "mixed network," being any combination of the types just listed.

The administration and governance of any network will depend, of course, on whether it is local, state, regional, national or international in scope. Charles H. Stevens claims that "network governance has not stabilized around a model, and no body of theory has emerged upon which a widespread practice can be built" (27) Network governance, however, is much more than a constitution or a set of documents which give rules, regulations and procedures to follow; most importantly, governance allows for setting up measurable goals and objectives so that the consortium, network or cooperative has a sense of direction and means for determining its progress. Joseph Becker has set forth what he considers essential in the design of any network:

> Participants should share a sense of common purpose, of course, but even more vital is their willingness to undertake legal, fiscal, and other contractual commitments to ensure and preserve the functional integrity of the network.
>
> Examples of commitments that network participants may be called upon to make include: provision of materials and information services to the constituency served by other parts of the network on the same basis as that provided to its own constituency; maintenance of an agreed-upon level of service in terms of dollars and people; payment of a proportionate share of the expenses incurred in network operation; an understanding not to withdraw from the network without payment of penalties; and, agreement on the responsibilities of central network authority (28).

A fine history of networking and examples of informal and formal arrangements among college and university libraries has been written by David Weber (29).

The requirements for successful networking have been commented upon by many. First of all, as noted above, it is absolutely necessary that the proper climate be established so that resource sharing can be conducted. Then the autonomy of each institution must be assured so that its local goals and missions will not be hampered in any resource-sharing arrangement. It also follows that all network members must participate in the development of the goals and objectives as well as the rules and regulations of the network. In addition the collection size and variety of the membership must be significant enough to warrant the cost of networking and the organization of the network must provide bibliographic access to the total collections as well as a quick and efficient document delivery capacity. There must be an incentive to cooperate and the benefits must be seen to be worth the money.

One great concern is the financing of any network, consortium or cooperative; in other words, what are the costs and benefits. H.W. Axford believes that much of the money needed for effective resource sharing "is lying dormant in internal systems and structures which are redundant, technologically obsolete, no longer cost effective, counterproductive, or which should never have existed in the first place" (30). Moreover, it must be realized that cooperation is not simply a new layer to be added to any library system, but requires that there be total re-examination of what we do. To date, libraries have received financial support for networking from various federal and state agencies, from federal revenue-sharing monies or direct federal grants and through a system of fee structures within the given network.

There is evidence that the number of networks is ever growing. The first edition of *Directory of Academic Consortia* listed 145 in 1973, and in the second edition of 1975 there were over 400 such consortia listed (31). On a regional basis one immediately thinks of SOLINET (South Eastern Library Network), NELINET (New England Library Network), SWELP (South Western Educational Library Project), MIDLNET (Midwest Regional Library Network) and WILCO (Western Interstate Library Coordinating Organization). Two of the more recent consortia among academic libraries are RLG (Research Libraries' Group) and its West Coast counterpart being developed by the University of California at Berkeley and Stanford University.

As to the evaluation of the success of resource sharing and networking, little is yet known: "The practical application of evaluation methodologies and criteria to actual resource sharing and networking decisions is just beginning . . . Current efforts to apply, test, and compare evaluation methodologies and performance criteria to make decisions systematically or to better understand the impact of resource sharing or networking activities are fragmented" (*32*). It is evident that in order to assess the success of resource sharing and networking a systematic approach by all concerned should be made whereby tests used, methodologies applied and results realized should be made public and available to all.

On a nationwide basis, the National Commission on Libraries and Information Science (NCLIS) is seeking the establishment of a National Periodicals Center. Among the reasons are, first, that there is no coordinated national system for interlibrary loan of periodicals and serials, and the result is that there is no workable system whereby requests for materials might be more equally distributed among the present library systems; second, a large proportion of interlibrary loan requests, among academic libraries, are for periodical articles, and libraries are simply not able to acquire a large proportion of the world's periodical output; and third, more and more money is being allocated to maintain periodical expenses, thus alarmingly reducing amounts available for the purchase of books. Of course, it is envisaged that the National Periodicals Center would not stand by itself, but would serve as a back-up for requests not filled at a local, state or regional library system. Most important of all, it is essential that collection development decisions must support and be responsive to such a national system. And again, bibliographic access to any system, as well as an efficient document delivery system would be required.

RESOURCE SHARING AND TECHNOLOGY

As stated above, "a network . . . is defined as a formal organization of three or more autonomous organizations interconnected to achieve their common purposes through the joint use of communications and computer technology." The common purpose for us will be resource sharing. How it might be done will be our concern here.

For any network, consortium or cooperative to engage successfully in resource sharing it is imperative that there be an interinstitutional sharing of the basic records dealing with acquisitions, cataloging (library holdings), and interlibrary loan. Therefore computers and an effective communication system become of foremost importance in designing and operating resource sharing systems:

> ... for contemporary librarianship, networking connotes both a formal organization, or agreement, and the electronic exchange of bibliographic data. ... The minicomputer, especially in combination with the increasingly available software packages, can now offer turnkey capability in data processing for medium-sized and smaller libraries, at a cost most can afford, and is, in fact, today being utilized in both public and academic libraries (33).

In any resource-sharing network, the selection of computers and systems to be used must be compatible and this is where library governance is especially important in that the network must achieve unity in its direction for accomplishing its purpose and in establishing set procedures that all must follow.

Through computers and other communication devices which we have, due to advances in technology, library network governance has undergone numerous changes and will surely continue to do so. The complexities that new technology brings make it imperative to develop formal rather than informal structures. We are now in what we could call the era of information management. It is necessary, therefore, that there be effective organization and planning on the part of the institutions using new technologies so that effective resource sharing may become a reality. In other words, traditional information networks must adapt to the changes brought about by the advances in technology. The problems are many and varied: if there is going to be a sharing of bibliographic data for access, some form of authority control must be established; one computer system must be able to communicate with another computer system and thus there must be some regularization of data/language translation, as well as the ability for an individual system to communicate with not only one other system, but a multiple-system network. The overall problem between networking and technology has been succinctly stated by Bret Butler:

> The management of sophisticated cooperative efforts among libraries representing very disparate organizations and a multitude of funding bases is a problem for which answers become less clear as the participation of the organization in the network becomes more central to the operation of the individual library (*34*).

As a result of the development of new technologies, we may well be on the way to what F. Wilfrid Lancaster has called a "paperless society" (*35*). While dealing mainly with the world of science, Lancaster warns that we may soon arrive at a point whereby we are no longer able to deal satisfactorily with "what can be communicated by printing, mailing, storing and retrieving pieces of paper" (*36*) and that "the year 2000 may in fact be a more or less direct electronic analog of the present system" (*37*). Lancaster has noted that "the growth of machine-readable data bases, and of on-line access to these, has had the effect of: improving the availability of information resources, drastically reducing geographic distance as a barrier to communication, making information sources as readily accessible in a small community as they are in a major city, and significantly reducing the cost of access to these resources" (*38*). This is indeed possible if Lancaster's assumptions are correct, namely, that "computers will continue to increase in power and decline in cost, that methods of data transmission will become more efficient and less costly, that new storage devices will make it economically feasible to hold extremely large volumes of text in a readily accessible form, and, most important of all, that computer terminals will be reduced in price . . . " (*39*). Of course in a computerized system there will still be problems to solve such as handling material that is not now in a data base and may never well be and such as preventing machines from limiting the information available because of the mode of processing.

In summary, it appears that resource sharing will be with us whether we are dealing with the vast collections already housed in libraries or in a future "paperless society." No one library is, or probably ever will be, self-sufficient to handle the information needs of its clients. Information needs will be great, or perhaps greater, in the future and the questions of how to organize, to administer and to maintain some division of responsibility for information will become even greater no matter what its form will be. The individual library will still need records of what it owns, what is needed and what is available to it from elsewhere, be it physically or electronically produced. As we move further into the electronic age resource sharing will probably become increasingly important since new technology will allow us rapidly to access collections, data banks and data bases. With new technology the organization of networks, consortia and cooperatives will become more complex and one may foresee large state, regional, national and international networks with the capacity to handle and share great masses of information. Persons involved in collection development will not be concerned only with the development of individual collection policies, but with access and document delivery, that is to say, not only in information as such, but in the technique by which it is best acquired.

REFERENCES

1. Hendrik Edelman and G. Marvin Tatum, Jr., "The Development of Collections in American University Libraries." *College and Research Libraries* 37 (1976): 227.
2. Richard De Gennaro, cited in Allen Kent, "The Goals of Resource Sharing in Libraries." In *Library Resource Sharing*, Allen Kent and Thomas J. Galvin, eds. (New York and Basel: Marcel Dekker, Inc., 1977), p. 16.
3. "International Information Networks and Their Role in the Transfer of Educational Experience." *Unesco Bulletin for Libraries* 32 (1978): 237.
4. Thomas J. Galvin, "Introduction." In Kent and Galvin, *Library Resource Sharing*, op. cit., p. 1.
5. Ibid., pp. 1, 18, and Allen Kent, "Resource Sharing in Libraries." In *Encyclopedia of Library and Information Science*. (New York and Basel: Marcel Dekker, Inc., 1978), 25:295.
6. Kent and Galvin, *Library Resource Sharing*, op. cit., p. 13.
7. *Titles Classified by the Library of Congress Classification: National Shelflist*

Count. (Berkeley: General Library, University of California, 1977), p. vi.

8. Frederick C. Lynden, "Resources in 1977." *Library Resources and Technical Services* 22 (1978): 312-313.

9. *Collection Analysis Project. Final Report and Recommendations.* (Boston: M.I.T. Libraries, 1978), p. 50.

10. Ibid., pp. 50-56.

11. *Collection Analysis Project.* (Tempe: The Arizona State University Library, Arizona State University, 1978), p. 137.

12. Thomas J. Galvin and Marcy Murphy, "Progress Towards Goals in Library Resource Sharing." In Kent and Galvin, *Library Resource Sharing*, op. cit., p. 77.

13. H.H. Fussler and J.S. Simon, *Patterns of Use of Books in Large Research Libraries.* (Chicago: University of Chicago Press, 1961.)

14. Pauline Atkin, *A Bibliography of Use Surveys, 1950-1970.* (London: The Library Association, 1971.)

15. "Guidelines for the Formulation of Collection Development Policies," revised edition, 1978.

16. Ibid., p. 3.

17. Ibid., p. 10.

18. Juanita Doares and Erle Kemp, *RLG Coordinated Collection Development Program Manual, Coordinated Collection Development Policy Statement.* (New York: Research Libraries Group, 1977.)

19. Ibid., p. 2.

20. Ibid., pp. 3-4.

21. Robert F. Moran, Jr., "Library Cooperation and Change." *College and Research Libraries* 39 (1978): 269.

22. Galvin and Murphy, "Progress Towards Goals," op. cit., p. 70.

23. John P. McDonald, "Problems Needing Attention: Reactions." In Kent and Galvin, *Library Resource Sharing*, op. cit., p. 167.

24. Cited by Roderick G. Swartz, "Progress Towards Goals: Response." In Kent and Galvin, *Library Resource Sharing*, op. cit., p. 119.

25. Charles H. Stevens, "Governance of Library Networks." *Library Trends* 26 (1977): 219.

26. "The Goals of Resource Sharing." In Kent and Galvin, *Library Resource Sharing*, op. cit., p. 28.

27. Stevens, "Governance of Library Networks," op. cit., p. 219.

28. Joseph Becker, "Information Network Prospects in the United States." *Library Trends* 17 (1969): 313.

29. David C. Weber, "A Century of Cooperative Programs Among Academic Libraries." *College and Research Libraries* 37 (1976): 208.

30. H. William Axford, "The Negative Impact of Intrinsic Incrementalism, Chronic Overlayism and Pernicious OCLC-itis on the Development of Effective Resource Sharing Networks." In Kent and Galvin, *Library Resource Sharing*, op. cit. p. 155.
31. Galvin and Murphy, "Progress Towards Goals," op. cit., p. 67.
32. Eleanor Montague, "Evaluation Studies of Resource Sharing and Networking Activities: Quo Vadis?" In Kent and Galvin, *Library Resource Sharing*, pp. 289, 292.
33. Galvin and Murphy, "Progress Towards Goals," op. cit., p. 78.
34. Bret Butler, "State of the Nation in Networking." *Journal of Library Automation* 8 (1975): 217.
35. F. Wilfrid Lancaster, "Whither Libraries?, or Wither Libraries." *College and Research Libraries* 39 (1978): 356.
36. Cited in Lancaster, "Whither Libraries?" op. cit., p. 346.
37. Ibid., p. 353.
38. Ibid., p. 351.
39. Ibid., p. 352.

Managing Library Collections:
The Process of Review and Pruning

Paul H. Mosher

If there were librarians who worked in a library with unlimited funds to procure library materials, a library with the bibliographic control and expertise to find and procure the five or six hundred thousand items published in each and every year, a library with the staff to process them, a library with the space to hold them, and the capacity to do these things forever, those librarians would have no need of this chapter (or this book!). All others do.

This chapter will briefly cover the function of reviewing library collections for relegation to storage, discard, and the spinoff of identifying candidates for conservation or preservation treatment. The chapter is primarily addressed to academic librarians who are involved in collection development and management functions; the identification of titles for pruning and preservation is a major function of collection management. It is understood that after being identified for action, titles may be subject to review by faculty or other users, and that they must then be processed by other library units. It is the process of identification which is part of the collection development function and will be treated here.

Emphasis in this chapter is on the practical and useful over the theoretical and formulaic, but argument will also be made—sadly but forcefully—that there is no single simple, accurate, trustworthy, mechanical method which can safely be used for relegation to storage or discard, and that safe and satisfactory pruning always requires time and a combination of at least two methods.

The bibliography on weeding or pruning is enormous, and is increasing rapidly each year. The present chapter must, for this reason, be selective; however, reference will be made to some books and articles that extensively review the literature and methodology in a bibliographic note at the end of this chapter. These titles should form part of the arsenal of any librarian involved in collection development and management and will amplify many points or issues dealt with here.

TERMINOLOGY

The terms used for the process under consideration are almost as numerous as the bibliography on the subject, and they run from the organic (weeding, pruning) through relatively neutral terms (retirement, deselection), to the positively mechanical (stock control). It will be necessary, therefore, to identify the terms to be used before proceeding further.

The phrase "review of collections" will be used as the larger, more generic process inclusive of the others; it is the process by which decisions to take specific actions are carried out. *Pruning* will be used for processes either of "relegating" to storage or "discarding" titles from the collections. The term *deselection* will also be used as roughly equivalent to pruning when the program- and content-related aspects of collection review are emphasized. The term *weeding* will be avoided because it has pejorative connotations which are often not warranted, though the term has entered into common parlance and will never go away. Mechanical terms like *stock control* will also be avoided, not because they are inaccurate, but because this chapter emphasizes the relationship between the essentially organic nature of library collections, of collection development and management, and the changing and evolving nature of academic programs served by academic libraries. Without adequate knowledge of institutional programs and goals, the relationship of library collections to these, the content of books, and even the nature of academic disciplines and the relevance of library collections to them, no program of collection review can be entirely successful.

HISTORICAL BACKGROUND

"In terms of long-range perspective, responsible judgement suggests that there is no feasible choice before libraries other than a wide and continuous program of selective book retirement. This is imposed upon us because shelf space is limited and ultimately our space in libraries will be filled" (1). These words, written by the librarian of the Yale Divinity School to Lee Ash in 1963 represent a scarcely novel view; even before the American colonies separated from England our academic libraries had begun to search for answers to overcrowding. Thomas Hollis wrote from London to Harvard College in 1725 that "if you want more roome for modern books, it is easy to remove the less usefull into a more remote place, but do not sell any, they are devoted" (2).

Harvard University paid the price of developing a significant research library collection even before the end of the last century. D.C. Gilman of Cornell University wrote to President Charles W. Eliot of Harvard in 1891 that "It is not safe for a librarian to destroy any book, lest it should presently be in demand. What, then, can keep the shelves from encumbrance? Only constant elimination, convenient storage, frequent rearrangement. The books less wanted must be stacked away, half a mile away, if you please, and the books most valued must be brought forward. Constant readjustments are essential to the healthy vitality of a library" (3). Harvard followed Cornell's advice; in 1893 Librarian Justin Winsor stored 15,000 volumes in various basements of buildings around Gore Hall, which served at that time as Harvard's library building (4).

President Eliot's concern over the growth rate of Harvard's main library collections continued, and he wrote in 1899:

> One who watches the rapid accumulation of books in any large library must long for some means of dividing the books that are used from those that are not used, and for a more compact mode than the iron stacks supply of storing the books that are not used . . . The devising of these desirable means of discrimination and of compact storage seems to be the next problem before librarians (5).

Eliot worked with the Harvard faculty to identify a core collection size which would maximize use, and questioned whether any single university should store the millions of books which seemed destined for the future (Gore Hall then housed 367,000), and suggested with characteristic foresight that the nation would need regional storage centers for less-used research library materials (Eliot suggested New York, Chicago, and the Library of Congress) (6).

Thus, neither the concept nor the practice of weeding library collections is new. All libraries which possess growing collections, without possessing unlimited space, eventually must take steps to reduce the size of their collections. Some libraries, such as Yale, have undertaken large-scale review of their collections with an eye to removing less used volumes to storage and discarding never used, obsolete or duplicate books. And they have done so with success (7).

The concept of selecting and removing books from a central or active academic library collection for storage elsewhere is thus over a quarter of a millennium old in the United States—yet at the 1977 ALA Collection Development Preconference in Detroit, participants still said that while some of them had gone through processes of "pruning," "weeding," "relegation," or other forms of collection review, and while all recognized the proximate need of doing so, they equally agreed that the topic was the most difficult and sensitive issue dealt with at the preconference. Public librarians have much more commonly—and more openly—pruned their collections than academic librarians. Roscoe Rouse questioned a significant sample of U.S. libraries of various types in 1971, and he found that *every* public library respondent had pruned, while 60 percent of the academic library respondents reported pruning activity (*8*). More pruning has gone on in academic libraries than is commonly admitted—rather like smoking among women in Victorian England—but it has often been done late, under pressure, and with reluctance or trepidation rather than foresight and planning; it has most often been carried out as the result of space or fiscal pressure, and has more often concentrated on volume of material pruned or net cost savings which had to be delivered rather than appropriateness of individual decisions of long-term impact on academic programs served. Thus the process of pruning in libraries is truly the "ungrasped nettle" (*9*). Ford's epithet is confirmed by Wilmer Baatz of Indiana University who, in a recent study of collection development practices of nineteen Association of Research Libraries members, noted that "weeding has been minimally done" (*10*).

The pruning of library collections—especially in a research environment—remains one of the most sensitive functions of the librarian. The task is politically as well as substantially sensitive—"How can anyone alive know what will be grist for the academic mill in 2080? How could librarians of 1880 possibly have anticipated what sorts of material social historians or social anthropologists would be making use of today?"

The plea of cosmic and historic ignorance is a perfectly valid one, of course, within limits of the necessities of money and space, but it is also often an excuse for not making decisions. It is easier *not* to have to examine collections for pruning purposes; decisions to prune are fraught with potential consequences.

WHY PRUNE? BENEFITS AND PROBLEMS

While Fremont Rider's prediction that research library collections will double in size every sixteen years has been shown to be inaccurate (they tend to reduce their rate of growth after they exceed three million volumes or so), he has not been shown to be wrong in showing that libraries fill storage space rapidly and inexorably—and most libraries have discovered that the cost of new prime collection space accelerates at a rate even more intolerable than the growth rate of collections.

If it can be accepted that we simply cannot afford unlimited collection growth, and that *no* library possesses "comprehensive" collections—positions now taken by both the Library of Congress and the New York Public Library—then it must be accepted that primary or active collections must be trimmed or pruned in some way over time to provide room for more important recent acquisitions. Given the problems of collection growth, space, and cost by academic libraries today, the question becomes not *whether* to prune, but *what* to prune, how, and how to deal with the consequences.

Libraries must prune for a variety of reasons: chief among them being finite space and growing collections in a fiscal environment which cannot provide prime collection space when called for by collection expansion, and budget constraints that demand serial cancellation as the area of greatest per-item cost savings. There are less negative arguments as well: for smaller academic institutions the greater utility and quality of collections for curricular support has long been recognized (*11*). There are other reasons which are implicit in the literature; many librarians, library scholars and university administrators seem to have "hygienic" reasons for pruning or modifying collection size. Libraries with millions of volumes seem to some Calvinist or Puritan souls wasteful or excessive per se, quite apart from any proved needlessness or waste.

There are sounder reasons than this, and a major one is historical: the collections of most academic and all research libraries have been built up over time through a quite unsystematic accumulation of gift and purchase—often by means of large collections acquired en masse, as well as generations of unsystematic and inconsistent faculty and library purchases often made with neglect, and occasionally arrogant disregard, of long-term institutional programs or goals—and in the absence of carefully formulated collection development policies to guide acquisition efforts. The holdings of other nearby libraries—even on the same campus—were also often neglected. Thus, any collection can benefit from occasional programs of collection review to eliminate the undesirable and redundant results of history, though effort must be taken as well to protect appropriate and unique historical strength and richness which also have resulted from the "manifest destiny" of past collection building.

The process of collection review and its results (relegation to storage, discard, and preservation) have their offsetting problems (popularly called "trade-offs") as well. Research libraries hold special problems for the collection manager—they defy simple models and easy solutions because they are large and complex organizations serving even larger and more complex organizations. While it is reasonable to say for a public or college library (whose faculty has no significant actual research responsibility) that recorded and unrecorded use define the needed collection, the addition of research and publication programs presents complications, especially if these programs involve historical or critical components which require historical materials or texts.

There are, in addition, the staff time necessary to carry out the deselection process, record changes, and transport of materials, and other costs involved in changing records, providing space for material to be stored, and the cost and delay of obtaining material elsewhere if it is demanded later. There is also, inevitably, cost to the present and future users which must be calculated carefully, for our libraries do exist, in the long run, to serve them. Methods used to deselect and store should be cognizant of their present and future needs; many faculties and libraries still bear the scars of too hasty and insensitive pruning efforts of the past.

None of these problems is, in fact, an absolute reason not to prune, but each is a reason for doing so in a timely and conscious way, consistent with policy and institutional goals, and as sensitive as possible to user needs.

MACRO-METHODOLOGY:
PLANNING AND STRATEGY

A sound and ongoing or periodic program of collection review is a service for library users. Pruning which is carried out as deselection— the counterpart of selection, and according to a program-centered, rational and consistent collection development policy statement— reduces undesirable redundancy in collections, maximizes prime stack space, and prevents panic decisions with inadequate time for planning and preparation. *In the long run*, it is cost and personnel effective.

It has been said with wisdom that the best and most effective pruning decision is made in the selection process (*12*). As mentioned above, pruning is desirable in most libraries because of redundant, unprogrammatic and inconsistent development of historic collections. In most cases these factors are not in themselves adequate reasons to spend time and money to rectify them; however, collection growth rates, lack of adequate expansion space, and cost of new prime library space make reduction of collection growth rate in this prime space highly desirable.

As the reverse of selection, review and pruning processes should follow institutional goals, and should be subject to the same collection policies by which collections are selected, acquired and evaluated; collection development is a process of maintaining balanced, consistent, user-responsive collections based on curricular and research programs of universities and colleges. Goals for collections are now increasingly based on *quality*, which means *utility* rather than *quantity*, as has too often been the case in the past. Utility implies program-related economy and careful management to maintain a responsive, minimally redundant or superfluous, set of collections. In addition, the process of review of collections, which should involve long-term and systematic reading of shelves by subject or discipline specialists, is excellent education for bibliographers, and allows identification of embrittled or disbound books, and other candidates for conservation/preservation activity at the same time.

It is also important to recognize major program differences in devising criteria for identifying deselection candidates. For example, Figure 1 indicates some schematic differences between library

FIGURE 1.

MAJOR COLLECTION DEVELOPMENT PROGRAM VARIANTS

(Schematic)

Sciences/Technology
Shorter-life collections
Serial, report-intensive
Data-information intensive
Lab research-driven
Use-intensive
2% retrospective acq.
More use/citation intensive

Social Sciences

Science-like
Psychology
Sociology
Economics
Linguistics
Most education
Most communication

Humanities-like
Anthropology
Econ. History
International Studies
Political Theory
Some education
Some communication

Humanities
Longer-life collections
Historical or source-
    dependent
Monograph/monograph
Series-intensive
Browsing-intensive
In-library use-intensive
Heavy use of retro-
    spective materials
20% retrospective acq.

167

collections by major discipline which may be helpful in thinking of these larger program issues. The figure is schematic, and does not necessarily represent behavior at any specific institution; individual institutions will need to devise their own scheme based upon local circumstances, and use those findings in collection development policy preparation and in devising pruning criteria for that library's collections.

The point of identifying local program variants and variables—including interdisciplinary activity—and building them into collection review planning as well as the collection development policy statement cannot be overemphasized. MIT is not the same as Smith College, nor is California State University, Hayward, the same as the University of North Carolina, Chapel Hill. Engineers work differently, and use different library materials in different ways than classicists. Much of the literature on pruning has come from studies of the behavior of science and technology materials, and is written by social- or information-scientists who, in the process of trying to discover prospective, empirical, universally applicable laws of library materials behavior, oversimplify the complex and diverse nature of academic programs and the collection use that supports them. Seymour, Cooper, Sandison and Line, and others argue for careful study of the goals, use behavior, and collection needs of local programs before initiating a program of review of collections (13).

A review and pruning program for any academic library should take into account local programs and variables, and should as well consider the content and nature of the books or journals themselves. Many recent writers have concluded that pruning decisions cannot be made en masse, but must be made title by title, and experience substantiates their arguments (14).

Normally, in identifying candidates for pruning, *more than one method should be used*, and it is advisable to include a more mechanical technique, such as past circulation data or citation frequency, along with more judgmental or subjective considerations such as local program need or knowledge of subject literature. While most writers on the subject agree that past use is the best predictor of future use, it is clear that no single method can predict all forms—or likelihood—of potential use in an academic environment; for example, to use two extreme illustrations, if a college had no program in Italian history or literature, it is possible that the Singleton edition and translation of Dante's *Divine Comedy* might not have circulated; or without a history of science program, the journal *Isis* might have been little used. But to discard or store these basic and fundamental works would be poor service indeed for long-term academic needs. It would be well to have a bibliographer familiar with the field involved in the selection of candidates for pruning, and to have appropriate faculty review the list of candidates suggested. In almost every case, more than one criterion or method, selected for appropriateness and sensitivity to program need as well as economy, should be chosen.

THE CORE/NON-CORE DESELECTION MODEL

In *Weeding Library Collections*, Stanley Slote recommends the macro-methodology of dividing library materials into two groups, a core collrection which will serve 90-95 percent of current use, and a weedable collection which consists of the larger group of library materials which provides the remaining 5-10 percent of use. Slote calls this two-stage process "positive" and "negative" selection, with the latter being the opposite of the high-use core—everything left after "positive" selection (*15*). This type of approach is very useful.

For example, Stanford University, serial pruning strategy in the science/technology libraries uses a slightly modified core/non-core model. First, a core of essential journal titles is selected which, under any circumstances, must be readily available. Since journals are often noncirculating, citation counts in-library use, and faculty consultation are used to establish the core list. Then, from the remaining list of non-core titles, a lowest-value title list is identified using the same methods, and allowing plenty of time for consideration of the lowest-value list by faculty and librarians. Titles remaining in this list then form the first rank for cancellation and discard of back issues.

MINIMIZING TRAUMA:
THE TIME FACTOR

Pruning activity has potentially traumatic effect on library users and other library units if they are not informed as to what is going on and have no opportunity for appropriate input in the planning and execution stages of the review process.

While the literature shows that faculty have been minimally helpful during the phase of identifying candidates for pruning, they can be invaluable in reviewing items chosen, and can prevent mistakes from taking place that are costly or impossible to repair after the fact.

Storage decisions too often have to be made after it is already too late—when collections already overrun existing space, and substantial numbers of titles must be moved rapidly to accommodate incoming volumes. This often leads to class or group storage decisions which have impact or implications unforeseen in the rush of more short-term decision making. These late-blooming consequences can include impact on teaching or research needs of faculty and students, can depress requests for needed items through a process of self-fulfilling prophecy (an important but unanalyzed monographic series cannot be requested because it cannot be found), and can have serious political repercussions for the library (faculty have been known to bear vendettas against librarians for years over poorly planned and abrupt storage moves). In addition, hastily planned and executed moves can have serious impact on the processing and circulation functions of the library; sound planning, good communication, thoughtful timing, and careful coordination are needed to make any substantial program of pruning successful.

A carefully planned and phased program of collection review should:

1. Identify and allocate appropriate and bearable collection development, acquisitions, circulation and cataloging staff time to accomplish the desired end. Time required is usually months or years when dealing with large or research collections unless extraordinary funding and staffing are available.

2. Devise appropriate forms and procedures.

3. Calculate impact of volume of selection decisions on staff and space and phase processes to take these into account.
4. Educate participating staff in the program and its goals, appropriate functions or activities, and program timing and phasing.
5. Involve faculty in reviewing plans or lists of items selected for storage or discard.

Again, to use Stanford University as an example, a program and forms have been devised (see Micro-Methodology: Review and Pruning Techniques) to identify candidates for pruning so that the review process can take place well in advance of, and independently of, the processing and moving activities necessary to deal with the items. This allows processing units to schedule their own activities when appropriate staff, time and space are available to actuate the decisions. A period of ten years has been set aside for the whole review process, which will resemble, but is not the same as, Yale's selective book-retirement program.

IMPACT OF COLLECTION SHARING

It is a truism that even the greatest research libraries are no longer islands, but are entering into programs of resource sharing and cooperative collection development in efforts to control rates of collection growth and maximize the utility of their collections to researchers.

These programs will have their impact on pruning and storage programs as well. Cooperative collection management planning should include cooperative storage and pruning arrangements, and such activity should be provided for by mutual policies and be coordinated within consortia to reduce unwanted redundancy and to avoid storage or discard of titles which may have greater utility for the consortium than for individual libraries.

TO STORE OR TO DISCARD?

Historically, smaller academic libraries have discarded, and larger research libraries have stored; policy, such as it existed, was based on the hypothetical needs of posterity rather than measured or projected use of individual volumes or classes of material. The long lack of consistent, policy-guided, subject-responsive collection building in U.S. research libraries has already been addressed; college libraries have generally fared better in this regard than university libraries. With the added complexity of research components, libraries become increasingly unwilling to discard, and feel that inadequate knowledge of future research needs paralyzes the nerve of judgment, selection, and discrimination.

Choice of pruning method, whether storage or discard, must be a decision made on the basis of local or cooperative policy, need and circumstance. Resource-sharing arrangements of consortia, if they include shared bibliographic control and adequate delivery, make discard decisions more feasible for items in the lowest priority category. While books should be stored rather than discarded in cases where minimal future use is predicted, storage without atmospheric control or without good bibliographic access and delivery can bring about a self-fulfilling prophecy; a book can be so inaccessible that it cannot or will not be used. Storage should be used as an extension of primary shelf space and not as a scarcely disguised substitute for discarding books.

Seymour lists the following criteria for discarding, rather than storing, titles:

1. If allowing a book to remain in the collection would produce a "negative value."
2. If the book can be obtained elsewhere at similar or lower cost than that of maintaining it in the collection.
3. If financial and physical resources do not exist to provide continuing housing and maintenance of the item (16).

MICRO-METHODOLOGY:
REVIEW AND PRUNING TECHNIQUES

No single, simple, sure, cheap method exists for reviewing or pruning all types of materials in academic libraries, but some techniques are easier and cheaper than others. Generally, the process is simpler and more straightforward in science and technology collections (which is why nearly all of the more quantitative and mechanical techniques have been devised for or tested on them), and more complex and problematic in humanities collections, and is also more straightforward in public library, undergraduate or college collections than in research collections.

In any program of collection review, the following observations will be helpful:

1. Use methods appropriate to the library's goal and to the disciplines or subjects under consideration.
2. Be practical. If pruning obsolete multiple copies, noncurrent texts, or superseded editions from the collection is the objective, it can best be done by a simple and rapid shelf reading; no complex methodology is required.
3. Use more than one method; be sure to use subject expertise and knowledge to supplement and correct the results of more mechanical techniques. The time saved by inappropriate short-cutting will probably have to be repaid many times over in dealing with user dissatisfaction and other problems.
4. Do not hesitate to use faculty to help provide subject expertise missing in the library staff, and to check proposed candidates for pruning. Librarians and faculty are colleagues working toward common goals, and interchange is usually mutually beneficial.

SERIALS:
SOME SPECIAL CONSIDERATIONS

Since the number of new serial titles continues to rise, and since serials back-runs occupy so much space, serials are prime candidates for pruning activity. The process of serial pruning may be conveniently devided into two categories to make the work clearer and easier:

1. Ongoing and continual culling of recent subscriptions designed to avoid continuing little-needed and unnecessary duplicate sub-scriptions, and a built-in review process to reexamine subscriptions after the first year or two to see whether use and need are evident and whether anticipated content level is maintained. This is a program which should be worked out at each library by the collection development officer, the serials unit chief, and the library bibliographers.

2. Review of existing, longer-term subscriptions. (Dead or discon-tinued runs can be treated as monographs. See below.) Studies have shown that this review process should be carried out for complete runs rather than individual volumes, and that serials containing historical, textual (primary source) or critical material may need to be reviewed according to monographic standards as well. Indeed, a science journal backrun correctly evaluated as superfluous for the science collections may be discovered to have value as history of science material needed by readers in the humanities.

REVIEW AND PRUNING TECHNIQUES

1. *Measurement of Past Use.*

   It is generally agreed, certainly for science/technology materials and less so for humanities materials, that past use is the best *single* predictor of future use. This factor can be measured by:

   a. *Circulation Counts.* These are very useful if consistent, long-term circulation records exist. Titles may be pruned if they have *never* been circulated, or have not circulated for a long period of time. This method can be used for serials and monographs.

   b. *Shelf Time.* When the time between uses exceeds an established standard an item is considered for pruning. As Elmer Grieder first suggested in 1950, this is a fairly accurate technique for predicting future use (*17*). This method is used for serials and monographs.

c. *In-Library Use.* This is difficult to measure with accuracy, but it is considered by a number of authors as a vital corrective to other data, since in-library use to circulation ratios can be as high as 5:1, especially in libraries which support a high level of long-term, in-library research (*18*). In-library use is usually made by having staff users mark uses or reshelvings of books on spines or forms attached to books. The method is used for serials and monographs.

d. *Interlibrary Loan Records.* Maintained by the interlibrary loan unit, these records can provide out-of-library circulation data on items. Records of borrowing of serials by the British Library Lending Division have been used by libraries as a measure of serial title utility. Similar records of a U.S. National Periodicals Center, if it is established, may be useful in this way. This method is most often used for serials, but can be used for monographs.

e. *Citation Analysis.* Citation analysis ranking lists can be compiled from national citation indices (most common) or from citations by the library's user group. This method, used only for serials, has been shown not to reveal many uses of items for reasons other than formal citation in published works, but can be valuable if used in conjunction with another technique.

2. *Shelf Review.*
This is a useful process for most libraries, either on an ongoing or an occasional basis. During the shelf-review process, titles can be identified for storage, discard, and for conservation/preservation treatment. Action can be initiated at once, or it can be deferred to a later date (see Book-Slip Method below). Depending upon collection and collection development staff size, the stack can be divided among appropriate staff by Library of Congress class (the conspectus used in the collection development policy statement will be useful in this case). Pruning decisions can be made on a number of bases:

a. *Routine Maintenance.* Items can be selected for discard if they are:

1) multiple copies of a title.
2) noncurrent textbooks.

   3) old editions replaced by current revisions (*19*).
   b. *Deselection.* Titles may no longer conform to academic program
      need, based on considerations such as:
      1) behavior of discipline.
      2) curriculum and faculty subject interest profiles.
      3) language.
      4) format or nature of material.
      5) circulation data in book.
      6) lack of reference, source or critical value.
      7) number of better books on subject on shelves.
      8) holdings of other institutions.
      9) faculty consultation.
      Basically, the deselection criteria are similar to—or the reverse
      of—those used to select titles according to the collection
      development policy statement. This method is used chiefly for
      monographs.
3. *Book-Slip Method.*
   Slips identifying items as candidates for storage, discard, or
   preservation are placed in volumes during shelf review by librarians
   (see Figure 2). Slips are left in books for a minimum of one year,
   and longer if possible. Faculty and processing staff are notified as
   the process takes place. As processing units have time, but not
   before the minimum fixed date, they withdraw books from the
   stack for processing. This is a useful procedure because time
   available to librarians for pruning purposes usually does not
   coincide, chronologically or in amount, with the time processing
   staff may have available for processing materials so identified or
   the availability of space for the movement of such books. This
   means that it is desirable to have a review process by which books
   may be identified at one time for action planned or phased for
   some later period.
4. *Patron Consultation.*
   This technique can be used to identify pruning candidates, or to
   verify or double check the validity of other methods. While in
   most cases librarians are the final decision-makers in the review
   process, consultation may prevent costly and serious mistakes.
   This method can be used for serials and monographs.

Colored Strip	Colored Strip	Back Legend for Each Slip
DISCARD	**TRANSFER TO STORAGE**	**WHY HAS THIS ITEM BEEN IDENTIFIED?**
Date identified: _____	Date identified: _____	Stanford's Libraries are filling up—some slowly, and some more rapidly—with books, journals, microforms, reports, documents, and a myriad of other materials. In some cases space is already running short, while in other cases we have time for a longer term effort to reduce the rate of collection growth.
Librarian: _____	Librarian: _____	
Call number: _____	Call number: _____	

PROPOSED ACTION: This item has been proposed as a candidate for discard from this library's collections.

If you feel that this action is not appropriate, please note your objection below and turn this slip at the Circulation Desk on your departure from the stack area.

☐ **Please consider sending this book to storage rather than discarding it.**

Reason for keeping in active collection:

PROPOSED ACTION: This item has been proposed as a candidate for relegation to an auxiliary (less active storage collection at another location.

If you feel that this action is inappropriate, please note the reason below, and remove and leave this slip at the Circulation Desk on your departure from the stack area.

☐ **Please keep this book in its present collection**

Reason for keeping in active collection:

Without efforts to prune collections so that active, most convenient space is occupied by most-needed, most-used materials, we are faced with having to double current library space every 20 or 25 years at unbearable cost. In addition, the accumulation of obsolete or unneeded duplicate titles grows over the years, occupying much-needed, active shelf space with materials we no longer need.

177

If you would like to discuss this further, please leave your name and phone number or address below:

Name: _____

Phone No. _____

Address: _____

_____

_____

_____

SUL 316 2/79

If you would like to discuss this further, please leave your name and phone number of address below:

Name: _____

Phone No. _____

Address: _____

For these reasons—and others—we have begun a long-term process of shelf review by subject bibliographers or faculty of titles in their areas of expertise. They are attempting to identify candidates for remote storage and discard, and wish to allow ample time for user response before taking action. If you feel that this title or item should not be removed for the stated purpose, remove this slip, note the reason if possible, and turn this slip in at the Circulation Desk.

THANK YOU.

SUL 315 2/79

FIGURE 2

Sample Slips for Book-Slip Method

BIBLIOGRAPHIC NOTE

There are a few titles which have provided the backbone of this chapter and which should be read by anyone who expects to carry out pruning activity. The most recent of these is the "Guidelines for the review of library collections," contained in the 1979 ALA publication, *Guidelines for Collection Development* (20). These guidelines contain a helpful bibliography. The basic methodological handbook is by Stanley J. Slote, *Weeding Library Collections* (21). It is useful in providing detailed guidelines and procedures, but can sometimes seem arbitrary and idiosyncratic. Parts 1 and 2 of Michael Buckland's *Book Availability and the Library User* are important, and the book contains an excellent and exhaustive bibliography (22). Lee Ash, *Yale's Selective Book Retirement Program*, describes a long-term, systematic and successful effort of pruning in a large, old research library collection, and Fussler and Simon's *Patterns in the Use of Books in Large Research Libraries* will continue to be a classic for many more years although it has been challenged or corrected on a number of points (23). J.A. Urquhart and N.C. Urquhart have published results of a large-scale study of academic library materials use and selection of titles for relegation which is helpful for those seeking sophisticated but practical methodology (though results, findings and conclusions are sometimes contradictory, and the work appears to be somewhat incomplete) (24). The impact of the future on the process of review is predicted by a number of authors in *Farewell to Alexandria*, a set of proceedings edited by Daniel Gore (25). Carol Seymour has published a thoughtful and analytical survey of the more important literature on the subject through 1971 (26).

REFERENCES

1. Lee Ash, *Yale's Selective Book Retirement Program*. (Hamden, Conn.: Linnet Books, 1963), p. 63.
2. Alfred Claghorn Potter, *The Library of Harvard University: Descriptive and Historical Notes*. 4th ed. (Cambridge, Mass.: Harvard University, 1934), p. 14.

3. Quoted by Kenneth J. Brough, *Scholars Workshop: Evolving Conceptions of Library Service*. Illinois Contributions to Librarianship, No. 5 (Urbana: University of Illinois, 1953), p. 125.

4. Ibid., p. 124.

5. Ibid.

6. Ibid., p. 125.

7. Ash, op. cit.

8. Roscoe Rouse, "Within-Library Solutions to Book Space Problems." *Library Trends* 19 (1971): 301.

9. Geoffrey Ford in Appendix 3 of Durham University Libraries *Report*, cited by J.A. Urquhart and N.C. Urquhart, *Relegation and Stock Control in Libraries* (Newcastle-upon-Tyne: Oriel Press, 1976), p. 1.

10. Wilmer H. Baatz, "Collection Development in 19 Libraries of the Association of Research Libraries," *Library Acquisitions: Practice and Theory* 2 (1978): 116.

11. Miriam Matthews and Mary Murdoch, "Improving the Book Collection," Parts I, 'Quality Through Weeding," and II, 'Weeding in Action,' *Oklahoma Librarian* 11 (1961): 57-58; 79-81.

12. Rouse, "Within-Library Solutions," op. cit., p. 302.

13. Carol A. Seymour, "Weeding the Collection: A Review of Research on Identifying Obsolete Stock," Part I, Monographs; Part II, Serials. *Libri* 22 (1972): 137-148, 183-180. Marianne Cooper, "Criteria for Weeding of Collections," *Library Resources and Technical Services*, 12 (1968): 339-351. Maurice B. Line and A. Sandison, " 'Obsolescence' and Changes in the Use of Literature with Time," *Journal of Documentation* 30 (1974): 284, 318.

14. Lee Ash, Carol A. Seymour, and Alan Singleton, "Journal Ranking and Selection: A Review in Physics." *Journal of Documentation* 32 (1976): 258-289.

15. Stanley J. Slote, *Weeding Library Collections*. (Littleton: Libraries Unlimited, 1975), p. xv.

16. Seymour, "Weeding the Collection," op. cit., p. 139.

17. Elmer M. Grieder, "The Effect of Book Storage on Circulation Service." *College and Research Libraries* 11 (1950): 374-376. The significance of Grieder's findings is discussed and amplified by Michael Buckland, *Book Availability and the Library User*. (New York: Pergamon Press, 1975), Introduction and Parts 1 and 2.

18. Ibid., p. 138; Urquhart and Urquhart, *Relegation*, op. cit., pp. 19-21.

19. Donald A. Woods, "Weeding the Library Should Be Continuous." *Library Journal* 76 (1951): 1196.

20. American Library Association, Resources and Technical Services Division, Collection Development Committee, *Guidelines for Collection Development*,

David R. Perkins, ed. (Chicago: ALA, 1979), pp. 20-30, 70-77.

21. Slote, op. cit.
22. Buckland, op. cit.
23. Ash, op. cit.; Herman H. Fussler and Julian L. Simon, *Patterns in the Use of Books in Large Research Libraries*, The University of Chicago Studies in Library Science (Chicago: University of Chicago, 1969).
24. Urquhart and Urquhart, op. cit.; this book also has a useful bibliography.
25. *Farewell to Alexandria; Solutions to Space, Growth, and Performance Problems of Libraries*, Daniel Gore, ed. (Westport and London: Greenwood Press, 1976.)
26. Seymour, op. cit.

PART III

COLLECTION DEVELOPMENT PROCESS

The Selection Process

Jean Boyer Hamlin

The selection process may be viewed as having two aspects. It may be considered as the process within the whole collection development operation which results in decisions on which materials (or types of material) will be acquired, and which will not. These decisions are dependent upon a variety of considerations, from the broad mission of the institution to the detail of which programs and types of users are to be served. The other aspect of the selection process is that it may be considered as the means by which selection decisions are made within the organization. In a small operation with only one librarian there may be no one with whom to consult, and no need to consult because all responsibility is vested in this one person. In a large, complex organization like a multibranch public library or an academic research library, consultation with various individuals or groups within and outside the library is essential if appropriate selections are to be made.

THE SELECTION PROCESS AS PART OF
COLLECTION DEVELOPMENT

Through the years since the term *collection development* has become common there has been a tendency to confuse collection development with selection, and to assume they are one and the same. By at least some librarians the term *collection development* has been understood simply as a grander term for the same old thing, namely, acquisitions. Further confusion has been created by the overlap between selection and ordering functions in the traditional use of the word *acquisitions*. Thus it is important that there be, first of all, a common understanding of the relationship between selection and collection development. At the American Library Association Pre-Conference on Collection Development in July 1977, Hendrik Edelman addressed this issue in his paper, "Selection Methodology for Collection Development in Academic Libraries." He emphasized the fact that collection development is a planning function, that selection is the decision-making process which implements the collection development goals, and that acquisitions is the implementation of selection decisions. The selection process, then, consists of working through a decision-making procedure, and in all but the smallest libraries, a decision-making organization.

THE DECISION-MAKING ORGANIZATION

In the public library responsibility for selecting the materials needed for the various types of users (adult, young adult, child) may be divided among several individuals or groups as well as among a number of different locations (branches or departments); in an academic library selection responsibility for various disciplines may be divided among a number of locations, and different formats may be handled by different people (the Documents librarian selects documents, the Serials librarian selects serials of a general nature or in all fields, bibliographers or reference librarians select monographs in particular fields). This can, of course, also occur in large public libraries with departmental structures. In academic and school libraries there is the obligation to work with academic departments, individual faculty members, students, administrators, and special interest groups on campus. In a special library, consultation with the technical experts, etc., within the organization is often expected. For the selection process to be effective under these conditions of dispersed or shared responsibility there must be some form of coordination, and some common understandings, no matter how general, to serve as the bases for selection decisions. Even the person with sole responsibility for the library operation has to have some particular objectives in mind in order to be able to make appropriate selection decisions.

THE POLICY STATEMENT

It has been traditional in public libraries and in many school systems to develop written policy statements on book selection. Academic libraries have begun to devise such statements only in recent years, and in most cases they are designed for, and serve a completely different purpose from the book selection policy statements in public libraries. In public and school libraries the threat of censorship is ever-present, and many policy statements are written to protect the library's right to acquire materials to which patrons may object and also the right to make certain materials available to all users, children as well as adults. In academic libraries policy statements are more likely to be known as collection development policy statements; they tend to be quite elaborate documents describing in detail the types of material to be collected, and the levels of collecting intensity, for the disciplines and programs for which the library has responsibility. Although such policy statements are by no means universal, the selection process in academic libraries is now far more likely to be based upon written policies than it was in the past. The absence of such a statement does not necessarily mean there is no planning as there are almost always some general understandings and agreements on which selection decisions are based.

WHAT SELECTION ENTAILS

Whether there are detailed policy statements, broad written guidelines, or simply unwritten institutional understandings, the selection process must accomplish the goal of assuring that the materials appropriate to the needs of the institution or community are acquired for inclusion in the library's collection. For this function to be performed effectively a number of skills must be brought to bear. A selector must have:

1. A good understanding of the types of material needed, based on an intimate knowledge of community or institutional needs.
2. Knowledge of sources to use in locating suitable material.
3. Ability to choose between a variety of materials and formats in order to acquire those most suitable.
4. Ability to determine the quality of materials.
5. Ability to balance quantity and costs with the financial resources available.
6. Ability to recognize the value of gifts, free or ephemeral materials for certain types of collections.

THE PEOPLE WHO PERFORM THE SELECTION FUNCTION

In small libraries with one librarian all the selection will most probably be done by that person. The selections may be subject to review by a higher authority before approval for purchase is given; e.g., in a school the principal or superintendent may give the final nod; in a small public library the members of the board may be involved. In large public libraries the selection may be done by department heads, branch heads, a selection committee, or individual staff members. Final approval may be by the chief librarian but is more likely to come from a division head or the book selection committee. In general, all selection is done by librarians although a few materials are acquired as a result of patron requests and recommendations.

In college and university libraries the picture is much less clear. During the past two decades there has been a swing away from the situation in which almost all the selection was done by faculty with little or no input from librarians, to almost the reverse situation whereby most selection decisions are made by librarians with some input from faculty and students. The ideal situation, which is tending to become the most common, is the one in which faculty and librarians work together as colleagues. Librarians recognize particular faculty expertise in subject specialties, and faculty acknowledge that librarians have the knowledge of the book market and patron needs essential to coordinate the whole process. Many librarians also have special subject knowledge and handle alone subjects where faculty are unavailable or uninterested. Complications can arise when the responsibility for the selection of materials in different formats is given to different people within the library. In an academic library thinking is most often oriented by subject or discipline, and skillful coordination is required to see that the right materials are acquired to support a particular academic program when one person selects monographs, and others select serials, documents, reference materials, microforms, and so on. It is important that each of these persons have the same vision of the resources that should be available to support a particular program. Because of these concerns it has become increasingly common for academic libraries to create the position of coordinator for collection development activities. This function was in a quieter, less hectic age, often performed by the library director. It was also performed by the Acquisitions Department, which may have had little or no contact with the users of the collections. In special libraries the selection is primarily the responsibility of the librarian(s). The amount of input into selection decisions from outside varies widely from none at all, where the librarian is simply expected to know what is needed, to the type of organization which functions with an advisory group of specialists either working together as a committee or separately as individual advisers.

SELECTION METHODOLOGY

It is important to recognize that there is no one single methodology. There are various ways to approach the selection of library materials, some of which are more likely to be used in one type of institution than in another. There may be several different methods in use at the same time in a given library, and they may change over time depending upon an institution's stage of development, rate of growth, and financial situation. Methods that will work when there are ample funds and the institution is in a period of growth will be less suitable or even impossible when money becomes tight and programs are curtailed. The approval plan used by academic libraries is an example of a method which is less suitable when there is less money. Thus a library which had been developing retrospective collections or special collections of one kind or another may be forced to curtail such activities if programs are dropped or financial support is reduced. Conversely, a new program or interest, coupled with an injection of funds for library materials, could lead to the need to select and acquire materials very quickly. It might then become necessary to attempt to purchase existing collections rather than attempt to build one up slowly over time.

CURRENT MATERIALS

All libraries, with a few very rare exceptions, have to acquire currently published materials. In general these materials are the easiest to deal with because there are many sources of information for librarians to use: reviews, publishers' announcements, accessions lists, indexing and abstracting services, receiving the books themselves on approval. Some states and school systems have developed book-inspection centers where librarians and teachers may go to look at books and other types of library materials, so that selection decisions may be based on a personal inspection of the actual book, record, or cassette. This method is particularly useful when materials are acquired selectively, when speed is not vital, and when the ability to defend the inclusion of a particular item in a collection may be called into play. Public libraries, small college libraries, and school libraries tend to use reviews and books on approval as their basic sources of information. Larger college and public libraries, university research libraries and special libraries use publishers' announcements and standing order or approval plans more often. This enables them to acquire materials more quickly, but still permits the later use of reviews in trade and subject journals as a check on the original selections. Public libraries pay attention to best-seller lists, most other types of libraries do not. Not all materials are readily obtained in this way; special types of material require special techniques and sources. In the case of government documents, some libraries may elect to become depositories, usually larger public and academic libraries, thus receiving large quantities of material without having to pay for them or to select them individually. Smaller libraries select and purchase such items on a title-by-title basis. Technical reports, corporation reports, patent lists, and other publications of government departments and business corporations have to be sought through published guides when they exist, and through newsletters, journal reports, house organs, etc., when no published guides are available. A less common need for smaller libraries, but vital for academic research libraries and special libraries, is to locate material such as local documents or newspapers from a particular town or locale in a foreign country. This may be very difficult since it is highly unlikely that these publications will ever appear in national or trade bibliographies, or if they do, they are undoubtedly out of print by the time they show up in such lists. It is this kind of selection activity which crosses the fine line between selection and acquisition, and it is here that the specialist book dealer becomes a vital source of information and supply. This leads to a further point which can be made about the selection process: there is a distinction between the selection of material known to be available (most often current materials, but reprints and secondhand items can fall in this category), and a decision to attempt to obtain a certain title or type of material known to be desirable for the collection but which may not exist, or may no longer exist. Examples would be: a newspaper or statistical compilation from a particular locale which would enhance a collection specializing in that area; a book which is now out of print and has not been reprinted. In general, this latter activity requires a more active and aggressive approach, as opposed to the more passive activity of reviewing what is received in the mail or crosses one's desk. This distinction should not be carried too far, but it has some significance for collection development in research libraries where both activities must be kept in balance.

TITLE-BY-TITLE DECISIONS (MICRO-DECISIONS) AND EN BLOC DECISIONS (MACRO-DECISIONS)

Most of the discussion so far has centered around the activity of title-by-title selection, although there have been brief references to approval plans, standing orders, and other methods of acquiring materials in quantity. It is now important to realize that in a number of libraries most of the material acquired may be there as the result of a one-time decision.

Examples of such decisions are:

1. those based on type of publication, e.g., the decision to acquire government documents, technical reports;
2. those based on subject, e.g., the decision to acquire all books of contemporary American poetry, regardless of price, quality, or quantity;
3. those based on source, e.g., the decision to acquire all publications of a particular association or institution;
4. those based on current publishing output of a particular publisher or certain subject fields, e.g., standing orders and approval plans.

While these examples may result in the acquisition of widely different types of material they all have in common the fact that one decision made at one time will continue to bring certain materials into the collection until steps are taken to stop the process. This is also true of journals and other serials, but there is a difference between a one-time decision on a journal and a one-time decision on the other types of materials noted above. A journal is a single title in many parts published over time, which is likely to be predictable in content and quite probably predictable in quality.

Another type of en bloc selection is the acquisition by purchase or gift of a special collection: e.g., Senator X's private papers, Professor Y's Latin American collection. This type of selection has some similarity to the title-by-title decision, however, because as a rule there is an opportunity to examine the collection and the library is not making a commitment to purchase what is not yet published. In large academic research libraries and large public libraries with research collections it is quite common for the majority of materials to be acquired through such macro-decisions and for the individual title selection to be a supplementary activity which fills the gaps. It has even been said that book selection is not an appropriate term to use in connection with an academic research library, that in these libraries selection refers not to the selection of individual books but to selecting fields and areas within which to collect books. Another way of making the same point is to say that large libraries acquire so much of the world's publishing output through these macro-decisions that selection consists of deciding what not to acquire.

THE SELECTION OF INDIVIDUAL TITLES

The selection of individual titles is influences by a number of considerations. After receiving a piece of information on available material in the form of an announcement, review, etc., the librarian must decide whether to acquire it. At this point it is usually desirable to first verify that the library does not own it or has not already ordered it. Taking this step at the beginning can save a lot of agonizing over doubtful titles. The considerations influencing the decisions will vary slightly by type of library; but, in general, they are similar, and attention to them is critical to good selection. They may be outlined as follows:

1. whether the item falls within the general parameters of subjects or areas to be covered (school, academic, special);
2. whether it will be of interest to library users (public, recreational collections);
3. whether the library already has sufficient materials on the subject, or of this particular type and, therefore, does not need another;

4. whether the library can afford it (this consideration may well be first when the item is particularly expensive, such as a new encyclopedia);
5. whether the library should acquire it if there are likely to be patron objections (public, school) or if there is a high probability that the material will be a potential target for theft, vandalism or mutilation;
6. whether there is sufficient information to determine quality, or at least make a good estimate of probable quality;
7. if a journal, serial, multivolume series, whether the library wishes to enter into a continuing commitment;
8. if a multivolume series or large microform set containing previously published material, how much duplication there is with existing holdings; then it will be necessary to decide what level of duplication is acceptable in order to acquire the additional material included in the set;
9. it may be necessary on occasion to consider how material will be handled in the library; e.g., if it is difficult for the library to handle small newsletters, for example, it might be better to avoid them altogether.

The process is somewhat different when a title is found in a bibliography or some other source which is not necessarily describing available material, but listing all material on a particular subject or by a particular individual. In this situation the decision to try to acquire a particular title may come at the outset. The fact that it is listed in the bibliography and that the library is trying to have as complete a collection as possible determines that the particular item is desirable. It is then necessary to determine whether the title is still in print, and if not, to begin a search through reprint and microform catalogs. If all these sources fail, it becomes necessary to look through appropriate secondhand dealers' catalogs, to visit bookstores specializing in this particular type of material, or to advertise the library's needs in the secondhand market. With this type of selection one serious problem is that if a copy of the item does become available it may be at a very high price and the library has to make the decision whether to acquire it or not at the end of what might have been a long and arduous process. This is in contrast to the selection of material known to be available, when price considerations occur at the beginning of the process.

SELECTION FROM A DEALER'S CATALOG

Dealers' catalogs can be of several types: those which list secondhand materials only, those which carry a mix of old and current materials, and those which specialize in current materials of a particular kind, e.g., current publications from the Soviet Union, or new art books. The catalogs which list current publications from other countries are often the only reliable sources of information for selecting and acquiring such materials. The catalogs which mix the old and the current are less useful to libraries, because most libraries already have an abundance of other sources from which to identify current titles. However, regardless of the type of catalog in use, an experienced selector should be able to bring to bear the considerations outlined above in a split second of attention focused upon a particular entry in the catalog. It is assumed that the catalog being worked on has been chosen because it is expected to contain some items needed by the library, so that the process is one of identifying those particular items and ignoring all others. During the same instant a skilled person should be able to ask and answer all the following questions in his or her mind:

Is this title of interest to our library? Why?

Does it address a subject or fill a need not now taken care of?

Is there a chance the library will need this in the future although it is not needed now?

Will it enhance the collection now in the library, or does it simply duplicate what is already there?

How do I know if it is any good?

Is the price one that the library can afford?

If the price is very high is it still important for the library to get it?

If I cannot decide whether to get it or not, whom can I consult with expertise in the subject?

The most basic attribute of any selector in this situation and in any other selection activity is a thorough knowledge of the library's present collection. The underlying purpose of the selection process is to acquire material appropriate for a particular library and its mission. The most significant title in a subject is of no intrinsic value to a library which does not need to cover this subject in its collection. Likewise, knowing the literature of a subject is not sufficient in itself. It is the knowledge of the library's need for the literature of the subject that is all-important.

SHORT-TERM NEEDS AND LONG-TERM NEEDS

It is usually easy to ascertain the short-term needs of a library. Academic and school libraries obviously have the needs of the curriculum as a guide, and selection of materials to support curriculum needs is normally a straightforward matter of identifying types of material and particular titles required by individual faculty members and students. In public libraries, where collections are recreational as well as informational, it is also a fairly straightforward matter to predict patron interests and needs in a particular community. It is common to weed public, school and college; i.e., nonresearch collections, because use of the material rather than preservation over the long term is the underlying concern. In selecting for a research collection the likelihood of use of a particular title is a lesser consideration than the obligation to develop a comprehensive collection providing the material necessary for the conduct of research. Under these circumstances materials which might be of little value in isolation assume a worth and importance, because they are brought together to form a collection. This kind of collection is developed for the long-term needs of the institution. It is sometimes possible to predict long-term needs with a fair degree of certainty, but libraries such as special and university libraries can discover that suddenly they are expected to provide materials which were previously out of scope for their collections. This can happen when a business undertakes to enter an entirely different product market, or when a university hires a new faculty member in a field previously ignored by the university.

THE SELECTION OF JOURNALS AND SERIALS

In making the decision to acquire a journal or other type of serial a library is undertaking a long-term commitment of special significance. It is normally necessary to renew subscriptions before the cost for the next year is definitely known, and it has become increasingly common for libraries to be caught with a commitment to continue journals for which they were unable to budget adequately. This is a regular occurrence in many academic libraries. It thus is very important to ensure that new subscriptions are undertaken only for those journals likely to be really needed. It is possible to make selection decisions from reviews, from lists of recommended titles, or from the lists of journals indexed by particular periodical indexes. In an academic library, however, the source for a faculty recommendation on a new title is more likely to be a publisher's announcement.

Announcements often contain a detailed description of the expected scope and content, and a listing of the members of the editorial board. Even with this detailed information at hand many libraries go one step further and request a sample issue for personal inspection.

In special libraries the rising costs of continuing commitments are also likely to cause concern, but special collections are usually more narrowly focused than academic library collections and the problem is thus less acute. In small recreational collections the selection of journals is simply a matter of deciding upon a few popular titles of interest to that particular community. For somewhat larger collections, as in schools and larger public libraries, titles are selected from the list of titles indexed by a general periodical index like the *Reader's Guide to Periodicals*.

SOURCES FOR SELECTION

In selecting materials for these different types of institutional needs it is necessary to choose among a large variety of sources, since some selection aids are more appropriate for one type of library collection than another. What follows is a short summary of types of selection sources, with some discussion of where they are found to be most useful.

1. *Reviews* appear in the library press, in newspapers, in general-interest periodicals, and in journals for particular subjects. They are widely available and widely read. In general, the reviews in library publications and the daily press are current and up to date. Many of the journals in particular disciplines provide scholarly and critical reviews of high quality, but there is often a serious time lag between publication of a title and a review. One of the great problems with reviews is that despite their wide availability, the actual number of titles reviewed is only a small portion of the world publishing output. Some titles are reviewed by many publications, but many others are never reviewed at all. For example, until recently there were no reviewing sources for small press publications or for publications of the alternative press. Reviews tend to be most useful for selecting materials for current, popular, and recreational collections. Academic libraries and other libraries developing research collections use the reviews appearing later in scholarly journals as a check on earlier selections.

2. *Lists of selected titles* issued by libraries, by library publishers, and by school systems, etc. These lists may be current, such as accession lists from libraries, or standard lists such as those produced by the H.W. Wilsom Company. Accessions lists are more likely to be useful to libraries in which the collection is smaller and less comprehensive than that of the library issuing the list. Annotations make these lists even more useful as selection aids, but most libraries do not go to the trouble and expense of annotations. Standard lists serve as buying guides for new libraries and as sources for filling gaps in existing collections.

3. *Bibliographical tools*, such as national bibliographies and trade lists, are often used as selection sources in academic, special and large public libraries. They are less commonly used for selection in smaller libraries, because the people making the selections are not as likely to want to make judgments based solely on a bibliographical description of a title.

4. *Publishers' announcements* in the form of flyers, small brochures and catalogs are a useful source for all libraries. Many contain

detailed descriptions of the contents, biographical information on the author, and other information of real value in making a selection decision. They have the advantage of being timely, are usually easy to handle, and they can be discarded easily when no longer useful. They are widely used by academic, special, and large public libraries, because when honestly written they provide better information than any other source, with the exception of reviews.

5. Many academic libraries use *dealers and jobbers* who supply books from many different publishers, and who provide notification of available titles in the form of lists, cards, multiple-order forms, or even magnetic tapes. Used as selection aids, these notifications are usually at least as current as the national and trade bibliographies, and frequently have the added advantage of being selection aids and order forms all in one. The decision-making process here is similar to that involved in the use of bibliographical tools, as only the basic bibliographical information is normally included. Dealers and jobbers tend to specialize in supplying a particular type of library and limit their notifications to items preselected as suitable for that type of library. School libraries and small public libraries may try to match their dealers' offerings against reviews before making a decision.

6. *Indexing and abstracting services* can be useful selection aids, especially in academic and special libraries. The list of publications indexed is always a good initial buying guide, and many indexes include current books and conference proceedings as well as journal titles.

7. A somewhat newer form of selection aid is the *off-line printout* produced as a result of searching a computer data base in a particular subject or field. It is possible to identify in this way materials suitable for research and special collections, but it is not a desirable method for smaller libraries where acquisitions are highly selective.

8. Receipt of *books on approval* provides a means of selecting from the best possible source of information, the book itself. Over the past decade many academic libraries have entered into approval plans whereby large numbers of items are received automatically. Smaller libraries tend to handle books on approval only in the case

of an occasional doubtful title.

9. To locate material for *special collections of an unusual nature*, e.g., a collection reflecting contemporary culture, it is often necessary to resort to unusual methods. There are often no selection sources at all, and the person responsible for the collection has to write to organizations, visit their headquarters, attend rallies, collect street handouts, and in general be imaginative in devising possible means for acquiring the desired materials.

WHEN TO SELECT AND WHEN NOT TO SELECT

A discussion of the selection process would not be complete without drawing attention to the fact that it is equally important for a selector to know what not to select. With an exploding information market and a climate of fiscal restraint more libraries must rely on each other to provide what each cannot do alone. Today's selectors require more than a knowledge of the book market, and of their own particular library's collections. They must be aware of what patron needs it would be possible to fill by providing access to the material rather than acquiring it. A wide and intimate knowledge of other library collections, especially within the immediate region, is essential.

BIBLIOGRAPHY

Allen, Kenneth W., and Loren Allen. *The Organization and Administration of the Learning Resources Center in the Community College.* (Hamden, Conn.: Linnet Books, 1973.)

Bonk, Wallace J. and Rose Mary Magrill. *Building Library Collections*, 5th ed. (Metuchen, N.J.: Scarecrow Press, 1979.)

Broadus, Robert Newton. *Selecting Material for Libraries.* (New York: H.W. Wilson, 1973.)

Edelman, Hendrik. "Selection Methodology in Academic Libraries." *Library Resources and Technical Services* 23 (Winter 1979): 33-44.

Haro, Robert P. "Book Selection in Academic Libraries." *College and Research Libraries* 28 (1967): 104-106.

Jenks, George M. "Book Selection: An Approach for Small- and Medium-Sized Libraries." *College and Research Libraries* 33 (1972): 28-30.

Kosa, Geza Attila. "Book Selection Trends in American Academic Libraries." *Australian Library Journal* 21 (1972): 416-424.

Opello, Olivia, and Lindsay Murdock. "Acquisitions Overkill in Science Collections—and an Alternative." *College and Research Libraries* 37 (1967): 452-456.

Saunders, Helen E. *The Modern School Library*, 2nd ed., completely rev. by Nancy Polette. (Metuchen, N.J.: Scarecrow Press, 1975.)

Sinclair, Dorothy. *Administration of the Small Public Library*. (Chicago: American Library Association, 1965.)

Spiller, David. *Book Selection: An Introduction to Principles and Practice*, 2nd ed. rev. (Hamden, Conn.: Shoe String Press, 1974.)

Strauss, Lucille Jackson. *Scientific and Technical Libraries; Their Organization and Administration*, 2nd ed. (New York: Becker & Hayes, 1972.)

Wofford, Azile. *Book Selection for School Libraries*. (New York: H.W. Wilson, 1962).

Wulfekoetter, Gertrude. *Acquisition Work: Processes Involved in Building Library Collections*. (Seattle, Wash.: University of Washington Press, 1961.)

Mass Buying Programs in the Development Process

Robert D. Stueart

INTRODUCTION

Probably no twentieth-century trend in libraries has generated more heated discussion or debate than the concept of mass buying programs. That the idea has difficulty being accepted is reflected in library literature, through journal articles, symposia, monographs, etc., where even the term has never gained a place of respectability and where indexing sources such as Library Literature cross reference to "Acquisitions—Order processing" and the Library of Congress's Subject Headings simply list the topic under "Acquisitions."

Mass buying programs are simply the selection portion of collection development which has evolved into an automatic acquisitions program variously called blanket order plans, mass buying plans, approval plans, profile plans, standing order plans, lease-purchase plans, or gathering plans. These plans are all collection development *tools* and have played and will continue to play, although on a reduced scale, a very important role in the collection development process, particularly for larger libraries.

The most important issue relating to these plans is one which Merritt identifies as "the quality of the collection produced, not the promised increase in efficiency of ordering procedures" (*1*), and that is the issue which will be addressed in this chapter.

HISTORY

Most attempts, as with much of collection development as it has emerged, can be dated to that period of time immediately following World War II when research libraries were charged with gathering materials from other countries, particularly of Western Europe but also other countries whose languages were unfamiliar to most librarians and which had no organized national bibliographies. It was also during this time that major efforts were made to hire area specialist bibliographers to begin a systematic development of non-Western area materials. As these early programs developed they were designed to supply large quantities of materials primarily to research libraries and without the library's direct involvement in selecting individual titles.

The first important plan established in the United States was the briefly lived Cooperative Acquisitions Project for Wartime Publications (CAPWP) (1945-1948) established through the Library of Congress to acquire scholarly materials from occupied Europe. The 115 libraries which originally participated in the plans were required to keep all materials sent to them. From this original group more than half dropped out because of costs and quality of some materials. It was, despite this high attrition rate, as Raney points out, the first time that American libraries had agreed to collect current publications which "were selected, acquired and distributed to them by an outside agency" (*2*).

The CAPWP was the forerunner of the now defunct Farmington Plan for gathering West European materials, which over its life had a much greater impact on collections in academic libraries, and was the first truly national program for resource development. From 1948 until the Association of Research Libraries abandoned its effort in 1972 the plan operated with participation of about 60 academic and research libraries through book dealers and national libraries in many countries. One of the primary reasons for its demise was that many of the libraries were beginning to place limited blanket orders for materials directly with European dealers. The Farmington Plan's major purpose was "to make sure that at least one copy of each new foreign book and pamphlet that might reasonably be expected to interest a research worker in the United States will be acquired by an American library, promptly listed in the Union Catalog at the Library of Congress and made available by interlibrary loan or photographic reproduction" (3).

The Latin American Cooperative Acquisitions Program, started by Stechert-Hafner in 1960 through the instigation of SALALM (Seminar on the Acquisition of Latin American Library Materials) with broadly the same purpose for Latin American materials as Farmington had for West European, also ceased in 1972.

A spin-off of the Farmington Plan for materials from East and South Asia, Latin America, Africa, Eastern Europe, and the Middle East was started in 1952 and shortly thereafter, in 1954, the Agricultural Trade Development and Assistance Act, commonly known as PL 83-480, was passed to acquire materials from non-Western countries with U.S. trade deficits.

Because these prototype gathering plans were primarily methods for implementing national cooperative programs rather than developing collections for individual libraries, none allowed libraries the privilege of returning items they felt were not appropriate for their collections. All, however, have paved the way for current blanket order or approval plans by rejecting the title-by-title approach to developing "comprehensive" research collections. The current de-emphasis or in some cases termination of those early blanket order plans is a clear indication that the explosive growth of the 1960s and early 1970s has given way to a much more cautious approach to acquiring materials.

One other program, although it supplies materials only to the Library of Congress, which must be mentioned because it does provide bibliographic information and has saved libraries millions of dollars, is the National Program for Acquisitions and Cataloging which is a direct outgrowth of those previously mentioned plans.

During the late 1950s a domestic blanket order plan developed between the Philadelphia Free Library and the J.B. Lippincott Company with the thought that such an agreement would guarantee that the library would receive prepublication copies of all trade publications issued by that company. Known as the Greenaway Plan, this appears to be the first domestic plan and has continued, in a much expanded form, with many public libraries receiving advanced materials from a number of publishers, including Abingdon; Braziller; Chilton; Dodd, Mead; Drake; Harcourt Brace Jovanovich; Hawthorn; Little, Brown; Norton; Random House; Sheed Andrews and McMeel; Simon and Schuster; Stein and Day; and Third Press.

By the mid 1950s a number of academic libraries were beginning to explore the same arrangement with university presses because they would "a) receive books within a few days of publication; b) receive wanted books we might otherwise have overlooked; c) receive a slightly better discount than by ordering selectively; and d) cut through a large part of the paper work of ordering selectively" (4).

In 1957 William B. Ready at Marquette University started a more comprehensive program titled "Books on Trial" which was the immediate predecessor of the present-day approval plans which allow for return of materials deemed not suitable by the librarian. Marquette began to reply on its dealers to supply the books which it felt would normally be acquired for an academic library since the library staff was confident that the books chosen would have been received eventually if they were ordered title by title.

Originally being taunted as "plans designed to put more books, at larger discounts, and less staff costs, into the library" (5) these approval plans proved to be most attractive to those libraries which were building comprehensive collections and of considerably less value to medium-sized or smaller libraries.

Aided by a great infusion of federal dollars, many more approval plans emerged during the late 1960s and particularly after the Higher

Education Act of 1965. Expanding enrollments and curricula as well as what seems to have been a benevolent view of libraries by funding authorities also contributed to the acquisitions budgets during that period.

However, by 1975 almost half of the 212 libraries responding to a selection procedures questionnaire, prepared by the Resources Section, Resources and Technical Services Division of the American Library Association in conjunction with the Joint Committee of the Association of American Publishers, reported they did not have blanket orders with publishers (6). Many more had at one time had blanket order plans. There is no doubt that approval plans have moved from the point of being fads, through the shakedown period and into a position of acceptance and, indeed, importance as a method of building collections.

DEFINITION

There are differences between the terms previously mentioned, which should be addressed before a full discussion can ensue. Generally, the terms *gathering plan* or *mass buying plan* are accepted generic terms which cover programs. This includes all types of purchasing agreements entered into by a library and a vendor or publisher in which the seller is given responsibility for preselecting and supplying automatically current books which meet criteria specified by the library. But there are shades of difference between "approval plans" and "blanket order plans" with "standing orders" and "lease-purchase" plans being even more specialized arrangements which may be pertinent to both.

"An approval plan is an agreement between the library and a vendor, who is given the responsibility of selecting and supplying all current monographs published in the subject area, levels and countries specified by the library" (7) in its profile. The right is retained by the library "to examine incoming books and to return those which, for one reason or another are judged unsuitable for the permanent collection" (8). Approval plans are just that—materials sent "on approval."

On the other hand, a "blanket order is a request (usually placed with the publisher rather than the vendor) specifying that everything the firm published be supplied, and it does not, in most cases, include unquestioned return privileges" (9). It is nonselective and a library must be willing to relinquish the selection responsibility to the vendor. Such arrangements are usually appropriate in narrowly defined fields in which there is a need for heavy and extensive coverage, such as research monographs published by university presses, or, in some cases, for materials, such as government documents, which cannot be purchased in any other way. Blanket orders are more a function of the size of the institution than are approval plans, i.e., libraries with larger budgets can more easily afford to place blanket orders than can libraries with more limited budgets.

Standing orders serve basically the same purpose as blanket orders with publishers, but are most often entered into for the purchase of monographs in series. Such orders are placed either with the publisher or with a vendor, although some societies only allow standing orders directly through them.

Finally, lease plans or lease-purchase plans are programs which have developed with vendors to provide school, public and academic libraries with current, popular, heavily used materials. Libraries enter such programs on a lease basis, returning materials when they are no longer needed or, on a lease-purchase agreement, are allowed to retain materials which they, after receipt, decide they would like to add to their permanent collection. Schools use such plans for nonbook materials as well as monographs.

The foundation of all such agreements is that there is a core of materials which, given the needs of library users and sufficient staff and time, would normally be selected for inclusion in the library's collection. They also presume that, given adequate directions in the form of a library's profile, a vendor or publisher can preselect a large percentage of those materials for the library. It is also recognized that there should be only a small percentage of materials which will be selected by the seller which are not acceptable to the library and that there will also be a small percentage of materials which will be culled by the seller but which the library deems appropriate. These exceptions should be minor because otherwise the plan becomes unworkable—expensive, inconvenient, unattractive, and impractical. In this case, the plan needs a major overhaul and the "profile" must be redefined or the program must be abandoned.

THE PROFILE

Of all the elements found in such mass purchasing plans, the most crucial one is that of the profile—sometimes called "personality profile" of the library or "profile parameter." This is the statement which details the subject matter, language, publisher, type of binding, geographic area, price, format and intensity of collection to be covered. This carefully detailed and formulated listing of criteria for exclusion as well as inclusion requires constant monitoring by both the seller and the library staff, and is subject to adjustment as needed. This profile then becomes a thesaurus for the seller to follow.

The construction of such a profile requires a sustained cooperative effort on the part of both parties in order to come to an understanding of what is expected. Before such an effort can be undertaken, the library should develop a current, written, collection development policy. This necessitates discussion and agreement from all segments —vendor, acquisitions librarian, subject specialists and faculty—and forces the library to go through a collection evaluation and planning process which may not have otherwise occurred.

Any such profile of agreement must be written with the library's budget in mind—a hamburger-and-coke budget cannot begin to satisfy a champagne-and-caviar taste. Contrary to one popular belief, there is no magic figure for a nominal dollar amount of an approval plan. Although most plans cater to larger academic and public libraries with substantial budgets and although economic constraints have reduced some of those, it can generally be argued that those limitations do not negate approval plans.

Once the profile has been established, the vendor monitors all currently published materials in the categories described and automatically ships all which, in their estimation, fit the profile. Because of this responsible task assigned the vendor, it is desirable to select a vendor with extensive contacts in the publishing world, and one who has an experienced bookman on the staff.

The final element in refining the profile is that the library accepts or rejects those materials selected and requests additional materials which were not initially selected. It is generally agreed that a "miss" rate, either of returns or of additional orders, of more than 10 percent is economically unacceptable, and is a clear indication that the profile needs adjusting. This process is not a speedy one, and may require six months or more before the shakedown is completed. Experience has considerably refined the whole system and the introduction of computers has enabled the system to introduce more stringent parameters and descriptors.

THE PLANS

There are literally hundreds of mass buying programs in existence today, and those libraries which participate have plans ranging from one to as many as 125. A simplified, but useful, step-by-step approach to developing an approval plan is provided by Grieder (*10*).

The two largest vendor approved plans in existence are those offered by Baker & Taylor through its "Current Books for Academic Libraries" and the plans offered by Blackwell North America which rescued the plans first offered by Richard Abel and Sons until the company folded in late 1974. Both of those systems are now automated and the profiles are computer stored, with over 3,000 descriptors, and can be quickly adjusted as needed. Both programs allow for general or in-depth selection. Bro-Dart, Inc. which bought Stacey's, the first scientific and technical publisher to offer an approval plan, has now abandoned its "Books Coming Into Print" program. The only other major general approval plan, one which is not automated, is that offered by Coutts Library Service.

There are many specialized programs, such as those for music and art, which are serviced by special dealers or publishers such as Alexander Broude, a music publisher and dealer who supplies American music (scores) as well as that from all around the world, through a gathering plan. Other specialized plans—for music and/or art—are plans offered by Harrassowitz, Boonin, Abrams, Wittenborn and the Worldwide Museum Exhibition Catalog.

A number of publishers offer a selection of approval plans under a variety of titles: Silver Burdett's "Standing Order Plan"; Scribner's "Automatic Shipment Plan"; Norton's "Advance Copy Play"; McGraw-Hill's "Library Service Plan"; Macmillan's "Service Order Program for Public Libraries," (as well as for other types of libraries); Holt, Rinehart and Winston's "Review Copy Plan"; and Morrow's "Automatic Order Plan"; to mention a few.

About 45 university presses, which are members of the Association of American University Presses, offer standing orders with return privileges for their publications and usually offer between 20 and 25 percent discount for materials purchased on such plans.

Many publishers now offer "Greenaway Plan"-type blanket orders for current popular trade materials at 60 to 75 percent discounts to libraries which subscribe. These programs are intended primarily for public libraries and the materials are nonreturnable. Other special nonreturnable plans are those like the National Education Association publications which are offered in three categories: 1) all print and audiovisual; 2) print only; and 3) audiovisual only.

Series standing orders have presented a particular challenge for libraries, publishers, and vendors in relation to their inclusion or exclusion from approval plans. These series—reprint series, publishers' monograph series, society publications series or annuals, irregularly published handbooks, and directories—can often be duplicative of materials already in the collection or being provided through the vendor on an approval plan or conversely through the publisher on a standing order plan. Many libraries which participate in approval plans have transferred their standing orders with publishers to the approval plan vendors. Others have maintained those standing orders with agreement from vendors that no numbered series will be sent except for the first one in the new series or unless the library specifically requests it. A large percentage of the European scholarly materials, particularly those from Germany, fall into this numbered series category. Societies, such as the American Chemical Society with its Advances in Chemistry and its symposium and monograph series, present a special problem with their series publications which are available only through them.

Finally, lease plans or lease-purchase plans are also providing libraries with copies of best-sellers and other heavily used titles. These titles are selected by vendors and are returnable either immediately or after they have lost their usefulness. They may also be purchased by the library. This type of plan started in public libraries, but now many academic libraries use them as well. The two most popular suppliers are Bro-Dart, Inc. with its McNaughton Plan and Josten's.

ADVANTAGES AND DISADVANTAGES

There are both advantages and disadvantages to approval plans, much depending on the size of the institution, the subjects to be covered and the intensity of that coverage. Some of the advantages which have been mentioned are:

1. Much broader coverage of selected areas is possible, in contrast to the sometimes sporadic selection practices of faculty. These plans have also taken up the slack since faculty seem to have less time to select.

2. Since the materials being acquired are current imprints, it means that oftentimes the most popular books are available at a time when the user wants them and there is certainly less danger of their going out of print, this often being a problem when there is a delay in ordering certain types of materials through regular acquisitions channels. Also, materials which may be important to research collections but have little apparent immediate value are obtained.

3. The ability to examine the book "in hand" provides the best possible selection tool the librarian could have. This fact obviates the idea of giving over the principle of selection to the vendor, since the materials received on approval plans may be returned. It also means that with book in hand, bibliographic checking is minimized and precataloging by LC or OCLC becomes a clerical task.

4. Such approval plans allow diverting of faculty and librarian

selection talents toward collection development, thus allowing more time for selecting retrospective materials, examination of the collection for gaps, and deselecting materials which are no longer pertinent to the collection.

5. Working with one dealer, the library receives certain special benefits such as more personalized service and discount advantages. The vendor also assumes the time-consuming task of gathering materials and making the control bibliography for the library's information. Thus, acquisitions can be streamlined through such features as: dealer slips that can be used as invoice; simplification of filing and bibliographic control (no multiple records needed); and because most services are now automated, the library can receive preprinted announcement forms for books not shipped on approval but of potential interest. The three main computer techniques, then, are title selection, accounting and keeping the library informed.

6. Through the development of a selection policy, augmented by the profile, a priority approach to acquiring materials is established, there being in every library a core without which the institution cannot effectively function. It has been estimated that up to 60 percent of materials purchased by libraries really "buy themselves," i.e., the library cannot do without them and one way or another they should be added to the collection.

7. The problem of securing coverage in exotic languages or in countries with no or inadequate national bibliographies may be solved. In many geographic areas, the only way of ensuring efficient implementation of the acquisitions policy is through approval plans with vendors who know the scene.

The disadvantages, or problems, most often cited with approval plans are: "coverage and profile, vendor's discontinuing the plan, service problems, and discounts and pricing" (11). Enumerated, some of these disadvantages contradict those already cited as advantages:

1. The plan can be expensive and beyond the budget of the smaller libraries.

2. Approval plans fail to supply multiple copies of heavily used materials and, therefore, they must be special ordered. There is

also an uncertainty of receiving individual titles requested by faculty members.

3. The length of time necessary to establish a program is time consuming. Even then, the profile is often inadequate and the vendor is inexperienced in interpreting the profile.

4. Selection, at least the preselection portion, is out of the hands of the librarians. This places an overdependence on the vendor.

5. There can be a general dissatisfaction with books received: peripheral materials, reprints not needed, areas not in profile, and duplicates received due to simultaneous publication in two or more countries.

6. Mechanical problems relating to delay in receipt of materials and need for more interim control.

CONCLUSION

Selection of materials through an approval plan starts with the profile and ends with the volume on the shelf. The rationale for such plans has already been presented, but there are a number of items which must still be considered.

There is no doubt that approval plans work most effectively with huge numbers of materials available from high-production countries which have both trade and university presses. Larger libraries, because of broader and more in-depth coverage needs have benefited the most. According to McCullough, "there is a tendency toward increasing use of approval plans as the size of the institution and of the monetary resources allotted to the library increase" (*12*).

However, Myrick's (*13*) study indicates that budgetary constraints have had no significant impact on approval plans. Certainly they have not solved the problem now being faced by shrinking materials' budgets which are coupled with inflation and decreasing outside funding, just as they have not solved the problem of inadequate staff, nor that of accelerating publications rate. But in realizing the obvious benefits that can accrue by utilizing carefully selected approval plans "the profession should make an effort whenever possible to assist libraries which are unable to take advantage of standing-order plans (because of anachronistic fiscal regulations) by educating municipal officers and lay library officials" (*14*).

On the topic of budgets, these approval plan arrangements have usually led to the abandonment, at least partially, of the departmental allocation system and what may have been the faculty's strong control over materials budgets. Although there is only sketchy current information, the amount which was at one time being spent on approval plans was quite substantial. Lane's (*15*) study indicated that the most any Association of Research Libraries' member was spending on approval plans was 35 percent of the budget, with an average of all ARL libraries of 13 percent of their budget on foreign materials approval plans, and with an average of 14 percent on English language approval plans. This is quite a substantial part of the book portion of the budget when one considers that perhaps 50 percent of the budget is spent on serials subscriptions. This 50 percent is a good estimate since the 1977 McCullough (*11*) study indicates that of 65 institutions in their study with book budgets over $500,000, 58 had monograph budgets of less than $250,000.

An important point to reemphasize is that approval plan vendors do not make the final selection for the library, but rather the librarian or faculty member makes it with book in hand. As to lists of materials not sent, some vendors send copies of *Publishers' Weekly*, *British National Bibliography*, *Deutsche Bibliographie* and other bibliographies which have been marked by the vendor. This process should insure that very few materials are likely to be missed. It also places more emphasis on competent collection developers who can closely define a profile and monitor it with the book in hand rather than someone else's review. These books, once received, are reviewed with some regularity by all concerned, thereby insuring that the quality of the collection is controlled by the library. Probably the most important yet abused part of approval plans is the communication process between the library and the vendor. Even with a clearly defined profile which is carefully followed by the vendor, it is most important to have some sort of personalized follow-up. For this reason, some vendors now call their approval plan customers on a regular basis to iron out any difficulties which may be developing. Constant communication must be maintained to ensure that the library is receiving the desired materials and that the mechanics of shipment, receiving, billing, etc., are going according to plan. If the only communication between the library and the vendor is through books being returned, the vendor will probably tend to send less, thus causing an even greater problem for the future.

Just as periodical and nonperiodical serials subscriptions are coming under close scrutiny because of economic considerations, approval plans are receiving the same kind of scrutiny. They may also suffer some as shared acquisitions and networking begin to play a larger role. However, there is no doubt that the fad days of approval plans, when libraries rushed in without adequate planning, are over. Some of those who suffered the consequences and cast critical comments about approval plan viability are now beginning to reassess that situation. Approval plans are not for every situation, and certainly they have suffered some drop in popularity, but they are desirable plans for many situations and are a trend that has had and will continue to have an impact on collection development for some time to come.

REFERENCES

1. Leroy C. Merritt, "Are We Selecting or Collecting?" *Library Resources and Technical Services* 12 (Spring 1968): 140.
2. Leon Raney, "An Investigation into the Adaptability of a Domestic Approval Program to the Existing Pattern of Book Selection in a Medium-Sized Academic Library," 1972 (unpublished Ph.D. dissertation, Indiana University), p. 34.
3. Edwin Williams, *Farmington Plan Handbook*, (Bloomington, Ind.: Association of Research Libraries, 1953), p. 3.
4. Rolland E. Stevens, "No Librarian Will Defend a 'Get-'em All' Theory of Book Buying." *Library Journal* 85 (October 1, 1960): 3392.
5. Abigale Dahl-Hansen and Richard M. Dougherty, "Acquisitions Trends 1968." *Library Resources and Technical Services* 13 (Summer 1969): 376.
6. John Berry, "Publishing and Libraries." *Library Journal* 100 (June 15, 1975): 1192.
7. Harriet K. Rebuldela, "Some Administrative Aspects of Blanket Ordering: A Response." *Library Resources and Technical Services* 13 (Summer 1969): 343.

8. Raney, op. cit., p. 4.
9. Rebuldela, op. cit.
10. Ted Grieder, *Acquisitions: Where, What and How.* (Westport, Conn.: Greenwood Press, 1978).
11. Kathleen McCullough, Edwin D. Posey, and Doyle C. Pickett, *Approval Plans and Academic Libraries.* (Phoenix, Ariz.: Oryx Press, 1977), p. 2.
12. Ibid., p. 1.
13. William J. Myrick, Jr., "The Use of Approval Plans by Large Academic Libraries in Times of Fiscal Stringency: A Brief Report." *Library Acquisitions: Practice and Theory* (April 1977): 87.
14. Abigale Dahl-Hansen and Richard M. Dougherty, "Acquisitions in 1967." *Library Resources and Technical Services* 12 (Spring 1968): 180.
15. David O. Lane, "Total Effect of Approval Plans on the Nation's Academic Libraries." In *Economics of Approval Plans*, Peter Spyers-Divran and Daniel Gore, eds. (Westport, Conn.: Greenwood Press, 1971.)

Collecting Foreign Materials from Latin America

Carl W. Deal

INTRODUCTION

The study of Latin America in the United States has traditionally included the Spanish-speaking Caribbean countries and French-speaking Haiti. With the inclusion of several of the English-speaking countries in the Organization of American States and the growing interest in regional studies, many libraries have defined Latin America more broadly for collection purposes to embrace the entire Caribbean area for a total of some 35 countries in the Western Hemisphere. The Iberian Peninsula, consisting of Spain and Portugal, is also important, especially for studies of the colonial period from the discovery of the New World to the period of independence in the nineteenth century. Today it is not uncommon that a university administer its Latin American studies through a Center for Latin American and Caribbean Studies, and in several of these programs, degrees in Ibero-American studies are offered. Several directories identifying these programs are of assistance in locating colleagues and programs on other campuses (1).

Librarians who work with Latin American materials will find it rewarding to participate in the Seminar on the Acquisition of Latin American Library Materials, perhaps better known, and referred to throughout this chapter, by its acronym SALALM. Founded in 1956, SALALM is an international professional library organization with individual and institutional membership. Publication of the *Final Reports and Working Papers* of the annual SALALM conference, the quarterly *SALALM Newsletter*, and a special bibliographic series provides a critical mass of materials upon which librarians have come to depend. Another professional group, the Association of Caribbean University, Research, and Institutional Libraries (ACURIL), serves the Caribbean region. Its more limited publication program includes a newsletter, *Carta informativa*, as well as some annual conference proceedings.

PROBLEMS OF BIBLIOGRAPHIC CONTROL

Bibliographic control of publications throughout Latin America is often poor. It has been hindered by inadequate support to maintain regularly issued national bibliographies, and in many countries is characterized by the inability of national libraries to collect and preserve the books and published materials which form the national bibliographic record. Generally speaking, current bibliographic control in Spain is superior to that found in Latin America. Control in Portugal also has been better than that which is found in much of Latin America. This situation is due in part to the strict enforcement in the Iberian Peninsula of the laws of legal deposit; in Latin America these laws are often ignored. A more detailed explanation of some of these problems of Latin America was provided by Nettie Lee Benson in 1967 (2). While stressing the need for more enumerative or systematic bibliography and the preservation of materials in sufficient numbers to make that possible, she underlined some of the more important areas of accomplishment and deficiency. These were dealt with in greater detail by Irene Zimmerman in her state-of-the-art study, *Current National Bibliographies of Latin America*, and there have been few new developments since it appeared in 1971.

Among Latin American countries, it remains paradoxical that Argentina, one of the most active publishing nations, has not had a comprehensive national bibliography since 1938. Mexico's recent national bibliography still remains incomplete for 1966-1967, and Chile's excellent *Anuario de la prensa chilena* has not been completed beyond 1972. Although Brazil has revitalized its national bibliography, the most useful, comprehensive and up-to-date guide to current publications is the monthly acquisitions list of the Library of Congress Brazil field office. Among those countries with more complete bibliographic records, Cuba can be cited for maintaining good coverage since 1937. In oil-rich Venezuela, where a special government program for updating the country's bibliographic record is underway, efforts are being made to cover the gaps which remain for the years 1955-1966 and 1969-1974.

Of the Central American countries, only Costa Rica has consistently maintained its national bibliography, largely through the efforts of its national library association. In Bolivia a private bookdealer has produced an annual national bibliography since 1966 in the absence of an official government-funded program. Coverage for the Caribbean region remains uneven, especially in the absence of the *Current Caribbean Bibliography*, a regional effort which collapsed after 1973.

In the Iberian Peninsula, by way of contrast, both Spain and Portugal have maintained a more continuous record. *El libro español*, the monthly magazine of the Instituto Nacional del Libro Español, is an excellent record and price list of titles published throughout the country, with accompanying statistics on the number of titles published in each province. The Portuguese monthly *Boletim de bibliografia portuguesa* also appears with regularity, and can be supplemented by several commercial dealers' lists. Unfortunately, the *Boletim internacional de bibliografia luso brasileira* has ceased. From 1960 to 1972, it afforded reference to books and journal articles published anywhere in the world about Brazil, Portugal, and the Portuguese-speaking world.

PUBLISHING AND THE BOOK TRADE

Conditions governing the publishing and distribution of books from Latin America pose special problems for acquisition librarians. The lack of an adequate number of commercial publishers, the relatively small market for books in some countries, and the peculiarities of distribution of government and institutional publications are several problem areas with which librarians must be familiar. In the early 1970s three excellent and similar conferences held in the United States (1971), England (1972) and Luxembourg (1973) produced useful papers treating the characteristics and problems of the Latin American book trade (3). These problems and conditions are now predictable for book selectors, since there is a special SALALM working paper for virtually every country or region considered part of Latin America.

Earlier, at the University of Chicago Graduate Library School's 1965 conference, John P. Harrison presented a commentary (4) which is still largely valid today. He noted then that publishing in some countries is often done at the expense of the author and in small editions. This is true today, particularly in the less-developed provincial areas. Benson recognized this and noted that because book production is such a highly individual matter, acquisition is made difficult. The limited number of copies of most titles, the existence of pirate presses, the abundance of privately printed works, the lack of well-organized book information services, and an insufficient number of adequate libraries are all factors contributing to an incomplete bibliographic history of many titles.

For purposes of comparison one might consider the problems of literary publishing in the West Indies vis-à-vis those conditions in a developed country (5). Before the 1940s West Indian writers faced the hostility of an educated class oriented toward things European, an audience at home seriously limited by a high illiteracy rate, and a lack of organized outlets for their publications. At one extreme, the

West Indian writer types or mimeographs his work to peddle on a street corner, or "publishes" in a mimeographed periodical which incidentally is difficult if not impossible to acquire abroad. If the work is privately printed, the author may solicit advertisements to reduce printing costs, or may submit the work to a newspaper. With some luck the work may be accepted by one of the few commercial publishers in the area, but the prospects of becoming known abroad are bleak for these writers. The same scenario would apply in most Central American countries, as well as in many areas in South America.

On the other hand, in Argentina and particularly in Buenos Aires, authors can print their works privately, but there are larger and better established publishing houses that they can approach. A highly literate public—browsing through bookshops even late at night is a part of this great city's lifestyle—eagerly awaits the next work of a favorite writer or new literary figure. Newspapers with large national and international circulations review the arts and new books in special cultural and literary supplements. Writers in Mexico City, Rio de Janeiro, Barcelona, Madrid, Sao Paulo and other major cities enjoy similar favorable conditions.

While commercial publishers are responsible for much of the material available in literature, history, and the humanities, much of the research in social science appears in institutional publications of a university or a special research institute. With headquarters in Buenos Aires, the Consejo Latinoamericano de Ciencias Sociales counts among its members many of the leading social science research institutes in Latin America and reports its activities through its newsletter, *Carta de CLACSO*. The Institute of Social and Economic Research of the University of the West Indies, the Instituto Torcuato di Tella in Argentina, the Central Brasileiro de Análise e Planejamento in Brazil, the Instituto de Estudios Peruanos in Peru are a few important institutes to be considered. Other research institutes may have private or official government sponsorship, and publications are sometimes distributed through the regular trade as well as through the institutes. For this reason extensive correspondence is often necessary in order to identify the source of supply and to maintain a steady flow of materials.

In the field of economics, one must not overlook the publications of a number of regional common markets. The Latin American Free Trade Association, the Central American Common Market, the Caribbean Community, and the Andean Pact have produced important literature on regional economic development at one time or another. Their publications vary in accessibility, and direct correspondence to the proper offices will yield the best results when seeking information.

The publishing activities of Latin American universities provide an obvious and valuable source of material for potential acquisition. The most important university presses are located in the major cities. Presses of the University of Buenos Aires, the National University of Mexico, the University of São Paulo, and the Central University in Caracas have all published extensive catalogs. Moreover, joint publishing in universities and commercial publishers in Brazil is encouraged by the Brazilian National Book Institute. Direct sales from many presses abroad is deficient, however, and commercial bookdealers often have difficulties securing their titles. It is not uncommon for a university division or institute to maintain control of its publications, e.g., by offering them primarily for exchange, rather than to make them available through a central sales office.

A major problem in developing adequate research collections is acquiring government publications, which include parliamentary debates, annual reports of major ministries and their subordinate offices, presidential speeches, laws, development plans, statistical yearbooks, census publications, etc. Often available only as gifts, many of these materials are virtually unobtainable from abroad by conventional means, and often command exorbitant prices from commercial dealers. Official publications usually are not sold by a central government printing office, but must be obtained directly from the publishing office. The fact that many of these are produced solely as vanity publications, with slick covers, attractive illustrations and little textual material of research value has prompted some Latin American librarians to comment on the waste involved in such government publishing. Nevertheless, government publications constitute such a large part of research materials that they cannot be disregarded.

SALALM for years has maintained a standing committee on official publications, and a union catalog of these holdings in American libraries has been prepared (6). Under the auspices of this same committee, a guide to Latin American institutional and government agencies which currently maintained exchanges with American research libraries was produced in 1977 and 1978 (7). The addresses of agencies listed in this guide make it an excellent directory from which potential exchange partners may be selected. Since comprehensive catalogs are rarely produced, an extensive catalog of Portuguese official and institutional publications which appeared under the title of *Catálogo de publicações distribuidas pelas librerias do estado* in 1975 was welcomed, although it appears not to have been updated. Unfortunately, no country under discussion here produces a publication similar to the *Monthly Catalog of United States Government Publications*.

Materials from central banks, learned societies, museums, national libraries, and national archives, which are often quasi-official publications, are extremely important. Those published by central banks are the easiest to acquire, often available upon request as direct gifts (8). Several good sources for identification of these institutions are the *World of Learning*, various SALALM working papers, and publications like the SALALM and the Latin American Studies Association newsletters. An extensive directory of European centers for Latin American research and their publications is currently in preparation by Carmelo Mesa-Lago at the University of Pittsburgh, and should prove especially useful.

Finally, research collections must include publications by international agencies. The Latin American Center of Demography in Santiago, the Pan American Institute of Geography and History in Mexico City, the Inter-American Development Bank in Washington, the Inter-American Children's Institute in Montevideo, the Economic Commission for Latin America in Santiago and the Organization of American States in Washington are some significant publishers of newsletters, reports, journals, and monographic studies.

ACQUISITION TECHNIQUES AND
COLLECTION DEVELOPMENT

Concerned with the chaotic conditions of bibliographic reporting and the book trade in Latin America, a small group of librarians met in 1956 at Chinsegut Hill in Florida for the first Seminar on the Acquisition of Latin American Library materials (SALALM). In the 23 years since, SALALM has grown to more than 300 individual and institutional members, and its focus has been extended to include library development in Latin America, bibliographic problems, bibliographic instruction, materials for Spanish-speaking people in the United States, and problems of cataloging. Through its many committees the Seminar has played a major role in developing the Latin American Cooperative Acquisition Program and in organizing a cooperative cataloging program utilizing the OCLC data base. In supporting the *Hispanic American Periodical Index*, which now analyzes more than 200 periodicals, and in organizing the Latin American Microforms Project, through which some 20 libraries are sharing costs for major filming endeavors, SALALM has been very effective in increasing the availability of materials throughout the nation's libraries. Results of these projects and other activities are often reported in SALALM publications. Anyone interested in the development of a Latin American collection must refer to SALALM publications; these are available from its Secretariat (currently housed in the Benson Latin American Collection at the University of Texas at Austin).

Following World War II and prior to the establishment of SALALM, cooperative measures had been undertaken to improve the coverage of Spain, Portugal, and Latin America in research libraries. Most notably, the Farmington Plan—discussed in a previous chapter—included Spain and Portugal in the first 12 European countries to be covered. By 1949 the plan was in effect for Mexico, and in 1959 greater flexibility in collecting responsibilities made it possible to approach acquisitions from Latin America on a broad, country basis, as well as on the more narrow subject focus originally practiced. However, conditions prevailing in the book trade often required libraries to rely on more than a single dealer, to change dealers frequently, or simply to accept the limitations of staff and the time required to cope with any comprehensive collecting from the area. It was the impact of the Farmington Plan, and of a cooperative field trip conducted in 1958 by a representative of the Library of Congress for 11 additional research libraries, which led to the establishment in 1960 of the Latin American Cooperative Acquisition Project (LACAP) by the New York book firm of Stecher-Hafner.

LACAP really introduced the Latin American blanket order to research libraries. A book by M.J. Savary describes its functions from 1960 to 1968 in great detail (9). The study provides accounts of Nettie Lee Benson's first field acquisition trips for LACAP subscribers and fascinating reading on the Latin American book trade of that time. It was through her buying trips that Stechert-Hafner was able to set up its first group of Latin American bookdealers. These dealers, often inexperienced in working with North American libraries, selected multiple copies of books and sent them to Stechert-Hafner for distribution to clients. Client libraries were provided books according to profiles of subject interests which the libraries maintained up to date. Current lists of LACAP publications were widely distributed to libraries wishing to make individual purchases. A traveling agent for the firm was based in Bogotá and made periodic visits to dealers in other countries. Eventually, a LACAP office was established in Brazil from which materials at that time were in heavy demand. While some librarians faulted LACAP for supplying uncommonly large numbers of ephemeral material, others recognized this as an unavoidable disadvantage of any blanket-order arrangement.

The demise of LACAP in 1972 was a shock to the approximately 40 participating libraries, but LACAP had proved that a blanket order was feasible for Latin America. During the 15 years of its operation, LACAP provided valuable education and experience in dealing with blanket orders for both librarians and bookdealers in Latin America. It has not been difficult since then to set up and maintain blanket orders with individual dealers (some of whom worked for Stechert-Hafner) in the most important publishing countries. The contributions of LACAP will be recognized by generations of scholars who will benefit from collections which might otherwise never have been assembled.

The experiences gained through LACAP and from librarians' visits to Latin America proved that field trips are a rewarding and often necessary way to gain access to materials. The writer has readily obtained in the field materials from government offices which were not available by written request because the publisher had no budget for postage and shipping costs. A visit to one dealer in Caracas uncovered the fact that books had been accumulating for shipment for an entire year without any staff to prepare invoices and ship them. Talks with another dealer resulted in arrangements for a blanket order and subscription service which were satisfactory for both parties. On another occasion, duplicate copies purchased from a monastery library in Ecuador offset the absence of an antiquarian dealer in Quito. In the same city, a personal visit with an Ecuadorian colleague to a major government publisher resulted in the acquisition of several hundred books which were not readily obtained abroad.

Libraries which institute blanket orders will never know if they are adequate without monitoring shipments. Foreign dealers do not always understand American processing techniques or collection policies. They may wonder why translations of Shakespeare or Brecht are returned by one library and retained by another, and they will continue to send ephemeral material unless specifically instructed otherwise. On the other hand, with close correspondence, they will be additionally responsive with special offers or assistance in filling desiderata. Greater personal contact with foreign dealers can only lead to better service.

The beginnings of LACAP and the scene for collection development in the early 1960s were greatly affected by the expansion of the entire system of higher education in the United States. At that time libraries were being built from scratch and large collections could be bought with little concern for duplication. Large sums of money often had to be spent within a prescribed period, making large en bloc purchases desirable. One Brazilian dealer supplied superb collections of basic journals, sets and monographs to developing Latin American collections at SUNY's Albany and Stony Brook campuses and to the University of California at Riverside. The same dealer was simultaneously filling gaps for older established collections that could not afford the duplication of en bloc purchases. Today, no Brazilian dealer provides this retrospective service, and these materials have disappeared from the market.

The time is virtually gone when a dealer might acquire and readily sell an entire general collection to an American library. Not only are there few libraries which could amass the money to start a new collection focus now, but there is a great scarcity of retrospective materials as well. Mexico has virtually been picked clean, and the number of pre-1950 publications offered in the few dealers' catalogs available to American libraries is pitifully small. The same can be said for Brazil and many other countries. Retrospective materials are almost nonexistent from the Caribbean area, where fewer titles have been produced. From the Iberian countries, Argentina, and Uruguay, all very rich publishing areas, retrospective titles are more readily obtained.

Obviously, the success of any library's collection development program depends ultimately on the ability of the bookdealers to fill requests. Personal contact has always been important, and establishing personal contacts today is less problematic, in part because of the existence of SALALM and its bookdealers' subcommittee of the Committee on Acquisitions. This group, comprising librarians, publishers, and bookdealers who regularly attend the SALALM meetings, provides an excellent forum for studying problems of the book trade and for conducting business (10).

Librarians who want good service must be sensitive to the problems of bookdealers who suffer from inflation and the financial strain caused by long delays in the arrival of payments from the United States. Such delays, sometimes due to insensitive payment procedures of American libraries, can only result in higher prices and poorer services. In response to complaints of bookdealers, librarians should strive to see that checks are at least sent by airmail to shorten the waiting period for payment, and payment of large invoices should not be held up by the failure to locate one or two titles. One should not expect service on a request for only a few titles from infrequently used dealers. For this reason, libraries with only limited needs should attempt to fill them with as few established dealers as possible.

Selection policies and techniques vary from one library to another, but as a rule, many larger collections rely on blanket orders to bring in a core of material based on a collection or subject profile prepared for the dealer. In addition to monographs the profile may specify serial publications and monographic series—a practice preferred by some dealers to setting up individual standing orders. At the very least, however, it should include first issues of new periodicals for review purposes. Blanket orders must, of course, be supplemented by current and retrospective purchases from publishers' and dealers' catalogs. Some librarians actually shy away from blanket orders or use them as little as possible, preferring the more selective procedures of unit orders from dealers' and publishers' lists.

A word must be said about Latin American serial publications. By its broadest definition, a serial is any publication appearing regularly or irregularly, often interpreted to include annual reports, periodicals, quarterly journals, and monographic series. The difficulties of acquiring serial publications for both dealers and libraries are many; titles are often short-lived and produced in limited numbers; they are produced by a myriad of separate government agencies with no commercial distribution; some of a political nature are subject to censorship; and many are often impossible to acquire retrospectively. This explains the significant amount of microfilming reported annually in Suzanne I. Hodgman's very useful annual compilation of "Microfilming Projects Newsletter" which appears in the SALALM *Final Reports and Working Papers (11)*. For a scholarly presentation on periodicals, Zimmerman's *A Guide to Current Latin American Periodicals* is a standard although somewhat dated study.

Because so much material is available by gift or exchange, identification of this material and its acquisition often can result only from extensive correspondence. Follow-up letters, acknowledgments of receipt, claiming, etc., are costly in staff time to maintain, but no successful exchange program is possible without this commitment.

A written acquisitions policy is helpful, but selectors who work with Latin American materials will soon learn that one must take advantage of what is available at the moment. Policies must be flexible in order to permit opportunistic purchases even when they do not fit present priority. It should be stressed that whatever a library's preferred procedures and policies may be, good relations with bookdealers are essential. Such relations are fostered by prompt responses to their letters, quick payment of invoices, and clear definitions of library needs and procedures. Visits in the field by librarians or other faculty and correspondence conducted in the dealer's language are often advantageous, but certainly are not required in dealing with many firms.

COSTS OF MAINTAINING COLLECTIONS

Costs of developing and maintaining collections are relative to size. At the 1967 SALALM conference, Nettie Lee Benson defined a comprehensive collection as one containing between 650,000 and 800,000 volumes (12). She estimated that in one year 300 full-time catalogers and 100 clerk typists would be required to catalog a collection of this size. Acquisition of this material over a 30-year period would occupy annually a staff of three professional librarians and six library clerks. While the holdings of the Library of Congress on Latin America come closest to a collection of this magnitude, it is not uncommon for annual acquisitions rates of major research libraries to range between 6,000 and 8,000 titles. A survey of research libraries conducted in 1969 (13) provides some helpful information on the number of staff required for collections of various sizes, but the figures reported by many libraries seem quite low, both in terms of the sizes of their collections and the number of staff.

The costs to libraries of Latin American materials have not been thoroughly documented. While data in the United Nations *Statistical Yearbook* provide publishing figures and book costs which may be accurate for Spain and Portugal, they are not dependable for Latin America. However, an annual survey prepared by Robert C. Sullivan of the Library of Congress on the costs of monograph publications appears in the *SALALM Newsletter* as well as in the *Bowker Annual*. Collected from eight research libraries, the figures reported in Table

TABLE 1

Country	Number of Books	Average Cost	Percentage Change in Cost from 1976
Argentina	8,615	$6.45	+10.3
Boliva	1,071	$6.30	− 7.2
Brazil	8,115	$7.43	+14.0
Chile	1,348	$8.14	+26.4
Colombia	2,338	$6.51	+21.7
Mexico	2,932	$4.42	− 4.7
Peru	2,338	$5.23	−18.3
Venezuela	1,534	$7.47	+13.9

SOURCE: *The Bowker Annual Library and Book Information*, 23rd ed., 1978, p. 36.

1 are taken from the 1977 fiscal year survey and include only acquisitions from countries for which more than 1,000 volumes were reported. One must bear in mind that binding costs are included by some libraries, and that unit costs for blanket-order materials are normally higher than costs for individual purchases. Unfortunately, a similar survey of serials costs is not available.

A survey conducted in 1976 studies funding trends for Latin American materials from 1965 to 1976 in 14 research libraries. Noting that the area of greatest need was in securing money for acquisitions rather than for staff, the study concludes that inflation was the most serious problem. As a result of rising costs over the 10-year period, one-third of the respondents had redefined acquisitions policies (14).

In an effort to reduce rising costs, libraries have engaged in various cooperative projects. The Farmington Plan and the National Plan for Acquisition and Cataloging (NPAC) of the Library of Congress are covered in other chapters. In addition, three microfilm programs are of special benefit for Latin America, Spain, and Portugal. The Foreign Newspaper Microfilm Project, administered through the Center for Research Libraries (CRL) in Chicago, provides microfilm copies of daily and weekly foreign newspapers, many of which are from Spain, Portugal, and Latin America. The Official Foreign Gazette Project, administered from 1961 to 1970 by CRL and now jointly undertaken by the New York Public Library and by the Library of Congress, makes available the daily official gazettes of Spain, Portugal, and Latin America. Both of these projects make it possible for libraries to have access to a large mass of little-used material for which they need not provide storage.

The third project is uniquely Latin American and is similar to programs administered by CRL for Africa, South Asia, and Southeast Asia. Established in 1976 as the Latin American Microforms Project (LAMP), it now includes some 20 members. Also centered at CRL, LAMP is completing the extensive microfilming of the annual reports of the Brazilian provinces for the years 1832-1889 found in the state archives, as well as from copies in the National Archives and the National Library in Rio de Janeiro. Such a program would exceed the financial and administrative capabilities of a single library, and researchers for that period of Brazilian history will be served immeasurably better by this material.

LOCATION OF SPECIAL COLLECTIONS
IN THE UNITED STATES

Knowledge of the content and location of important holdings is useful for librarians involved in collection development—particularly in research libraries. The location and description of Iberian and Latin American collections in American libraries has, however, not been very complete. While information from many national surveys is neither comprehensive nor accurate on the size and content of Latin American holdings and collections, a study undertaken in 1970 indicates that of the 85 ARL libraries and 35 additional libraries maintaining institutional membership in SALALM surveyed, the 59 responding described positive interests in collecting from Latin America (15). An analysis of these responses identified the foci of these collections to be particularly on the social science and humanistic disciplines.

Among important general surveys which do provide some assistance are Down's *American Library Resources* and Ash's *Subject Collection*. Of the specialized surveys focusing on Latin America, the most useful are Russell H. Bartley's *Latin America in Basic Historical Collections . . .* and Ronald Hilton's *Handbook of Hispanic Source Materials and Research Organizations . . . .* The latter is somewhat outdated but identifies materials on Spain and Portugal as well as Latin American holdings. William V. Jackson's *Latin American Collections* describes the development and/or acquisition of 15 special collections in research libraries and also discusses the Latin American acquisition policy of the Research Libraries of the New York Public Library, which is a useful reference for collection development officers. Of even greater value is his *Library Guide for Brazilian Materials*, a subject guide to resources on Brazil held in U.S. libraries.

Another valuable aid is the series of catalogs published by the G.K. Hall Company which list holdings of general or specialized collections in more than a dozen research libraries, including the Benson

Latin American Collection at the University of Texas (the largest U.S. academic library collection). Two of these catalogs, of the Greenlee collection at the Newberry Library and of the Hispanic Society of America, concentrate on Portugal, Brazil, and Spain. While these extensive dictionary catalogs have limited value for current acquisitions, they are excellent references for overview of a particular subject and for interlibrary loan purposes.

GUIDES TO COLLECTION DEVELOPMENT

Space limitations prohibit the listing of many important guides which would be helpful for collection development. However, some of the most important ones described below will lead readers to a fair array of useful selection tools.

Irene Zimmerman published an article in *Choice* as a guide to sources for selection especially for the college library. Her article is augmented by David Zubatsky's articles in the *SALALM News-letter* (*16*), which provide addresses and other information on book-dealers in the United States and Latin America. An annotated selection of the more basic works published in Spanish and French was published in 1975 by SALALM, and a similar title published by the Consortium of Latin American Studies Programs for works in English appeared the same year (*17*). These latter titles were both prepared with the needs of smaller libraries in mind.

The bible for researchers, however, is the *Handbook of Latin American Studies* (*18*). Prepared annually by the Hispanic Division of the Library of Congress, it is an annotated source for books and journal articles in the social science and humanistic disciplines. Special editors for each discipline provide necessary reviews and annotations.

A second major annual index is the *Hispanic American Periodical Index* (HAPI) which analyzes more than 200 journals—largely Latin American—in the social sciences and humanities. Prepared through the efforts of contributing librarians, it is a key guide to a core of the most important Latin American journals. Also important, but more specialized, is the annual bibliography of the Modern Language

Association, which lists important current periodical articles and books in the fields of Latin American, Spanish, and Portuguese language and literature. In addition to the catalogs of agents and dealers identified by Zubatsky, two Bowker publications are essential selection tools. The two titles, *Libros en venta* and *Fichero hispano-americano*, are roughly equivalent to *Books in Print* and *Publishers Weekly*. While excluding information from Portugal, they include an extensive array of titles from Spain and Latin America with current prices and addresses of publishers.

In recent years a number of guides to library resources have been prepared by curators for their local collections. As a reference guide also useful for other libraries, that prepared by Barbara Stein at Princeton University (*19*) is admirable. Not only does it list key specialized sources for research in a particular discipline, it also includes the more general sources useful for all world areas which are standard guides in most medium- and large-sized reference collections. Librarians will also find the more recently published guide of Ludwig Lauerhass (*20*) especially helpful in identifying important periodicals. Both Stein and Lauerhass identify excellent general and specialized bibliographies which are useful for book selection and collection development.

One may easily conclude from the available literature and extensive experience of specialists reported through the Seminar on the Acquisition of Latin American Library Materials that collection development for Latin American materials is quite complex. At the higher levels of collection specialized staff are required. But for nonspecialist librarians, who must concern themselves with the area, there is a wealth of published material upon which acquisition policies can be based.

REFERENCES

1. Academy for Educational Development, Inc., *Area Studies on U.S. Campuses: A Directory, July, 1974.* (New York, Washington: 1975); Margo Smith, comp. *Directory of Latin American Studies Programs and Faculty in the United States.* (CLASP Publ. No. 8). Gainesville, Fla., Consortium of

Latin American Studies Programs, 1975; and Martin Needler, "The Current Status of Latin American Studies Programs." *Latin American Review* 6 (Spring 1971): 19-39.

2. Nettie Lee Benson, "Latin American Books and Periodicals." *Library Trends* 15 (January 1967): 589-598.

3. Theodore Samore, ed., *Acquisition of Foreign Materials for U.S. Libraries.* (Metuchen, N.J.: Scarecrow Press, 1973.) See especially the two papers by Suzanne I. Hodgman, "Acquisition of Current Materials . . ." and "Acquisition of Out-of-Print Latin American Materials . . ."; B.C. Bloomfield, ed., *Acquisition and Provision of Foreign Books by National and University Libraries in the United Kingdom.* (London: Mansell, 1972.) See especially chapters by Bernard Naylor on "Latin America" and Valerie Bloomfield on "The Caribbean"; and D.A. Clarke, *Acquisitions from the Third World. Papers of the Ligue des bibliothèques européennees de recherche seminar 17-19 September 1973.* (London: Mansell, 1975.) See especially papers by Bernard Naylor on "A Comprehensive Loan Collection . . ." and by Glen F. Read Jr. on "SALALM . . ."

4. John P. Harrison, "Latin American Studies Library Needs and Problems." *The Library Quarterly* 35 (October 1965): 339-339.

5. Alvona Alleyne, "Literary Publishing in the English-Speaking Caribbean." In *Final Report and Working Papers, Twenty-First Seminar on the Acquisition of Latin American Library Materials.* (Austin: SALALM Secretariat, 1978), pp. 222-248.

6. Rosa Mesa, comp., *Latin American Serial Documents.* (Ann Arbor, Mich.: University Microfilms, 1968-   .) Projected to be complete in 19 volumes; 12 have appeared to date.

7. SALALM Subcommittee on Gifts and Exchanges, *Latin American Publications Available by Gift or Exchange,* 2 pts. Marilyn P. Whitmore, ed. (Austin: SALALM Secretariat, University of Texas at Austin, 1977 and 1978.)

8. See papers by Manuel Carvajal, Rosa Mesa, Laurel Jizba, and Maxine Williams in *Final Report and Working Papers of the Twenty-First Seminar on the Acquisition of Latin American Library Materials,* 1978, for a discussion and lists of central bank publications in Latin America and the Caribbean.

9. M.J. Savary, *The Latin American Cooperative Acquisitions Program . . . An Imaginative Venture.* (New York: Hafner Publishing Company, Inc., 1968.)

10. For an especially good presentation of basic information, see the workshop report on "Bookdealers and Their Problems" which appears in the *Final Reports and Working Papers of the Nineteenth Seminar on the Acquisition of Latin American Library Materials,* 1974, pp. 243-268.

11. Suzanne I. Hodgman, "Microfilming Projects Newsletters." In *Final Reports*

and Working Papers, Seminar on the Acquisition of Latin American Library Materials. Has appeared annually in the *Final Reports* since 1973. Prior to that time, and since it first appeared in 1965, it was issued separately by the author. A cumulative index is in preparation. This is an especially rich source for selection and acquisition of out-of-print journals already on film. Available from the SALALM Secretariat.

12. Nettie Lee Benson, "The Development of Comprehensive Latin American Collections." In *Final Report and Working Papers, Twelfth Seminar on the Acquisition of Latin American Library Materials.* (Reuniones biblio-tecologicas, No. 14.) (Washington, D.C.: Pan American Union, 1968), vol. I, pp. 177-182. Reprinted in William Vernon Jackson, *Latin American Collections.* (Nashville, Tenn.: Vanderbilt University, 1974.)

13. Kent E. Miller and Gilberto V. Fort, "Staffing of Latin American Research Collections in the United States." In *Final Report and Working Papers, Fourteenth Seminar on the Acquisition of Latin American Library Materials.* (Reuniones bibliotecologicas, No. 19). (Washington, D.C.: Pan American Union, 1969), vol. II, pp. 15-31.

14. Carl W. Deal, "Funding Problems for Latin American Collections." *Foreign Acquisitions Newsletter* 46 (Fall 1977): 1-7.

15. Robert K. Johnson, ed. *The Acquisition of Latin Americana in ARL Libraries* . . . (Tucson: ARL Latin American Farmington Plan Subcommittee, 1972); and *The Acquisition of Latin Americana in Non-ARL SALALM Libraries and in Selected Non-SALALM Libraries.* (Tucson: Graduate Library School, University of Arizona, 1973.)

16. Irene Zimmerman, "Latin America in the Undergraduate Library." *Choice* 3 (December 1966): 883-887; and David Zubatsky, "Acquisitions of Research Materials from Latin America and Their Selection," Part I *SALALM Newsletter* I (January 1973): 3-37; Part II *SALALM Newsletter* I (September 1973): 15-18. While outdated somewhat Zimmerman provides a subject focus for selection sources, many of which are still standard tools.

17. Hensley C. Woodbridge and Dan Newberry, eds., *Basic List of Latin American Materials in Spanish, Portuguese and French.* (SALALM Bibliography No. 2.) (Amherst, Mass.: Seminar on the Acquisition of Latin American Library Materials, 1975); and Earl J. Pariseau, *Latin America: An Acquisition Guide for Colleges and Public Libraries.* (CLASP Pub. No. 7.) (Gainesville, Fla.: Consortium of Latin American Studies Programs, 1975.) The section "General Reference Works and Bibliographies" in Pariseau provides an excellent group of reference and selection tools.

18. *Handbook of Latin American Studies* (Gainesville, Fla.: University of Florida Press, 1936-   ).

19. Barbara Stein, comp., *Latin America: A Guide to Selected Reference Sources, Bibliographies, and Introductory Texts in the Princeton University Library*. (Princeton, N.J.: Princeton University Library, 1977.)

20. Ludwig Lauerhass, Jr., *Library Resources on Latin America: Research Guide and Bibliographic Introduction*. (Library Resources on Latin America: Series A, No. 2.) (Los Angeles: UCLA Latin American Center and University Library, 1978.)

BIBLIOGRAPHY

Bartley, Russel H., and Stuart L. Wagner, *Latin America in Basic Historical Collections: A Working Guide*. (Hoover Institution Bibliographical Series LI). Stanford, Calif.: Hoover Institution Press, 1972.

Fichero bibliográfico hispanoamericano. New York (Buenos Aires): Bowker, 1961- .

Hilton, Ronald, ed., *Handbook of Hispanic Source Materials in the United States*, 2d ed. Stanford, Calif.: Stanford University Press, 1956.

Hispanic American Periodical Index, edited by Barbara G. Cox. Tempe (Los Angeles): Center for Latin American Studies, Arizona State University (UCLA Latin American Center Publications), 1974- .

Jackson, William Vernon, *Latin American Collections*. Nashville, Tenn.: Vanderbilt University, 1974.

——, *Library Guide for Brazilian Studies*. Pittsburgh: University of Pittsburgh Book Centers, 1974.

Libros en venta en Hispanoamérica y Espana, 2d ed. Buenos Aires: Bowker, 1974, 2 vols.

Zimmerman, Irene, *Current National Bibliographies of Latin America: A State of the Art Study*. Gainesville: Center for Latin American Studies, University of Florida, 1971.

——, *A Guide to Current Latin American Periodicals: Humanities and Social Sciences*. Gainesville, Fla.: Kallman, 1961.

Collecting Foreign Materials from Western Europe

Erwin Welsch

INTRODUCTION

Europe includes five of the ten largest linguistic groups in the world and produces almost half of all new titles published during a year, but is rarely considered a collection development or acquisitions problem (1). National bibliographies are, in most cases, venerable, speedy and comprehensive; the book trade is well organized; dealers correspond in English which is rapidly becoming the standard language for European scholars; and American libraries have long histories of collecting European materials (2). But European specialists in American libraries are not uniformly structured; some libraries—Harvard, Berkeley—assign European collection development primarily by language; others—Indiana, Wisconsin—by subject. The librarians have various titles and, hence, lack the easy identification of their colleagues in other area studies; few can be easily identified in the American Library Directory. The Library of Congress no longer has a division responsible for coverage. There is no general European studies association to which librarians could be affiliated: the Western European Language Specialists Group has concentrated on affiliation with the Modern Language Association and bibliographic instruction problems while librarians working with the Council for European Studies have been concerned almost entirely with the social sciences (3). The ALA Committee for Western Europe has not been active. The combination of assumed knowledge, lack of communication, and unclear identity results in less coordination and understanding of European collection development than is typical for other areas (4).

As Colin Steele observed of "Europe, the Neglected Continent," library and collection development problems have been ignored and little information is readily available (5). A search shows that few articles devoted to the continent have appeared in American library literature over the past 15 years. The *Foreign Acquisitions Newsletter* includes information about activities in the area and a list of new reference works in each issue but has published only two articles on Europe in this period (6). In a pioneering conference on foreign acquisitions held in Milwaukee and Madison in 1971, papers were given about Europe from both the dealers' and the librarians' viewpoint; the published proceedings contain a number of practical suggestions (7). A year later British librarians met in a similar symposium on foreign acquisitions but, remarkably, excluded continental Europe from its discussions (8). Two years later British librarians did thoroughly explore the subject; the published proceedings which included Steele's comments is still the most important publication in the field. Almost nothing has subsequently been published. The following survey is intended to supply basic information on European collection development, discuss types of publications that require special attention, and list useful selection tools. Because it is brief, it is intended to supplement, not repeat, information available in published sources and to provide guidance for new as well as advanced collections.

BOOK TRADE: CURRENT

The European book trade includes numerous firms with well-trained staff members, and is able to supply most books and serials with little difficulty. It could be viewed as having a north-south division: in the Mediterranean countries the national bibliographies are not as good, books are less expensive, dealers are less able to supply such publications as those of provincial presses, and different approaches, as well as more diligence, are required in collection development; in the north, booksellers associations are active in promoting the trade and assisting in the publication of comprehensive national bibliographies, bibliographic control improves, and such activities as book fairs provide access to even the smallest publishers. Although this generalization is unfair to such dealers as Casalini in Florence and others who provide excellent service, the chances of getting an obscure German title are better than getting one that was published in southern Italy.

Selecting a firm is a matter of chance and preference, but the following will help: booksellers associations may be able to provide lists of export firms but, for obvious reasons, do not evaluate their services (9); the list of firms in the *Farmington Plan Handbook* is somewhat dated, but that it is still useful is a testimony to the trade's steadiness (10); Steele and Walker's *European Acquisitions* provides lists and some comments on service; finally, verbal exchange of information with librarians with European experience is helpful. A good description of the trade in each country has been published as volume one of *Book Trade of the World*; it includes useful addresses, such as those of the trade associations, and articles written by specialists (11).

Costs for collection development also vary according to the north-south division, with books costing most in the north. Although there are variations—Italian scholarly monographs and art books can be ferociously expensive, while the two-dollar paperback can still be found in Scandinavia—the pattern generally holds true. It is also important to remember that there are varying collection development costs for different subjects. For example, the most recent edition of *Buch und Buchhandel im Zahlen*, the authoritative source of information about the German book trade, shows the following costs: all books, about $11.00; Literature, about $14.00; History, about $20.00; and Art, about $26.00. Since these averages include paperbound as well as hardcover, the very popular as well as the most scholarly, they should be adjusted upwards in most American libraries.

Another factor in purchasing European books is that, unlike American practice, discounting is almost uniformly illegal for domestic sales; in some countries the book trade is specifically exempt from antimonopoly laws to prevent competitive pricing. Since book prices almost always include a consumer tax of some kind (20-25 percent in Denmark!) which is *not* applied to export sales, books may actually be cheaper if purchased by mail than within the country. Dealers should, and most commonly do, pass along this savings to the foreign buyer, but since this is not uniformly true for all countries, one should be certain to ask and to check.

One opportunity to obtain books inexpensively is through remainder sales which are held regularly in some countries or through certain dealers in others. Regular trade dealers should have no hesitation about supplying information on such sales and, in many cases, forwarding the catalogs to prospective buyers.

Blanket orders must be used with caution: 1) books are expensive and return is difficult; 2) they do not include nontrade materials such as government publications or those of research institutes which are precisely the ones that are difficult to obtain; 3) unless specified and a means of avoiding duplication with serial orders can be found, they do not include books in series; since most European scholarly books are part of a series, this is a serious omission; 4) the duplication problem is becoming more severe as publishing becomes multinational and an increasing number of publishers open offices in other countries; duplicates can rapidly become an expensive and serious problem since some—the German Springer Verlag, the Dutch North Holland, and the Norwegian Oslo University Press, for example, publish in the country of origin, England, and the United States. Dealers are available in all countries who will handle blanket orders; in some cases such as Scandinavia there are dealers who will handle all publications from the area and others who will, for example, supply all French- or German-language publications wherever published. But in almost all cases blanket orders are not needed in order to be certain that a library receives a book before it goes out of print. There are two important exceptions: East Germany and Italy. East German publications are printed in limited numbers and must be ordered in advance in order to assure receipt; a blanket order for these publications with a West German dealer might accomplish this goal, although separate orders will do the same thing if books are selected from advance notices. Italian books are difficult to obtain, because the national bibliography is quite late and books quickly go out of print; Casalini offers both a blanket order service and sends printed cards for books to be published but not included in the blanket. While blanket orders may be useful in these cases and bring in some books that might otherwise be missed, their advantages should be carefully weighed against the problems described (12).

Finally, libraries that purchase few European books might find it more advantageous to acquire them through an American or English dealer who will take care of correspondence and other problems. There are firms in the United States with the expertise and several English dealers have a long history of providing such service. Since there have, unfortunately, been instances of re-export dealers who have added very high fees for their services, libraries that acquire in this manner must be careful about cost, but should be willing to accept, as part of the system, occasional service charges.

BOOK TRADE: RETROSPECTIVE

Libraries must purchase books no longer in print to replace materials, enrich already strong collections, or meet the changing needs of research programs. The antiquarian trade is one means of acquiring such items. Most antiquarian book dealers have a humanistic background which tends to make them both more interested in, and knowledgeable about, books in those fields. True, some have made themselves expert in such fields as the history of science, but the humanistic orientation makes it difficult to find certain types of materials. With few exceptions, government publications, except such basics as statistical yearbooks or parliamentary proceedings, are difficult to find; a few dealers do specialize in political literary pamphlets and ephemera, but these, too, are elusive items. In most cases it may be necessary to acquire microcopies of such items if they are to be acquired at all.

There is available in *European Bookdealers* a good, although by no means complete, list of dealers and their specialities (*13*). It also includes information, supplied by the dealers, on their services and whether they issue catalogs. Antiquarian booksellers' associations can supply lists of dealers and identify their specialities. The annual published by the *Antiquarian Bookman* is also helpful.

There are two ways of visiting antiquarian dealers: personally or by mail through their catalogs. Librarians planning a visit to Europe MUST, unless it is to be just a casual visit, write in advance for confirmation. Several dealers do not permit personal inspection of their stocks. Even dealers that do allow it may, and frequently do, show only a portion of their stock; they commonly maintain separate warehouses containing their most prized books. Through persistence and knowledge, one might gain access to stock not on the open shelves, but in many cases it is a reserved honor. The more common method of perusing a dealer's stock is through reading his catalog. Systematic reading of catalogs can be an education in itself, facilitated by the many dealers who now describe works in English. Most dealers will send catalogs upon request, but will stop if nothing is purchased; others may charge, and still others may refund cost against purchases. They are important contacts with the trade.

Locating a badly needed book quickly is problematic. Antiquarian dealers in several countries do have centralized search services, usually through a trade publication—the *Börsenblatt* in West Germany, for example—or a specialized periodical (*14*). But service is uncertain in what has become a sellers' market since many dealers no longer respond to these advertisements. Similarly, desiderata lists, once the staple of European collection development, now yield generally poor results. Several of the larger new-book dealers maintain antiquarian stocks, have search services, or will keep an order on file in the event a copy turns up, but at a price; some, notably Touzot and Harrassowitz, report on orders that are years old. Librarians should also remember that a search request is virtually a commitment to purchase.

SPECIAL PROBLEMS

Government Publications

Libraries building scholarly collections in history and the social sciences must have sound collections of government publications; even smaller libraries must acquire statistical yearbooks and government annuals for student papers and faculty research. Unfortunately, no continental European country maintains a centralized printing and distribution agency comparable to the Government Printing Office in this country or to Her Majesty's Stationery Office in England. Document printing and, to a certain extent, distribution is divided among the various branches of government. France is one country that is trying to centralize distribution through the agency known as "Documentation française" (29-31 quai Voltaire, Paris) which issues monthly and annual catalogs describing the government documents it publishes and/or distributes. But there are still separate printing firms for the "Journaux Officiels" (laws and parliamentary documents), the "Imprimerie nationale" (departments) and the "Institut national de la statistique et des études économiques" (statistical) which all issue catalogs of their publications. A similar situation obtains for other continental countries and, in the case of West Germany, which is highly decentralized because of its federal structure, the publishing agencies are even in widely separated cities.

Fortunately, bibliographic control is excellent. Most publications are listed in the national bibliography, either in a special section, e.g., France, or are included with other trade publications, e.g., the Nordic countries. Since many government publications go out of print quickly and are then very difficult to acquire, they must be ordered expeditiously. (Some governments also issue cumulated and comprehensive catalogs of government publications, but these usually appear late.) Smaller libraries can usually obtain the basic materials they need through the trade. Export dealers can supply parliamentary publications, statistical serials, government annuals, census publications, and such works as the French five-year plans. But larger libraries endeavoring to develop research collections will need copies of the various catalogs; the statistical is unusually important. Try contacting government agencies directly; some will supply publications upon direct request that they do not distribute through the trade. Direct orders to official printing houses vary in their results; these agencies are less familiar with library practice and less responsive.

Other important sources of information about continental Europe are the publications of international organizations: the European Communities; the Council of Europe; and the Organization for Economic Cooperation and Development. Each issues frequent publication lists available without charge (15).

Finally, it is important to remember—particularly for limited budgets—that most European governments distribute without cost various types of informational publications. Many can be obtained by writing to either the cultural attaché at the embassy or, if they have one, the information office, usually located in New York, the press and information office, or a special cultural agency, e.g., Inter Nationes (Kennedyallee, Bonn). These types of publications include periodicals, e.g., *News of Norway*; booklets on recent political developments, such as the English-language text of the treaty between East and West Germany; or press releases, such as those from the French Embassy. Naturally they are not critical of the governments issuing them, but used with care they can provide basic information.

The Alternative or Underground Press

Trade publications represent a major part of the culture of a country, but there also exists in Europe an important literary and political substratum which distributes its publications outside the mainstream through its own channels. It might be the "Kvindehusets bogcafé" (Woman's house book café) in Copenhagen which has available writings by Scandinavian feminists; the "Wohlthat'sche Buchhandlung" in Berlin whose "Der kleine Bazar" lists publications from the literary or political left; or the "Joie de lire" bookstore in Paris which now occupies two sides of a street on the Left Bank and serves as much as a headquarters for political groups as it does a distribution center for their publications. Usually located near universities— and easily found if one is in Europe—these stores are generally leftist and carry stocks intended to appeal to students but also works that can be considered as being factors in the shaping of Europe's intellectual elite. Collecting them for libraries from this side of the ocean is quite difficult and varies with each country. Germany is, perhaps appropriately, the best documented and has a dealer in Harrassowitz who can supply most of the publications on a blanket order (*16*).

Locating appropriate bookstores and sources of supply is difficult. The best way is to read little magazines, periodicals, or newspapers that are published by groups whose publications might be of interest (these range from *Westpennest*, which has been published by a literary collective in Austria since 1969, to *Legionaeren*, a periodical briefly published by poets in Denmark lacking access to other publishers) and to look for advertisements for similar books and periodicals and also for the names of bookstores which commonly advertise in periodicals of this type. They are usually responsive to foreign orders and, in a number of cases, even issue brochures or lists of new publications. In a few fields there are well-established distributors. For example, "Pinkus Genossenschaft" (Froschaugasse 7, Zürich) publishes an extensive listing three times each year which comprehensively covers books and pamphlets in the fields of labor history and socialism (*17*). Another means is through identifying relevant publishers who either distribute ideologically, e.g., Maspero in France, Sihrkampf and Luchterhand in Germany which are on the left, or who specialize in avant-garde literature, e.g., even such a small country as Denmark has at least three—Arena, Modtryk and Jorinde og Joringel. But in general this is a difficult collecting field that requires diligence, knowledge and speed in order to develop a collection. Acquiring books once they go out of print—usually quite quickly—is difficult (*18*).

Dissertations

These recently completed works by European scholars can be important sources of information on areas of current research interest or even magisterial 3,000-page works that culminate a life's work. Some are published—most frequently as part of series from either commercial publishers or in a university series—and may be obtained through the trade. Those that are not may be acquired through several means: direct request, usually as part of an exchange program through the university's library (which usually issues a list of dissertations completed each year), but since numbers are limited they quickly go out of print; through the University Microfilm program of filming dissertations and abstracting them in *Dissertation Abstracts International*, although this is only possible for the period since the program began in 1970; or buying a film copy from another source, usually a lengthy process. It is important also to consider the dissertation acquisition program at the Center for Research Libraries which can successfully furnish upward of 60 percent of requested titles on loan immediately and will purchase, for its members, any title requested (*19*).

The German Democratic Republic

GDR publications need special attention because: 1) most are printed in small numbers and need to be ordered in advance to be as certain as possible of supply; 2) some publications, particularly certain government documents, are forbidden export through regular channels; 3) many works, such as those of church groups, although published and eventually listed in the national bibliography, are *not* listed in the GDR selection aids used for advance ordering; and 4) periodicals, especially popular titles, are in very short supply. There is no way of entirely circumventing some of these problems in collection development, for even the largest research libraries share them, but awareness helps.

"Buchexport Leipzig" (Postfach 701, 701 Leipzig) and the "Zentralantiquariat der DDR" (Talstrasse 29, Postfach 1080, 701 Leipzig) supply both new and antiquarian books and periodicals. Elsewhere in the GDR there are antiquarian dealers—notably the Zentralantiquarian in Leipzig and the Norddeutsches Antiquariat in Rostock—that issue catalogs, but new books must be ordered through Leipzig, or a West German dealer.

The "Panorama DDR" agency (Wilhelm Pieck Strasse 49, 1054 Berlin) distributes, usually free, a large number of English translations of important documents of the Socialist Unity Party (SED) as well as pamphlets such as *Education in a Socialist Country* (1976).

Selection tools include: 1) *Wissen und Können*, an irregular series of subject guides; 2) *Nova*, a weekly listing of books in subject classifications; and 3) *Buch der Zeit*, an illustrated monthly featuring a few titles with lengthy descriptions (and English summaries). All are available free from Leipzig. Two periodicals are published for the trade in the GDR: 1) the *Börsenblatt für den deutschen Buchhandel* (about $35/year); and 2) the *Vorankündungsdienst* which is comparable to *Nova* in its stress on prepublication ordering, but is intended for the GDR book trade.

It is possible to establish exchange programs with libraries in the GDR. Not necessarily a cheaper way of obtaining materials—and in staff time actually quite expensive—but it can be effective and, for some titles such as important university scholarly serials ("Wissenschaftliche Zeitschriften"), it is the only way of getting them (*20*).

Political Parties and Pressure Groups Publications

Included in this category are the publications of all groups attempting either directly, e.g., political parties, or indirectly, e.g., employers' associations, to influence government policy and practice. They include election pamphlets (best acquired through direct request), conference proceedings (frequently very substantial and usually acquired as serials through the trade), and manifestos (irregularly issued; frequently published first in the party newspaper; and obtained through direct request). National bibliographies cover these publications irregularly in all countries. A valuable work that suggests the type of materials available and provides addresses is Mary H.F. Arnett, *A Checklist of the Publications of West European Political Parties and Interest Organizations* (Pittsburgh, 1975).

Publications of Academies, Research Institutions, Etc.

European scholars commonly communicate research findings through the publications—usually serial in nature—of academies of science (some dating from the mid-eighteenth century), of independent scholarly societies, or of research institutions attached to universities. Since academy publications are the foundation of sound research collections, research libraries have long-established serial subscriptions or exchange arrangements which bring in all the publications of a particular institution. Since most of the publications are mixed—a volume of a *Sitzungsbericht* from a german academy may contain articles in a dozen fields—smaller libraries which cannot afford serial subscriptions, but want certain publications may have difficulty identifying and obtaining them. Fortunately, virtually all are listed in appropriate sections of the national bibliographies, and checking carefully will yield results since most are available through the trade. Another approach is to check through the directories of scholarly societies, e.g., F. Domay, *Handbuch der deutschen wissenschaftlichen Akademien und Gesellschaften* (1977), and those that have international coverage, e.g., the Minerva series (*21*), and to write directly to the academies. Another approach is through subject. Using the social sciences as an example, one could check through such works as the *Register van sociaalwetenschappelijk Onderzoek* (the Netherlands), *Forschungen in den Sozialwissenschaften* (Germany), or *Social Science Research in Sweden* for the names of institutions or scholars working in fields of interest and write for catalogs of publications or other information. Another source of information is the government agency which dispenses research funds in each country. Although most are predominantly concerned with pure science, many sponsor social scientific and humanistic research as well. Through their lists of funding it is possible to identify important research institutions. For example, the "Centre Nationale de la Recherche Scientifique" publishes an *Annuaire sciences de l'homme* which describes funding for social science research and related disciplines in France and also issues other publications; the "Deutsche Forschunngsgemeinschaft" publishes its *Bericht* annually and issues a number of other publications; similar publications with mixed coverage exist for each country; direct request to the agency is always a possibility.

The publications of other research institutions or those affiliated with universities represent a gray area where suggested modes of acquisition are not always effective. For example, one publication devoted to uncovering the publications of institutes and of local governments (which are even more difficult to acquire) is appropriately titled *Graue Literatur* (Gray Literature) for these publications exist almost in a publishing and bibliographical vacuum. Appropriate institutions can usually be identified through university catalogs, but this is arduous; a subject approach is probably more effective. Some publications are listed in the nontrade sections of national bibliographies and, once identified, it is possible to request information and publication lists. The guides to research institutions mentioned above are useful. Comprehensive listing of these publications is not common; the French have made an effort through *Les Publications universitaires* which is a pioneering effort to identify all the nontrade works issued by French universities; there is nothing comparable for any other country (*22*). Even after identification, there are problems adding these: few trade dealers will handle requests, and many research institutions will not respond to requests or offers of exchange. It is a difficult category of collection development although one limited, in large part, to larger research libraries.

Music and Art Books
While only large research libraries try to develop special collections in some of the areas described in the preceding sections, virtually every library has a collection of music and art books. The following two brief descriptions written by specialists outline some of the basic problems associated with developing collections in these two areas.

Fundamental to an understanding of the acquisition of European music and sound recordings is the notion that the publication or manufacture of these commodities knows no national or linguistic boundaries. Libraries select scores for the availability of any edition of the required work or, ideally, for the quality of a particular edition; the same principles apply to sound recordings. Since music publishers and record manufacturers will rarely deal directly with libraries, they must rely on dealers. The marketing of published scores is often done through trade arrangements made between publisher and distributors, who may be publishers themselves. Librarians have a choice of utilizing domestic dealers who usually maintain stocks of a multitude of publishers, or of ordering from European dealers, most of whom order scores only as they receive requests for them and sometimes "batch" order, which results in delay. The problem of utilizing a domestic dealer comes when he does not have an item in stock and when the U.S. distributor maintains only partial stock of items listed in the publisher's catalog. Other factors that must be weighed include: 1) postal service problems; 2) the necessity of establishing a close working relationship with the dealer; 3) the difficulty of determining availability since tools comparable to a *Books in Print* are few; and 4) the absolute necessity of maintaining as complete a file of publishers' catalogs as possible since they are issued only on a most erratic basis.

Sound recording importers make their choices of what will be imported basically on what will sell over the counter and rarely consider the needs of the library community. It is virtually impossible to find European record dealers willing to handle all of the copyright and other complications involved in selling a sound recording to a library overseas. Even when a dealer could be found, the transaction is complicated by the all too frequent need to exchange defective copies of sound recordings. There are local dealers in most American cities capable of supplying recordings listed in Schwann (and some records that are not— and also willing to accept returns since they are familiar with the defect problem; there are also dealers who sell nationally by mail and provide good service (*23*).

Exhibition catalogs are the chief stumbling block in all art library acquisition programs. They are also the most important current tool and now, often, the only tool of the art historian. The catalogs are commonly printed in insufficient number and thus often go out of print before the exhibition closes. The museum will frequently restrict sales to those who visit the galleries, thus effectively excluding the catalog from library collections. Often a show will travel and its catalog will be available to dealers only after the last closing, and then in short supply. Moreover, museums seldom advertise their catalogs, making access even more difficult. While there are no solutions, there are ways to lessen the severity of the stumble. Large libraries with $3,000 to $6,000 to expend on German-language catalogs can rely on the excellent services of Harrassowitz for good general coverage, although they are unable to emphasize areas of special collection interest. Museum exchange programs, when they can be set up, are spotty at best, particularly American-European programs. Quarterly announcement services, such as the *Belser Kunstquartal*, are helpful to the librarian but require a very patient agent to track down the catalog. Outside the German-language countries it takes a bloodhound to ferret out these sources. There are commercial firms that claim worldwide coverage; Worldwide Books, Inc., in Boston also provides among its services a quarterly index, *The World-Wide Art Catalogue Bulletin*, which many libraries use as an access tool instead of doing full cataloging, much as the *Monthly Catalog* serves as cataloging for U.S. government publications. In whatever national bibliography catalogs may surface, it is almost inevitably too late for the librarian to acquire them in-print and in time to satisfy reader demands.

Contemporary "livres d'artiste" are of even greater elusiveness for the conscientious art librarian. Unlike their eighteenth- and nineteenth-century counterparts, these volumes go well beyond illustration and as frequently come from printmakers' studios as from printers' workshops. Sometimes commissioned by small clubs of connoisseurs (particularly in France) and sometimes the flower of the creative impulse, these works never appear in national bibliographies and only rarely in the catalogs of the most knowledgeable bookdealers and then only if they subscribe to the edition or know the printmaker. This is not a surprising situation since these "oeuvres" are not intentionally commercial (although many printers and printmakers live comfortably from the sale of their works) and since they are printed in small editions—often as few as 25. There is no solution to this collecting problem and yet the art librarian has the responsibility to provide examples, if not complete productions, of such presses in the library collection. The best that the librarian can do is to collect completely the works of some printers and printmakers with whose work he or she is sympathetic. Then, with the utter and complete knowledge of the contemporary art scene which is expected of all art librarians, collect spottily and as quickly as possible whatever other "livres d'artiste" he or she can locate and afford. These books, as original works of art, are often very expensive (*24*).

CONCLUSION

While developing a collection of diverse materials from continental Europe may not involve some of the technical difficulties characteristic of other areas, it still offers, as the preceding paragraphs have tried to show, many of the challenges that make librarianship an exciting profession: the need to use a library budget effectively in the face of dollar devaluation against European currencies; the search for art catalogs, underground publications, and unique materials that give a collection character; and the need to represent adequately the diversity of a dynamic continent that has helped shape American civilization and provided the models for its social programs. All these are worthy of diligent scholarship.

NOTES AND REFERENCES

1. UNESCO *Statistical Yearbook 1976* shows that about 200,000 of 568,000 titles were published in continental Europe, defined in this paper as including Austria, the Benelux countries, Denmark, Federal Republic of Germany, Finland, France, the German Democratic Republic, Greece, Iceland, Italy, Norway, Sweden, and Switzerland. Statistical information on European books acquired is infrequent, but R.J. Fulford noted that the British Museum in the early 1970s acquired each year about 350 monographs from Belgium; France, 2,000; Germany and Austria, 3,000; Greece, 300; Italy, 1,300; Netherland, 1,500; Scandinavia, 1,600; and Switzerland, 600; these totals exclude serial monograph receipts which, for Europe, are extremely significant. R.J. Fulford, "Foreign Acquisitions in the British Museum," in B.C. Bloomfield, ed., *Acquisition and Provision of Foreign Books by National and University Libraries in the United Kingdom . . .* (London: Mansell, 1972), pp. 115-124.

2. No comprehensive guide to European collections in American libraries has been published. Information is available in usual sources such as Lee Ash, *Subject Collections*, 4th ed. (New York: Bowker, 1978), and Robert B. Downs, *American Library Resources: A Bibliographical Guide* (Chicago: American Library Association, 1951) with decennial supplements 1950-1961 (1962), 1961-1970 (1972). The published catalogs of the G.K. Hall Company are also useful indications of library strengths, e.g., the 28-volume *Catalog of Printed Books of the Folger Shakespeare Library* (1970) which

has a somewhat misleading title since the Library has considerable strengths in many aspects of early society; the various catalogs of subjects (the First World War), departments (government documents), and special collections of the New York Public Library which have significant European materials; and for history and the social sciences, the very important *Catalog of the Western Language Collections* of the Hoover Institution.

3. The Council for European Studies *European Studies Newsletter*, 1972-   , has included articles on collection development and reviews of new reference works in European studies. The WELS Group publishes a mimeographed newsletter and meets regularly in conjunction with ALA meetings.

4. Stephen Blank, *European Studies in the United States* (Pittsburgh, Council for European Studies, 1975) alludes to a similar situation in the scholarly world; it also includes a chapter, "Library Resources on Western Europe in the United States," pp. 124-130, by Erwin K. Welsch which discusses problem areas in the social sciences.

5. Colin Steele and Gregory Walker, eds., *European Acquisitions and their Bibliographical Control*. Proceedings of an Exchange Experience Seminary at St. Antony's College, Oxford, 26 March, 1974. University of Lancaster Library Occasional Papers 9. Lancaster: University of Lancaster Library, 1975. The articles include useful bibliographies and descriptions of the book trade and dealers.

6. Erwin K. Welsch, "Acquisitions Programs for Social Science Materials from Western Europe," no. 34 (Fall 1971), pp. 19-23; and the same author's "Some Bibliographic and Resource Problems in Scandinavian Studies," no. 41 (Spring 1975), pp. 14-21.

7. *Acquisitions of Foreign Materials for U.S. Libraries*, compiled and edited by Theodore Samore. (Metuchen, N.J.: The Scarecrow Press, 1973.)

8. Bloomfield, op. cit.

9. For example, the German booksellers' association has published a very extensive guide: *How to Obtain German Books and Periodicals* (Frankfurt: Börsenverein des deutschen Buchhandels, 1977). Similar, if less detailed works are available from other countries.

10. Edwin W. Williams, *The Farmington Plan Handbook* (Washington, D.C.: Association of Research Libraries, 1961), includes a history of cooperative acquisitions programs for European books and a table of collecting areas which can still serve as a useful guide to American library collecting patterns.

11. Sigfred Taubert, ed., *The Book Trade of the World*: Volume I, Europe and International Section (New York: Bowker, 1972).

12. The chapter on Italy in Steele and Walker, pp. 48-80, is exceptionally well done. See also Robert Wedgeworth, "Foreign Blanket Orders: Precedent and

Practice," *Library Resources and Technical Services*, 14 (1970): 258-268, which includes a list of dealers.

13. *European Bookdealers: A Directory of Dealers in Secondhand and Antiquarian Books on the Continent of Europe*, 3d ed. (London: Sheppard Press, 1975.) 216 p. Commonly known as "Sheppard's."

14. Taubert, op. cit., lists them.

15. John Jeffries, *A Guide to the Official Publications of the European Communities* (New York: *Facts on File*, 1978) is the best guide. The *Government Publications Review* also includes articles on European documents and a section in each issue listing some new publications, but this list is useful only to smaller libraries. G.H. Spinney, "Documents in the Social Sciences," in volume one of the journal, pp. 53-60, summarizes acquisitions problems.

16. Information about German alternative presses is easiest to find. The "Mainzer Mini Pressen Messe" issued, from 1970 to 1974, three catalogs of the work exhibited at this counterculture's answer to the Frankfurt book fair. Recently there was also established the "Arbeitsgemeinschaft Alternativer Verlag" which issued its *AGAV-Katalog zur Gegenbuchmesse* in 1977. Several books have appeared on the phenomenon, e.g. Benno Käsmayr, *Die Sogennante Alternativepresse* (Augsburg: Maro Verlag & Druck, 1974), which includes a bibliography. There is little available on the phenomenon elsewhere in Europe.

17. *Bibliographische Information*, (Zurich: Pinkus, 1968-   ).

18. Vicki Hill assisted in preparation of this section.

19. Consult the Center's *Handbook*, Chicago, 1978.

20. Descriptions of American library collections on East Germany are contained in Paul L. Horecky and David H. Krause, eds., *East Central and Southeast Europe* (Santa Barbara: Clio Press, 1976).

21. *Minerva: Internationales Verzeichnis wissenschaftlicher Institutionen*, 33 Ausgabe (New York: de Gruyter, 1972), 1142 pp.

22. Jean Sgard, ed., *Les Publications universitaires*. (Grenoble: Centre de recherche sur l'edition, 1975, 3 vols.)

23. Written by Lenore Coral, Music Librarian, University of Wisconsin-Madison. For more information consult Carol June Bradley, *Reader in Music Librarianship* (Washington, D.C.: Microcard Editions Books, 1973); and the same author's *Manual of Music Librarianship* (Ann Arbor: Music Library Association, 1966).

24. Written by William Bruce, Art Librarian, University of Wisconsin-Madison. Offering no solutions but some help and sympathy are two works important to all art librarians: Gerd Muehsam's *Guide to Basic Information Sources in*

the Visual Arts (Santa Barbara, California: Jeffrey Norton/ABC-Clio, 1978), and Philip Pacey's *Art Library Manual, a Guide to Resources and Practice* (New York: Bowker, 1977).

The Role of Retrospective Materials in Collection Development

A. Dean Larsen

INTRODUCTION

Retrospective books are referred to in many terms. In this study, the phrase "retrospective books" is used broadly to include such terms as old, rare, antiquarian, used, and out-of-print books. Terminology can, however, be confusing. Not all old books are necessarily rare or valuable. On the other hand, recently published books can be both rare and valuable. A title published in 1950 on space exploration, for instance, may be a classic, while a seventeenth-century sermon may be virtually valueless. Furthermore, a book may be printed in a limited edition and, therefore, become rare almost at the time of printing.

Few, if any, libraries can ignore the problems of acquiring retrospective materials. An alive and growing library will continually be surveying its holdings to meet the needs of its public. It may be necessary to make replacements in heavily circulating subject areas, and new programs of study and research will create demands for materials not previously acquired. Larger research libraries will have the greatest need to develop an effective program for the acquisition of retrospective materials. Following World War II, emerging research institutions found it necessary to strengthen their libraries in order to meet the needs of rapidly expanding student bodies, growing faculties, and ever-increasing numbers of researchers. These changing conditions and the expansion of libraries which resulted are well known. More funds became available than ever before, and new techniques were rapidly developed. As a result, the postwar years saw not only great expansion in the purchase of out-of-print books, but also made necessary the development of a new reprint and microform industry.

The difficulty of securing out-of-print books is one of the principal problems faced by libraries. Since the end of World War II, libraries have acquired books—individual titles as well as collections—at the most accelerated rate in history. Titles that were once readily available at moderate prices have almost completely disappeared. When copies of such titles are occasionally offered for sale, the tremendous number of potential customers, including libraries, drives the price skyward. Inflating costs have forced publishers to print works in smaller numbers. Accordingly, new books seem to go out of print much more quickly than before.

The past few years have seen a slowdown in the purchasing of retrospective materials. This deceleration has been due primarily to the paradoxical condition of having budgets decrease while, concurrently, the costs of serials, binding, and new titles are increasing. Despite these factors, a library, to remain viable, must still look to the acquisition of retrospective materials in many, if not all, subject areas.

Richard Blackwell described secondhand-book selling as "the process of getting too few copies of too many titles into the hands of . . . too many customers" (1). What, then, are the methods which libraries must employ to acquire those materials which they are seeking? An in-print book may be simply ordered from the publisher or jobber. An out-of-print book must be located. This is not an easy job when one begins to consider the vast number of titles published since the time of Gutenberg—titles which are scattered throughout the world in untold thousands of private collections and in the stock of dealers specializing in the sale of out-of-print materials.

The collection development policy and acquisition plans of a specific library will determine the procedures and programs to be followed in the acquisition of retrospective materials. The depth of the retrospective acquisition program will determine the extent to which antiquarian catalogs, search services, reprint publishers, and micro materials will be tapped as acquisition sources.

ANTIQUARIAN BOOKSELLERS

The antiquarian bookdealer is the pinnacle of sources for the acquisition of retrospective materials. There are other methods of acquiring retrospective titles which will be discussed herein, but no one source is usually as important as the antiquarian dealer. Felix Reichmann classifies dealers into the following six broad categories:

1. The top-level, rare-book dealers who deal only in extremely choice and rare items;
2. The large-scale, antiquarian bookdealers who generally have a large stock and maintain their stock through connections with other dealers and auction houses, and who frequently buy large private collections;
3. Specialist bookdealers operating either from small shops or from their own homes and often by means of catalogs only;
4. Book scouts who make their living by searching out materials which are most often sold to other dealers;
5. Dealers in publishers' remainders;
6. Junk dealers who sometimes include books among their wares (2).

Libraries will most often seek the services of dealers in the first three categories, but if serious in acquiring retrospective materials in depth, must use all available sources and services as various situations might dictate.

There are a number of sources and methods for obtaining information about out-of-print dealers. The *AB Bookman's Yearbook* annually lists dealers by subject speciality. The *American Booktrade Directory* provides a geographical listing of dealers by state and city. The Sheppard Press regularly issues updated editions of *Bookdealers in North America*, the *Directory of Dealers in Secondhand and Antiquarian Books in the British Isles*, and *European Bookdealers, a Directory of Secondhand and Antiquarian Books on the Continent of Europe*. The International League of Antiquarian Booksellers issues periodically *International Directory of Antiquarian Booksellers* with listings by country and by specialty. These directories contain information on specialties, stock, and other important related items. Information on dealers can also be obtained from well-operated and established library acquisition departments of institutions with expertise in the acquisition of retrospective titles.

DEALERS' CATALOGS

Most often associated with antiquarian dealers is the "dealer catalog." There are as many varieties of catalogs as there are dealers. Some of these catalogs are classics of bibliography or printing. Others are short listings produced only in mimeograph or other inexpensive format. The library that does not make use of dealers' catalogs is missing out on one of the most important out-of-print acquisition tools available. The use of dealers' catalogs is not, however, without its drawbacks. Few, if any, libraries can afford to check all catalogs against their lists of desiderata. Such checking must, of necessity, be limited to those catalogs which, after examination by subject specialists or bibliographers, seem most likely to bear fruit. A quick perusal of these catalogs by someone well acquainted not only with the needs of the library but also with the library's holdings can be a most effective method in identifying needed and previously unidentified yet desirable retrospective items.

The library not only will have identified those broad subject areas it wishes to develop but also will have build desiderata lists of specific titles and editions. Most dealers' catalogs, however, cannot be checked against desiderata lists, as this procedure is usually too time consuming to be justified on the basis of the possible few items identified. Other methods for acquiring specific retrospective titles are usually more successful.

Much has been said regarding the necessity of speed in checking catalogs to insure acquisition of an item before it is sold to another library, dealer, or collector. It is true that competition for the most-sought-after items is keen, and the library which does the quickest checking and ordering will be the most successful in obtaining desired items. In certain instances, a telephone call or a cable to the dealer to reserve the most wanted items is a good practice to follow. However, not all items from a given catalog will always sell quickly. Helga Pietarski, in her article on out-of-print purchasing, reported that, although the most desirable items go quickly, it still takes two months on the average for a catalog to be sold out (3). This is further demonstrated by the experience of one library which, because of a lack of funds, made no purchases from catalogs for a number of months, and then made subsequent inquiries on the availability of wanted items. Approximately 30 percent of those items desired were still available.

Not all libraries have the same subject specialties nor the same desiderata in a specialty. Those libraries which consistently check catalogs against desiderata and make additional selections of previously unidentified items will be able to strengthen their collections measurably over a period of time.

Many antiquarian dealers are small merchants operating either from their homes or from small shops with the assistance of only one or two employees. For this reason, some may be slow in answering correspondence, and thus not always be willing or able to provide necessary services or meet the requirements of some library purchases. Anthony Rota discussed the problems dealers are having today in maintaining business in city centers because of the accelerating costs of rents (4). As a result of this inflation, many booksellers are being forced to move to the suburbs. Thus, the librarian who wishes to make visits to major booksellers in metropolitan centers may find it necessary either to spend a greater amount of time in traveling to the various shops, or to reduce the number of dealers he plans to visit. Mr. Rota also noted the problems dealers are encountering today in catalog production. The pattern of catalog publication is experiencing a rapid change due to rising publishing costs and increasing postal rates. Not only are fewer catalogs being issued, but the number of catalogs printed and the lists of persons and institutions to whom these catalogs are mailed are also being reduced.

As a library develops relationships with dealers and its interests and purchasing patterns become known, dealers can and will assist a specific library to build its collections. Dealers will quote items which may be of interest to the library before cataloging. In buying for stock, dealers will keep in mind the interests and specific wants of the libraries they serve. It is not an uncommon practice for a library to provide a checked bibliography which reflects holdings and/or wants. Through mutual agreement and trust, the dealer can then proceed to acquire items for his clients. Some dealers are willing to provide advance copies of catalog galley proofs to libraries that are principal customers.

LOCAL DEALERS

Libraries that have a dealer nearby can accrue many advantages by working closely with such dealers. Not only will the growth of a local antiquarian house be an advantage to the local community, but a local dealer can also provide many services to the library. For example, there is usually no better source for local history material if the library collects in this field. Such dealers can also offer appraisal service, provide a market for the sale of duplicates, and serve the library in numerous other ways. Too often the advantages of such cooperation between the local dealer and the library are missed.

PRICING

"What is a fair price for an antiquarian book?" is a question which may never be answered to everyone's satisfaction. Librarians have been heard to remark that a certain percentage markup by dealers is not justified. However, one must keep in mind that the dealer must pay the overhead costs of advertising, labor, catalog printing, postage, capital investment in stock, and so forth. Markup is usually greater on less expensive items and smaller on more expensive items. As the dealer does provide a service, a reasonable profit to the dealer must be expected. Supply and demand, of course, are also factors in the book trade as they are in most other businesses. Perez, in discussing an ALA out-of-print survey sent to selected dealers, stated that the most frequently mentioned basis for price assignment was book-trade experience (5). Pricing is based to some extent on past sales, and there are a number of guides which can be used.

Caution in judging variant pricing of the same item must be exercised, as the price of some titles may vary significantly because of condition, provenance, or binding. A book which is a presentation copy or has other distinctive features may also be higher priced. Librarians who have considerable experience in working with antiquarian bookdealers will have developed a sense for antiquarian book prices. If a library does considerable business with a particular dealer over a prolonged period, the librarian may note that although some books seem priced too high, others are real bargains. In the long run, these differences tend to offset each other. Felix Reichmann gives the following advice:

1. There is no such thing as the right price independent of time, space and the need (or the desire) of the prospective buyer. A price rejected by library "A" may be fully justified according to the acquisitions policy of library "B."
2. Never lose your temper because a price seems too high. Price quotations are not a personal insult nor do they inflict bodily harm.
3. Do not haggle about prices. If correspondence is necessary at all, inform the dealer politely that your need for the title offered is not so great that you feel you can justify its purchase—but thank him for the offer, nevertheless.

4. Bear in mind that the dealers' price is based on his own purchase price, his overall expenditures and his expertise. . . .
5. Whenever we judge a price as too high we accept one of the following underlying assumptions: (a) We can buy the same title in the same condition immediately at a lower price; (b) we do not need the title so urgently as to pay such a price (6).

There are a number of publications which may serve as guides to pricing. The user of such publications must keep in mind the possible variants in condition noted above as well as the currency of the publication being consulted. The *Bookman's Price Index*, compiled by Daniel F. McGrath and issued by the Gale Research Company, is an index to selected dealers' catalogs. Extensive details not essential to establishing condition or determining price are condensed or omitted. Other well-known guides, though out of date, include Van Allen Bradley's *New Gold in Your Attic*, Wright Howes's *U.S. IANA*, and Norman Head's *Bookman's Guide to Americana*.

Auction records are another important source for pricing information. Perhaps the most widely used is *American Book Prices Current*. The latest annual volume (84) reports the auction season from September 1977 to August 1978. Included are the leading auction houses in New York, London, Amsterdam, Los Angeles, Melbourne, Johannesburg, Edinburgh, Paris, Rome, Utrecht, Montreal, Baltimore, Leeds, Bath, Philadelphia, and San Francisco. Auction records of other foreign houses are also published and useful if the needs of the library warrant searching for prices to this extent.

AUCTIONS

Auctions are another important source for obtaining retrospective materials. Book auctions have a long history in Europe and the United States. The well-known firm of Sotheby in London dates from 1744, and numerous book auctions took place for over a half a century before its institution. Similar auctions in America date from the second decade of the eighteenth century. Recent years have seen an expansion of auction houses worldwide. Libraries can order auction catalogs to help them in their acquisition of retrospective titles. Obtaining catalogs from leading auction houses throughout the world, however, is an expensive and tedious task. It may be necessary, for example, to pay airmail rates in order to receive catalogs before the auctions actually take place.

Even with these problems, auctions must not be overlooked as a principal resource for the acquisition of retrospective materials. Many private collections pass through the hands of the auctioneer, and titles which have not been available for decades may come back into the general marketplace. Auction catalogs can, in and of themselves, be of value, as they may, like certain dealers' catalogs, serve as reference works. This is especially true if the collection described has been well developed by a serious collector. Although some auction houses handle primarily only rare items which may be of interest to only specialized or rare-book libraries, there are houses which handle less-expensive materials of use to the less-specialized collector.

Auction houses will accept direct mail bids from libraries, but there is much less flexibility at the auction if the librarian or his agent is not in attendance. Most libraries prefer to be represented by a dealer who can make judgments on the spot in line with instructions previously received from the library. Although it is necessary to pay the dealer's commission in such cases, this method obviously has many more advantages than a mail bid.

ADVERTISING

Another method of acquiring out-of-print titles is through advertising in journals published in the book trade. In the United States and a number of other countries, antiquarian book trade and collectors' journals run ads for both dealers and libraries. The principal American journal is the *AB Bookman's Weekly for the Specialist Book World*. It has a present circulation of approximately 8,000, with approximately 6,000 copies going to dealers both in the United States and abroad. AB accepts ads from both libraries and dealers, although it does not solicit advertising from libraries.

Many libraries prefer to submit their want lists to dealers or search services rather than use direct advertising. There are advantages and disadvantages to both of these methods. Through direct advertising, the library might receive more than one quote for a specific title. If there is a significant difference in price, the library may then select the least expensive offer. On the other hand, this system makes it necessary to keep additional records and to use professional staff members in order to make judgments, thus incurring greater internal costs. Most libraries seem to prefer submitting lists to dealers, and there is evidence that the cost of using this method is no more than that of direct advertising when internal processing costs are taken into consideration.

Another American advertising journal is *The Library Bookseller*, commonly known by the acronym *TAAB*. This journal lists only books wanted by college and university libraries. Lists submitted by library subscribers are printed at no cost to the library. The journal is supported principally by subscriptions from dealers who quote from stock directly to the library or, in some cases, advertise for those items listed. Advertising journals published in other countries include London's *The Clique*, the German *Börsenblatt*, the French *Bulleten de la Librarie Ancienne et Moderne*, and the Spanish *Elenchus*.

DESIDERATA LISTS

Another common method used in locating retrospective items is the submission of want lists to dealers. A library may select a dealer on the basis of previous experience with the firm. Dealers may also be selected on the basis of their extensive stock, their particular specialty or their reputation for fulfilling the needs of their customers. In most instances, it is best to submit the list to only one dealer. If the same list is submitted to a number of dealers at the same time, all the dealers might advertise for the same item, creating a false demand and inflating the price. A good practice is to give a dealer the exclusive right to supply items from the want list within a specified period of time.

Some libraries may be concerned that dealers will price items higher than normal when automatic sale is assured. This assumption is not valid, however, and libraries should have no fear of such occurrences if they submit their want lists to established, reputable dealers. No dealer who wants to remain in business will risk unethical pricing practices. The library may also choose to set price limits on items, above which limit automatic shipment is not to be made by the dealer. Arrangements should further be made to review periodically both the price limits and the dealer's performance. Stanford University Libraries took some exception to this practice as reported by Lynden and Meyerfeld (7). The Stanford experience, however, was based on the ability of the Stanford University Libraries to appoint a full-time person to the staff to manage out-of-print procurement. Libraries without a program of out-of-print procurement large enough to justify such a position or resources adequate to fund it will find the system described above to be the most practical.

Some libraries demand advance quotations from dealers and scouts because of institutional purchasing regulations or other factors. Book scouts are dealers who usually do not carry a stock of their own, but operate search services for libraries, dealers, or private collectors. Although most dealers will quote prices and wait for a confirming purchase order, this method is universally more expensive. The dealer must incur the additional clerical costs of preparing quotes, covering the cost of postage, advertising, and so forth. The dealer may also be hesitant to acquire an item which might possibly end up in his own stock if for some reason the library did not purchase it. Whenever possible, the method of mutual trust in allowing automatic shipment should be employed, as experience indicates that it is most successful. When dealers or scouts who may be traveling locate an item, they are able to purchase it and be assured of a sale. If a list is submitted to a dealer to be checked against current stock only, this fact should be clearly stated and the dealer instructed not to advertise.

Shirley Heppell, in her article on the use of multiple-submission want lists as a method of receiving a number of quotes for price comparison, reported that this practice was not an advantageous system to be employed by libraries (8). Helga Pietarski also discussed the practice of multiple-submission lists and came to the same conclusions (9).

BOOK FAIRS

Although there is a long history of book fairs, recent years have seen a tremendous expansion of book fairs worldwide. It is reported that most of the selling at such fairs is from dealer to dealer, followed by sales to private collectors and libraries. There are difficulties faced by the librarian at the book fair, the largest of which is usually the librarian's lack of sufficient knowledge of his collection to allow purchase of those items not owned. This generally means that only major items which he knows the library lacks may be purchased.

There are, however, many advantages to attending book fairs. For one thing, the librarian can become acquainted with the dealers who exhibit. He can also examine the stock which is on display and become better acquainted with each dealer's specialties. It is imperative that the librarian who is to succeed in the acquisition of retrospective books become well acquainted and form personal relationships with potential suppliers. There is no better chance to examine the stock of a large number of bookdealers at one time and discuss the library's desiderata than during visits to book fairs. As previously mentioned, many dealers are being forced to move to the suburbs to cope with the inflating costs of business. Librarians who attend book fairs gain the opportunity of visiting with a large number of these dealers without the expense and trouble of traveling to the various scattered locations where they keep their shops. Still it must be remembered that the only way to see a dealer's complete stock is to visit the shop itself.

DEALER VISITS TO THE LIBRARY

Many dealers make visits periodically to their principal library clients. These visits not only afford close relationships to develop between the library personnel and the dealer, but also allow the dealer to survey the library's collection strengths and collection development interests. Usually the dealer will also make offers to the library by bringing catalog slips, lists, and books for examination and selection by the librarians. Such visits can be a tremendous asset to libraries which have communicated beforehand to the dealer those areas they wish to strengthen.

COLLECTION BUYING

The acquisition of a subject collection en bloc is a method whereby libraries may develop a subject specialty in a short time. Collections are formed by both private collectors and by dealers. If a library is expanding in a new subject area and has few or no holdings in that subject area, collection buying can be a useful method in quickly acquiring retrospective titles. During the period following World War II, a number of libraries experienced a rapid growth through the purchase of collections. Libraries must, however, use caution and judgment in the selection of collections. Potential collection purchases should be thoroughly studies by subject specialists to determine both the depth and breadth of the collection.

A prime consideration in collection purchasing is the unit cost of titles acquired through this method. In addition to the initial purchase price, expenses are incurred when labor is expended to determine which books within the collection duplicate the library's holdings. The cost of disposing of unwanted items must also be weighed. This expense is twofold, involving not only labor spent in disposing of the duplicates, but also the loss sustained in selling duplicate or unwanted items at a wholesale price to other dealers (3).

Furthermore, the library must consider the relative worth of absorbing nonpriority titles which characteristically accompany such large collections. Related to this is the time-consuming and expensive process of evaluating titles which may be of secondary interest to determine whether or not they should be added to the library's holdings. All these expenses must be considered in addition to the initial price of a collection and added together to determine unit costs as a part of the analysis of a collection. A well-established library cannot usually afford to consider a general collection. More specialized collections may add strength to weak subject areas in the library's holdings.

REPRINTS

Perhaps the most logical starting place for the acquisition of out-of-print materials is the reprint. A rare-book library may, for one of many reasons, wish to acquire the original edition of a work if the acquisition of the text is not the principal factor in collecting the item. When the prime consideration is the text, however, reprints can often fulfill the need. Such reprints may also be desirable even if a library already has a copy of the original edition. Some reprints contain new apparatus, such as introductions and indices, which can be an invaluable aid to library patrons. A reprint edition may also fulfill general circulation and reference needs if the original edition of a work is too rare or fragile to warrant general use.

There are a number of published guides dealing with reprints. These guides identify a large percentage of the major reprint houses and many of their principal publications. The publishers of each of these guides use certain criteria to determine which items they will include in the publication. The publishers of *Guide to Reprints*, for example, limit the contents of their guide to reprints published by way of a photo-offset process in editions of 200 or more copies. Furthermore, they require that the reprint be near the physical size of the original work and that no changes be made in the text itself. Other publishers use different criteria in compiling their guides.

While using these guides, a library must also remain cognizant of the small or highly specialized publisher who may also issue reprint editions but who may not be listed in one of the major guides. This is particularly true in such fields as local history where even a local historical society, library or other agency may sponsor the reprint of an older work no longer generally available in the out-of-print market.

Some reprint houses have been criticized in recent years because of publication delays following the announcement of a reprint edition. In some instances, reprint houses have even failed to produce the work when insufficient prepublication orders have been received. Not all publishers distinguish in their catalogs those titles which are in fact available, those which are in production, and those which are merely contemplated. A number of reprint jobbers are available, and among their services are reports of the actual availability of titles.

MICROFORMS

Another method of producing out-of-print titles is through one of the micro methods. One of the most convenient means of obtaining books produced in this manner is through the "books on demand" service provided by University Microfilms International of Ann Arbor, Michigan. University Microfilms employs xerography to produce copies of works ranging from the fifteenth century to the present decade. A three-volume guide titled *Books on Demand* lists the 84,000 titles which were available through 1976. Supplements to *Books on Demand* will be published as University Microfilms expands its program to include thousands of other titles. Orders can be placed either by telephone or by mail for any of the items listed in the guide. Perhaps one of the greatest advantages of the "books on demand" system is the guarantee that all works will be delivered within thirty days of receipt of the order, eliminating the long delays sometimes experienced with reprint publishers.

Other microforms include microfilm, microprint, and microfiche, etc. A number of companies have and are producing subject collections in microform and can provide large collections of otherwise unobtainable material. Oftentimes printed guides and indices as well as catalog cards may be available. It is not usually possible to select individual titles from such collections, but some companies do offer discounts to libraries which may already hold original printed copies in their collections. As with reprints, one must not overlook the small firm that may have produced microforms in a specialized subject area. It is also possible to make or have made copies of another institution's original text. One must exercise caution in using this method to insure that infringement on the rights of the copyright holder is avoided.

A general guide to micro materials is *Microforms in Print*, published by Microform Review, Inc., of Westport, Connecticut. This guide is issued annually and contains subject, author and title listings. Subjects are listed according to Library of Congress subject classification. Each entry includes such information as author, title, volume, date, price, publisher, and type of microform. Also included in the guide is a directory to those publishers whose works appear in the listings.

GIFTS AND EXCHANGE

Gift and exchange programs can also be used effectively to procure retrospective materials. Though gifts cannot always be anticipated, they should not be overlooked as a means of obtaining retrospective materials. Interested library patrons, alumni and others can often be encouraged to contribute books from their own collections. Friends of the Library organizations and similar groups can also stimulate cash donations which allow the library to further pursue its retrospective purchasing plans. Libraries receiving numerous out-of-print books as gifts will occasionally find choice titles or rare editions among the donated items. Even those works which duplicate library holdings or do not fall within the collection interests of the library can be useful as exchange items or sold or traded to dealers and thus eventually contribute to the acquisition of needed retrospective titles.

Libraries which establish exchange agreements with other institutions can greatly benefit their retrospective acquisition programs. Exchange agreements are often thought to include only the current scholarly publications of universities, museums and other research organizations; but many libraries have exchange agreements for retrospective materials which have proven to be of great advantage. One western United States library, for example, exchanges on a regular basis localized western Americana with an eastern U.S. library for more general materials in history and literature. The method employed for selection is the exchange of xeroxed copies of title pages. Libraries may also choose to participate in such agencies as the Universal Serials and Book Exchange, Inc., formerly the United States Book Exchange, Inc. in Washington, D.C.

CONCLUSION

The acquisition of retrospective materials is one of the primary functions of a growing library. Retrospective works are not always easy to obtain, however, since unlike in-print titles which can be simply ordered from a publisher or jobber, out-of-print items must first be located before they can be purchased. The antiquarian dealer is usually the library's principal source for the acquisition of retrospective titles. There are several kinds of antiquarian book-sellers, each of which may be consulted at one time or another by the library depending on the nature of the item being sought. Some bookdealers will make periodic visits to libraries which are prime customers. The examination of dealers' catalogs and the submission of desiderata lists will aid the library in locating desirable items. The library which has a competent antiquarian dealer nearby with which it can closely cooperate is particularly fortunate.

There are also several other useful methods for obtaining retro-spective works. Auctions, for example, sometimes provide the library the opportunity to acquire retrospective materials previously un-available for decades. The library may further obtain out-of-print books by advertising in one of the numerous journals published in the book trade in the United States and abroad. Collection buying permits a library to develop a particular subject specialty in a short amount of time. Libraries interested in primarily the text of a retrospective work can satisfy their needs by purchasing reprint or microform copies of the work. Gift and exchange programs are also useful tools in obtaining retrospective materials.

REFERENCES

1. Richard Blackwell, "Acquisition of Non-Current Material: A View from Blackwell." In *Acquisition of Foreign Materials for U.S. Libraries*, Theodore Samore, ed. (Metuchen, N.J.: Scarecrow Press, 1973), p. 64.
2. Felix Reichmann, "Purchase of Out-of-Print Material in American University Libraries." *Library Trends* 18 (January 1970): 338.
3. Helga Pietarski, "Acquisition of Out-of-Print Books for a University Li-brary." *Canadian Library Journal* 26 (September-October 1969): 348.
4. Anthony Rota, "The State of the Antiquarian Book Market in Great Britain." Association of Research Libraries, *Foreign Acquisitions Newsletter* 44 (Fall 1976): 1.
5. Ernest R. Perez, "Acquisition of Out-of-Print Materials." *Library Resources and Technical Services* 17 (Winter 1973): 55.
6. Reichmann, op. cit., pp. 333-334.

7. Fred C. Lynden and Arthur Meyerfeld, "Library Out-of-Print Book Procurement: The Stanford Experience." *Library Resources and Technical Services* 17 (Spring 1973): 217-218.
8. Shirley G. Heppell, "A Survey of OP Buying Practices." *Library Resources and Technical Services* 10 (Winter 1966): 28-30.
9. Pietarski, op. cit., p. 348.

BIBLIOGRAPHY

Bonk, John Wallace, and Rose Mary Magrill, *Building Library Collections*, 5th ed. Metuchen, N.J.: Scarecrow Press, 1979.

Bradley, Van Allen, *New Gold in Your Attic*, 2d ed. New York: Fleet, 1968.

Cook, Sarah A., "The Selective Purchase of Out-of-Print Books: A Survey of Practices." *Library Resources and Technical Services* 10 (Winter 1966): 31-37.

Gregory, Roma S., "Acquisition of Microforms." *Library Trends* 18 (January 1970): 373-384.

Heppell, Shirley G., "A Survey of OP Buying Practices." *Library Resources and Technical Services* 10 (Winter 1966): 28-30.

Jacob, Emerson, "The Use of TAAB in Out-of-Print Book Searching." *College and Research Libraries* 17 (January 1956): 16-18.

Kim, Ung Chong, "A Comparison of Two Out-of-Print Book Buying Methods." *College and Research Libraries* 34 (September 1973): 258-264.

Lynden, Fred C., and Arthur Meyerfeld. "Library Out-of-Print Book Procurement: The Stanford Experience." *Library Resources and Technical Services* 17 (Spring 1973): 216-224.

MacManus, George S., "What Librarians Should Know About Book Buying." *Library Journal* 85 (October 1, 1960): 3394-3397.

Mitchell, Betty J., "Methods Used in Out-of-Print Acquisition: A Survey of Out-of-Print Book Dealers." *Library Resources and Technical Services* 17 (Spring 1973): 211-215.

——, "A Systematic Approach to Performance Evaluation of Out-of-Print Book Dealers: The San Fernando Valley State College Experience." *Library Resources and Technical Services* 15 (Spring 1971): 215-222.

Perez, Ernest R., "Acquisitions of Out-of-Print Materials." *Library Resources and Technical Services* 17 (Winter 1973): 42-59.

Pietarski, Helga, "Acquisition of Out-of-Print Books for a University Library." *Canadian Library Journal* 26 (September-October 1969): 346-352.

Reichmann, Felix, "Bibliographical Control of Reprints." *Library Resources and Technical Services* 11 (Fall 1967): 415-434.

_____, "Purchase of Out-of-Print Material in American University Libraries." *Library Trends* 18 (January 1970): 328-353.

Rota, Anthony, "The State of the Antiquarian Book Market in Great Britain." Association of Research Libraries, *Foreign Acquisitions Newsletter* 44 (Fall 1976): 1-5.

Samore, Theodore, ed., *Acquisition of Foreign Materials for U.S. Libraries.* Metuchen, N.J.: Scarecrow Press, 1973.

Smith, Eldred, "Out-of-Print Booksearching." *College and Research Libraries* 29 (July 1968): 303-309.

Wing, Donald G., and Robert Vosper, "The Antiquarian Bookmarket and the Acquisition of Rare Books." *Library Trends* 3 (April 1955): 385-392.

"Collection Officer" or "Collector":

The Preservation Side of the "Development" Responsibility

Pamela W. Darling

INTRODUCTION

Generalization Number 1: Most people reading this book will call themselves (or aspire to be, or be in charge of) "collection/selection officers," "collection development officers," "bibliographers," or perhaps "subject specialists"—but NOT "book collectors." Because one does not personally own the materials being selected and the collections being ammassed, which do not decorate the home nor can they be sold someday for private gain, one tends not to have a strong proprietary interest in them as objects of value.

Generalization Number 2: Despite the pride with which one may point to "the fine collection of X thousand volumes in Y languages . . . ," the unending pressure of balancing patron demands, publishers' blurbs and limited funds keep attention focused on *collection* as a verb, the processes of decision-making and acquisition, rather than on the noun, the ever-growing result of those processes.

Generalization Number 3: With the important exception of rare book or "special" collections, the physical condition of materials being collected has not been of particular concern: selection is made for content, with only a generic interest in form (is it a book, film, record, etc.?), because it has been assumed that the form would be appropriate and durable.

Generalization Number 4: It has finally become evident that the latter assumption is increasingly false, and librarians must adopt more of the proprietary concern of the collec*tor* if collec*ting* is to be worth the effort.

PRESERVATION AND COLLECTION DEVELOPMENT

Professional awareness of the deterioration of library materials has increased quite dramatically in recent years, as evidenced by a steadily growing number of articles, workshops, proposals, planning studies, and new programs, with newly created positions for preservation officers addressing various aspects of the "preservation problem." The relationship between collection development and preservation becomes clear when one looks at some of the factors contributing to this new awareness:

Sharp curtailments in book-buying power are altering the proportion of new to "old" materials in many libraries, forcing librarians to rely more heavily on retrospective collections to meet patron needs.* As a result, the ailing condition of older materials has become increasingly apparent, even as it is aggravated by more frequent handling. At the same time, pressure for space to accommodate affordable materials draws attention to stack areas clogged with moldering tomes.

---

*The author is indebted to Karen Esper, Collection Development Librarian at Case Western University Library for this valuable observation, though she is not to be blamed for what has been done to her idea.

Resource-sharing, through expanding interlibrary loan activity and agreements to parcel out collecting responsibilities, brings to light more deficiencies in existing holdings and intensifies the need to keep things accessible by keeping them in not only usable but even transportable physical condition. The availability of fewer copies to meet the information needs of more and more people places further physical strains on those materials and increases the rate of deterioration.

Certain trends in publishing draw attention to physical features. Who has not noticed the flimsiness of new books, the spread of the "soft cover," the declining quality of "hard covers," the "perfect binding" glue that cracks, the synthetic cover materials that rip, the vanishing margin, the paper that visibly ages within a few years? The flood of reprints and micro editions of older works also serve as reminders of the fragile condition of the originals. Although that market first burgeoned during the expansive sixties serving new colleges and "instant libraries," it flourishes now in large part because of the replacement needs of older collections. And simultaneous or even sole publication of new material in microform is becoming common, with many implications for selection, storage and access. While it is a truism to note that libraries today are more than just collections of books, the impact of the significance of these changing forms and conditions for approach to building collections has not yet been fully absorbed.

The physical odds are mounting. The extensive substitution of photocopying for note-taking, even in some cases for learning!, places unprecedented strain on bindings. The generations of patrons growing up in a world of disposables, including bus-station paperbacks, endless magazines, and mail-order catalogs, has a less than careful attitude toward individual books. With each passing year, a larger proportion of all permanent collections falls into the rapidly self-destructing category because of the cumulating effects of a century-plus of publishing on poor quality paper.

IMPLICATIONS FOR COLLECTION DEVELOPMENT

There are two major implications for collection development: First, more attention must be focused on the physical form, as well as content, in future acquisition. Like the book collector, the librarian must now consider both physical form or condition and intellectual content in determining the "value," or how much one is willing to pay for it, of a potential addition to the collection. Two different aspects of physical condition are important.

First, *permanence* refers to the chemical stability of material (paper, cloth, glues, etc.), that is, its ability to retain its basic nature and characteristics over time. Before the last century, most book paper was very permanent, because papermaking techniques resulted in a chemically stable product which reacts very little to changes in the environment. It has finally been recognized that new methods, particularly the use of alum rosin sizing, introduced to permit economic mass production have resulted in an unstable product, containing residual elements generally acidic or prone to become so in the presence of such environmental elements as moisture or sulfur dioxide. Such nonpermanent papers can change dramatically in appearance and behavior, from white to yellow or brown, from flexible to brittle, without even being touched.

Second, in contrast, *durability* relates to the physical stability or strength of material, its ability to withstand handling or physical abuse. Most early papers were durable, because the crude methods of beating cellulosic raw materials into paper pulp resulted in relatively long thick fibers which bonded together very firmly. Sharp knives in mechanical beaters speeded up the pulping process, but produced short fibers incapable of forming very strong bonds within a sheet of paper. Folding endurance, the number of times paper can be folded under uniform tension without breaking, is the most common way to measure durability. Nondurable papers break or tear quite easily—try the "fold-a-corner test" in your own stacks.

Permanence and durability factors need to be considered independently when judging the condition, as one may exist without the other. A very weak paper may be chemically stable and able to resist environmental attack. In the case of a rarely held item, the lack of durability will not be a serious drawback as it would for something to be heavily used. Conversely, a strong, durable paper able to withstand much handling when new may also be very impermanent and deteriorate over time. Such a lack of permanence would be acceptable for this year's phone book or this month's airline guide, but not for titles to be retained indefinitely, because lack of permanence eventually degrades durability as well.

Permanence and durability apply not only to paper but to binding methods and cover materials, to film (silver halide is more permanent than durable; diazo and vesicular are durable but less permanent), to storage devices (record jackets, slide mounts, reels, boxes, slip cases, mats), to practically everything. And the degree to which something retains its original characteristics and strength also depends on external factors; a very weak, acidic paper will remain white and flexible indefinitely if stored in a cool, dry, dark, inert atmosphere.

With these factors in mind, the selector/collector then must ask if the physical form and condition are appropriate to the storage conditions and to the use the item will receive, be that air-conditioned limited-access dark storage, display, occasional consultation, or heavy reference. Will it withstand such storage and use for five, fifty, or five hundred years? There is an impossibility lurking in this suggestion, since the librarians are most often *not* in a position to examine an item before deciding whether to get it. Some choices may be available (soft cover vs. hard, paper vs. microform) and there should then be a match between the probable permanence and durability of the alternative chosen and the particular storage environment, use patterns of our patrons, and desired retention period. But too often one must take it "as is" if it is to be acquired at all, so further steps become necessary.

A shrewd collector may spot a rare edition languishing within dirty, tattered covers, snap it up and send it off to a conservator to repair and restore, thus prolonging the life of the item, making it usable again, and usually, if done properly, considerably enhancing its value. Similarly, the librarian may have to take remedial steps as a part of the initial investment in a deteriorating item. Professional restoration is one option, for materials important enough to warrant the enormous expense involved. But there are many other options for materials in various conditions destined for various uses: prompt binding of paperbacks and periodicals; repair or rebinding of items received in damaged condition; boxing, mounting, matting or otherwise creating protective containers for fragile items; deacidification and buffering to prevent future embrittlement (since deacidification is still chiefly a laboratory process, not applicable to large quantities of routine acquisitions); format conversion, i.e., photocopying onto archival paper or microfilming, to preserve the content of badly embrittled books. Procedures for screening new materials and selecting the appropriate option should be built into regular processing routines.

Efforts must also be continued to persuade more publishers to improve the quality of new materials, through educational programs, the establishment of technical standards, and the application of economic pressures when practicable. Such efforts have met with reasonable success in the area of microforms; but with the far older technologies of book and papermaking there has been discouragingly little progress in reversing the downward trend in physical quality. It is not for lack of technical knowledge or practical application, for paper mills know how to make permanent/durable paper and some regularly do. Nor is it even for insurmountable economic reasons: permanent/durable paper is already priced competitively with non-permanent/durable but otherwise quality book papers, and could become even cheaper if demand rose to justify higher-volume production and switchover of more mills to alkaline methods. The main problem now lies in overcoming the ignorance or apathy of many publishers about the probable life expectancy of their products, and the sincere but mistaken belief of many others that they can't afford to produce materials that will last for a price that customers, including libraries, will pay.

Along with these approaches to prospective collection development is the second major implication of the "preservation problem": collection *building* cannot continue at the expense of collection *maintenance* or the foundations will collapse. The serious collector provides carefully designed storage areas for the treasures, protected from dust, light, atmospheric pollutants, fluctuations in temperature and humidity, and rough or excessive handling, and examines them periodically to determine the need for protective or remedial treatment to safeguard the initial investment. The library's investment is of a different sort, but the need to protect it is no less great, and libraries may fail their readers as much by letting older resources erode as by not adding new ones.

Thus libraries must provide proper storage conditions, educate staff and patrons in safe handling techniques, and develop appropriate mechanisms for systematically reviewing the condition of the collections, deciding what needs replacement, conversion or preservation treatment of some kind, and getting that done. The intellectual processes involved in initial selection must again be employed in the making of preservation decisions, since both activities control the content and form of the total collection. It costs money to preserve or replace, as it does to acquire in the first place, and it is essential to coordinate the collecting and maintaining ends of the process. Because a preservation decision is actually a second acquisition decision—"It will cost this much to keep this in usable form in the collection; if we didn't already have it, would it be worth that much to acquire it?"—staff responsibility for both should rest in the same place, and funds for both should come from the same pot.

To make this work, the collection/selection officer must have information about condition, feasible physical treatment alternatives, the availability of replacements, and approximate costs for each possibility. Some of this information may be in the form of general guidelines, if the paper is still flexible, rebinding is possible for X dollars per volume; microfilming our copy would cost about Y cents per page, but some will have to be sought for each item. Is a commercial reprint available? Are there other copies in better condition? Can this be restored for under $200 or should it just be cleaned and boxed? Thus librarians must educate themselves in the generalities and develop efficient procedures, i.e., searching, getting treatment estimates, for assembling the particular data needed for informed decisions about individual items.

Donors and other funding sources must also be educated about the critical need to provide for maintenance as well as development if the continuing quality of the collection is to be assured. A guided tour through the stacks is often all that is needed to create sufficient awareness, after which a range of preservation packages, from "this book was preserved through the generosity of____ " book plates to large-scale microform conversion projects, can be presented for support. Whatever the approach, librarians must force themselves and those who pay the bills to recognize the harsh truth that the cost of each item in the collection is not paid once and for all when it is acquired and cataloged.

The seeds of destruction were sown in library collections many years ago, and the harvest of rotting bindings and crumbled paper grows steadily. In jeopardy stands the written record of generations, and with it the efforts of all those collection/selection officers, bibliographers and devoted collectors who assembled those materials. Some way must be found to preserve what has been selected for the sake of those to come; and ways must be found to minimize future threats to the things currently being chosen to continue the development of library collections.